The
OXFORD
Children's
THESAURUS

The
OXFORD

Children's

THESAURUS

Compiled by
Alan Spooner

OXFORD UNIVERSITY PRESS

Oxford University Press, Walton Street, Oxford OX2 6DP

Oxford   New York
Athens   Auckland   Bangkok   Bombay
Calcutta   Cape Town   Dar es Salaam   Delhi
Florence   Hong Kong   Istanbul   Karachi
Kuala Lumpur   Madras   Madrid   Melbourne
Mexico City   Nairobi   Paris   Singapore
Taipei   Tokyo   Toronto

and associated companies in
Berlin   Ibadan

Oxford is a trade mark of Oxford University Press

© **Oxford University Press 1987**

First published 1987
Redesigned impression 1994
3 5 7 9 10 8 6 4 2

ISBN 0 19 910323 2 (net hardback)
ISBN 0 19 910322 4 (non-net hardback)
A CIP catalogue record for this book is available from the British Library

Printed in Great Britain by Cambridge University Press

Do you have a query about words, their origin, meaning, use spelling
pronunciation, or any other aspect of the English language? Then write to
OWLS at Oxford University Press, Walton Street, Oxford OX2 6DP

All queries will be answered using the full resources of the
Oxford Dictionary Department

Preface

I have designed this thesaurus to enable young people to make good use of the words they already know, and to help them to improve their knowledge and understanding of language generally. I hope that it is simple to use, but that at the same time it includes a wide enough vocabulary to make it interesting and thought-provoking.

Our language is an extremely complicated system. Clearly, a book of this kind cannot give all the information a young person needs in order to judge whether a word is likely to convey a particular shade of meaning, or to be appropriate to a particular spoken or written context. It will often be important, therefore, for young people to be helped in their use of the book, as in their general language development, by parents, teachers, and other experienced users of English. Indeed, I hope that teachers may find it a useful book not only for children to refer to, but also for them to work from in various kinds of language work in the classroom.

The basic vocabulary of the *Thesaurus* is the same as that of *The Oxford Children's Dictionary (Second Edition)*. This means that the two books can be used alongside each other easily and confidently. Very occasionally I have included in the *Thesaurus* a sense or form of a word different from that in the *Dictionary*: but I have done so only when I felt it would be helpful rather than confusing to do so.

I should like to record my debt to John Weston, with whom I collaborated on the two editions of *The Oxford Children's Dictionary*. Without his enthusiasm and hard work on the *Dictionary*, this *Thesaurus* would not have come about.

I should also like to thank members of the Oxford University Press: Tony Augarde and Rob Scriven for their supportive help and advice; and in particular Janette Brown who has done an enormous amount of hard and constructive work in preparing the book for publication.

AJS

Headwords
The first word of each entry (the *headword*) is printed in green so that you can find it easily.

Cross-references
If we don't have space for all the information you might want under a particular headword, we suggest that you look up another entry. This is called *cross-referencing*.

geranium SEE **flower**.
gerbil SEE **animal, pet**.
germ bacteria, (informal) bug, microbe, virus. ! *Bacteria is a plural word.*
germinate *Our seeds have germinated.* to grow, to shoot, to spring up, to sprout, to start growing.
gesture 1 action, movement, sign. 2 WAYS TO MAKE GESTURES ARE to beckon, to nod, to point, to salute, to shake your head, to shrug, to wave, to wink.
get 1 *What did you get for Christmas? What can I get for £10?* to acquire, to be given, to buy, to gain, to get hold of, to obtain, to procure, to purchase, to receive. 2 *Tell the dog to get the ball.* to bring, to fetch, to pick up, to retrieve. 3 *Did you get a prize?* to earn, to take, to win. 4 *Lucy got a cold.* to catch, to contract, to develop, to suffer from. 5 *Get Tony to do the washing-up.* to cause, to persuade. 6 *Let's get tea now.* to make ready, to prepare. 7 *I don't get what he means.* to comprehend, to follow, to grasp, to understand. 8 *What time do you get to school?* to arrive at, to reach.

Warnings
When you need to be particularly careful about how you use a word, a warning goes in brackets before the word or phrase concerned.

Notes
Occasionally, we draw your attention to some interesting fact or problem about a word. This goes at the end of an entry after a big exclamation mark.

Related words
An explanation in small capitals tells you that the words we give are not synonyms but are related in some other way.

Synonyms
Most entries give you *synonyms*, words which are similar in meaning to the headword.

Numbers
When a word has more than one meaning, or can be used in more than one way, numbers separate the main meanings or uses of a word from each other.

Examples
Phrases or sentences printed in *italics* are examples of how the headword can be used.

What is a thesaurus for?

A thesaurus helps you find the words you need to make your language more interesting and more effective in saying what you want to say. It gives you words with similar meaning to the word you look up, so that you can choose the best word for your purpose. It also helps you find words which are related in other ways: names of various foods, words to describe the weather, terms to do with medical treatment, and so on.

What will you find in this thesaurus?

Headwords

The first word of each entry (the *headword*) is printed in green so that you can find it easily. All the headwords are arranged in alphabetical order.

Numbers

When a word has more than one meaning, or can be used in more than one way, numbers separate the main meanings or uses of a word from each other.

Examples

Phrases or sentences printed in *italics* are examples of how the headword can be used.

Synonyms

Most entries give you *synonyms*, words which are similar in meaning to the headword. Synonyms hardly ever mean exactly the same, so you should think carefully about how you use them. Which is the word which gives *most exactly* the meaning you have in mind? Which words are more informal, and which more for-

mal? Which words are more old-fashioned, and which are more up-to-date?

Related words

Sometimes an explanation in small capitals tells you that the words we give are not synonyms but are related in some other way. *For example*: to nod and to point do not mean the same, but they are both ways to make gestures. So under **gesture** we say WAYS TO MAKE GESTURES ARE … and *to nod* and *to point* are listed there.

Cross-references

If we don't have space for all the information you might want under a particular headword, we suggest that you look up another entry. This is called *cross-referencing*. When you look up a cross-reference you will find synonyms or related words which may help you. *For example*: if you look up **geranium**, it says: SEE **flower**. Under *flower* you will find *geranium* listed with other words to do with flowers.

Warnings

When you need to be particularly careful about how you use a word, a warning goes in brackets before the word or phrase concerned. *For example*: (informal) means that the word or phrase which comes next is usually *informal*, or more likely to be used in conversation than in writing. Similar warnings mark words which are *old-fashioned*, *insulting*, etc.

Notes

Occasionally, we draw your attention to some interesting fact or problem about a word. This goes at the end of an entry after a big exclamation mark.

Definitions

A thesaurus does not give definitions of words, although it helps you to understand words by putting them with other words of similar or related meaning. If you want a definition of a word, you must look it up in a dictionary. *The Oxford Children's Dictionary (Second Edition)* gives definitions of all the words in this thesaurus.

A a

abandon 1 *The weather was so bad they had to abandon their walk.* to cancel, to discard, to drop, to give up, to postpone, to scrap. 2 *Abandon ship!* to desert, to evacuate, to forsake, to leave, to quit. 3 *They abandoned Ben Gunn on Treasure Island.* to maroon, to strand.

abbey cathedral, church, monastery, priory. SEE ALSO **church**.

abdicate *to abdicate the throne.* to give up, to renounce, to resign.

abdomen belly, stomach, (informal) tummy. SEE ALSO **body**.

abduct *Terrorists abducted the millionaire's son.* to carry off, to kidnap.

abhorrent *The idea of eating meat is abhorrent to vegetarians.* disgusting, hateful, horrifying, repulsive, revolting. SEE ALSO **unpleasant**.

abide 1 (old-fashioned) to remain, to stay. 2 *Mrs Brunswick can't abide people who smoke.* to bear, to endure, to put up with, to stand, to tolerate. 3 *You must agree to abide by our rules.* to conform to, to keep to, to obey.

ability *Tony has the ability to become a good artist.* aptitude, capability, capacity, competence, gift, intelligence, knack, know-how, knowledge, power, prowess, skill, talent, training.

able 1 *Are you able to play today?* allowed, fit, free, permitted. 2 *Lucy is an able player.* capable, clever, competent, effective, experienced, gifted, intelligent, proficient, qualified, skilful, skilled, talented, trained.

abnormal *It's abnormal to have frost in the summer.* curious, exceptional, freak, funny, irregular, odd, peculiar, queer, rare, singular, strange, uncommon, unconventional, unusual.

abode (old-fashioned) *my humble abode.* dwelling, home, house, residence.

abolish *Dad wishes they would abolish income tax.* to eliminate, to end, to finish, to get rid of, to remove.

abominable *The weather was abominable: it rained all week.* appalling, awful, beastly, brutal, cruel, dreadful, hateful, horrible, nasty, odious, terrible. SEE ALSO **bad**.

abortion SEE **pregnant**.

about 1 *Is Lucy about?* around, close, near. 2 *It costs about £1.* almost, approximately, around, close to, nearly, roughly. 3 *Tony's got a book about sharks.* concerning, connected with, involving, regarding, relating to, telling of.

abridged *an abridged book.* abbreviated, condensed, cut, shortened.

abroad overseas.

abrupt 1 *The lesson came to an abrupt end when the fire bell went.* hasty, quick, sharp, sudden, unexpected. 2 *His abrupt manner made us feel uncomfortable.* blunt, curt, impolite, rude, short, unfriendly.

abscess boil, inflammation, sore. FOR OTHER AILMENTS SEE **illness**.

abscond to elope, to escape, to flee, to run away.

absent *Who's absent from school?* away, off.

absolute *Our rehearsal was absolute chaos!* complete, perfect, pure, sheer, total, unrestricted, utter.

absorb 1 to soak up. 2 *to be absorbed in your work.* to be immersed, to be interested, to be preoccupied. 3 *an absorbing hobby.* fascinating, interesting.

abstain *to abstain from voting.* to do without, to refrain from.

abstract *That maths was too abstract for me.* theoretical.

absurd *It was absurd to give the goldfish a Christmas present.* amusing, comic, crazy, farcical, foolish, funny, grotesque, illogical, irrational, laughable, ludicrous, mad, preposterous, ridiculous, senseless, silly, stupid, unreasonable, zany.

abundant *The explorers found an abundant supply of fresh water.* ample, copious, generous, liberal, plentiful, profuse.

abuse *He abused the driver who had crashed into his car.* to be rude to, to insult.

abysmal *Our team gave an abysmal performance.* appalling, awful, dreadful, worthless. SEE ALSO **bad**.

abyss chasm, crater, hole, pit.

academic *Lucy is good at games, but Tony is more academic.* brainy, clever, intellectual, intelligent, studious.

academy SEE **educate**.

accelerate to go faster, to quicken, to speed up.

accelerator SEE **vehicle**.

accent *You can tell Mr Brunswick comes from London because of his accent.* brogue, dialect, language.

accept 1 *Please accept this small gift.* to receive, to take. **2** *Most people accept that the world is round.* to acknowledge, to admit, to agree, to believe, to think.

acceptable *Flowers make an acceptable present.* adequate, appropriate, passable, pleasing, satisfactory, suitable, tolerable.

access *There is no direct access to our school from the main road.* approach, entrance, entry, way in.

accessory *accessories for an electric drill.* attachment, extension, fitting.

accident 1 *Was anyone injured in the accident?* calamity, catastrophe, crash, derailment, disaster, misadventure, misfortune, mishap. **2** *We met by accident.* chance, coincidence, fluke, luck.

accidental *We didn't mean to break the window: it was accidental.* casual, chance, fortunate, haphazard, lucky, unfortunate, unintentional, unplanned.

accommodate *The refugees were accommodated in tents.* to board, to house, to lodge, to put up.

accommodating *The people at the information office were very accommodating.* considerate, co-operative, helpful, obliging, thoughtful.

accommodation SEE **holiday**.

accompany *The headmaster accompanied our visitors to their car.* to escort, to go with.

accomplice *The two sets of fingerprints show that the burglar had an accomplice.* ally, assistant, collaborator, confederate, partner.

accomplish *We accomplished our mission successfully.* to achieve, to carry out, to complete, to do, to finish, to fulfil, to perform.

accomplished *an accomplished pianist.* brilliant, clever, experienced, gifted, masterly, skilful, talented.

accomplishment *Have you got any special accomplishments?* gift, skill, talent.

accordingly consequently, so, therefore, thus.

accordion SEE **music**.

account 1 *Can you account for your behaviour?* to explain, to make excuses. **2** *The shopkeeper gave us the account.* bill, receipt. **3** *We wrote a detailed account of our museum trip.* commentary, description, diary, explanation, log, narration, narrative, record, report, story, tale.

accountant SEE **job**.

accumulate *We accumulate a lot of rubbish in our garage.* to assemble, to bring together, to collect, to concentrate, to gather, to heap up, to hoard, to mass, to pile up, to store up.

accurate *Make sure the measurements are accurate.* correct, exact, meticulous, precise, right, true.

accuse *You should have evidence before you accuse someone of a crime.* to blame, to charge, to condemn, to incriminate, to prosecute.

accustomed *We went home by our accustomed route.* conventional, customary, habitual, normal, ordinary, regular, routine, traditional, usual.

ache 1 *an ache in a bad tooth.* discomfort, pain, pang, soreness, twinge. 2 *Lucy ached all over after running in the half marathon.* to be sore, to hurt, to sting, to throb.

achieve 1 *See what you can achieve in an hour.* to accomplish, to carry out, to complete, to do, to finish, to fulfil, to manage, to perform. 2 *Did they achieve their objective?* to gain, to get to, to reach.

achievement *It's a great achievement to get into the county team.* accomplishment, attainment, feat, success.

acid 1 SEE **chemical**. 2 *Lemons taste acid.* sharp, sour, tangy, tart. SEE ALSO **taste**.

acknowledge *Logan won't acknowledge that Lucy runs faster than he does.* to accept, to admit, to agree, to grant.

acquaintance *I don't know him well: he's just an acquaintance.* friend.

acquire *Where did Mrs Brunswick acquire that hat?* to buy, to gain, to get, to get hold of, to obtain, to procure, to purchase, to receive.

acquit *The prisoner was acquitted because of lack of evidence.* to discharge, to excuse, to free, to let off, to liberate.

acre SEE **measure**.

acrid *an acrid smell of burning.* bitter, unpleasant.

acrobat SEE **entertainment**.

act 1 *a brave act.* action, deed, exploit, feat, performance. 2 *He's only putting on an act.* deception, hoax, pretence. 3 *He's acting like a fool.* to behave, to conduct yourself, to pretend to be. 4 *Tony loved acting in the pantomime.* to appear, to perform, to play. 5 *Give the medicine time to act.* to function, to operate, to work.

action 1 *a helpful action.* act, deed, exploit, feat, performance. 2 *Lucy prefers films with plenty of action.* activity, drama, excitement, liveliness, movement. 3 *Grandad saw action in the Second World War.* battle, combat, conflict, fighting.

activate *Press that button to activate the alarm.* to set off, to start.

active 1 *Our puppy is so active he wears me out!* agile, energetic, lively, vigorous. 2 *Mum is active in charity work.* busy, employed, engaged, involved, occupied.

activity 1 *School is full of activity near Christmas.* action, excitement, liveliness, movement. 2 *What is your favourite activity?* hobby, occupation, pastime, project, task.

actor, actress SEE **entertainment, theatre**.

actual *That old oak tree isn't the actual tree Robin Hood lived in.* authentic, genuine, real, true.

acute 1 *acute pain.* extreme, intense, keen, severe, sharp, sudden. 2 *An acute angle.* pointed, sharp.

adamant *Mrs Brunswick was adamant that Lucy should not go to Logan's party.* decided, determined, firm, resolute, resolved.

adapt 1 *They adapted our minibus so that handicapped children can use it.* to adjust, to convert, to modify, to transform, to vary. 2 *Mrs Angel adapted a play by Shakespeare for us to perform.* to alter, to change, to edit, to rewrite.

add 1 *Add these numbers together.* to combine, to join, to put together, to unite. 2 *What does it all add up to?* to amount to, to come to, to make, to total. 3 *Add up what we have collected so far.* to calculate, to count, to reckon, to work out.

adder SEE **snake**.

addict *Mr Brunswick is a snooker addict.* enthusiast, fan, fanatic.

addiction custom, habit, obsession.

addition SEE **mathematics**.

additional *We need additional information.* extra, further, more, supplementary.

address 1 *Write the address clearly.* directions. **2** *The vicar addressed the school.* to speak to, to talk to.

adenoids SEE **body**.

adequate *The food was just adequate.* acceptable, enough, passable, satisfactory, sufficient, tolerable.

adhere *Limpets adhere to rocks.* to attach yourself, to cling, to fasten, to stick.

adhesive 1 *We need some adhesive to stick our work on to cards.* glue, gum, paste. **2** *adhesive tape.* gluey, gummed, sticky.

adjacent *Granny lives in the house adjacent to ours.* closest, nearest, neighbouring, next.

adjective SEE **language**.

adjourn *The teachers adjourned their meeting when the bell went.* to break off, to defer, to postpone, to put off, to suspend.

adjudicate *A famous musician adjudicated our music competition.* to arbitrate, to judge.

adjust *Tony has to adjust the saddle when he rides Lucy's bike.* to alter, to amend, to change, to modify, to put right, to vary.

administer 1 *The head administers the school.* to administrate, to command, to control, to direct, to govern, to look after, to manage, to rule, to run, to supervise. **2** *Are teachers still allowed to administer corporal punishment?* to deal out, to give, to hand out.

admirable *The actors gave an admirable performance.* creditable, excellent, (informal) fabulous, fine, marvellous, praiseworthy, wonderful. SEE ALSO **good**.

admiral SEE **sailor**.

admire 1 *We admired the firemen's courage.* to approve of, to honour, to marvel at, to praise, to respect, to revere, to value, to wonder at. **2** *We admired the view.* to appreciate, to enjoy, to like, to love.

admit 1 *Persons under sixteen are not admitted.* to allow in, to let in. **2** *Lucy admitted that she broke the window.* to

accept, to acknowledge, to agree, to confess, to own up.

adolescence *People say that adolescence is a difficult time.* growing up, puberty, (informal) your teens.

adolescent 1 *adolescent behaviour.* juvenile, youthful. **2** *Most adolescents like pop music.* teenager, youngster, youth.

adopted SEE **family**.

adore *Lucy and Tony adore their grandad.* to dote on, to idolize, to love, to revere, to worship.

adorn *The table was adorned with flowers.* to decorate.

adornment decoration, ornament.

adrift *We were adrift in the middle of the lake.* afloat, drifting, floating.

adult 1 *That film is for adults only.* grown-up. **2** *Tony has some very adult ideas.* developed, grown-up, mature.

adultery infidelity, unfaithfulness.

advance 1 *As we advanced, the birds flew away.* to approach, to come near, to go on, to make headway, to move forward, to proceed. **2** *Computers have advanced a lot in recent years.* to develop, to evolve, to improve, to move on, to progress.

advanced 1 *The school is buying a more advanced computer.* modern, sophisticated, up-to-date. **2** *Tony's maths is more advanced than Logan's.* complicated, difficult, hard.

advantage *It's an advantage to be tall when you play basketball.* asset, benefit, gain, help, profit.

advantageous beneficial, good, helpful, profitable, useful.

Advent SEE **church**.

adventure *Exploring the caves was quite an adventure.* escapade, excitement, exploit.

adventurous bold, brave, courageous, daring, enterprising, fearless, heroic, intrepid.

adverb SEE **language**.

adversary enemy, foe, opponent, opposition, rival.

adverse *adverse weather conditions.*

contrary, hostile, opposing, unfavourable.

adversity *It's good to have friends in times of adversity.* calamity, catastrophe, difficulty, disaster, distress, hardship, misfortune, trouble.

advertise *We advertised our concert in the local shops.* to make known, (informal) to plug, to promote, to publicize.

advertisement (informal) ad, (informal) advert, bill, commercial, notice, placard, (informal) plug, poster, publicity, sign.

advice *Dad gave me some advice.* help, suggestion, tip, warning.

advisable *It's advisable to wrap up warmly if you have a cold.* proper, prudent, sensible, wise.

advise 1 *They will advise us when the TV is mended.* inform, notify, tell. 2 *What medicine did the doctor advise?* prescribe, recommend, suggest.

aerobatics SEE **entertainment**.

aerobics SEE **exercise**.

aerodrome airfield, airport, airstrip, landing-strip.

aeroplane SEE **aircraft**.

affair 1 *Don't interfere: it's my affair!* business, concern, matter, thing. 2 *The robbery at the police station was a strange affair.* event, happening, incident, occasion.

affect 1 *Alcohol does affect your driving.* to alter, to change, to influence, to modify. 2 *The audience was deeply affected by the music.* to impress, to move, to stir, to touch.

affectionate attached, fond, friendly, kind, loving, tender, warm.

afflict *He was afflicted by boils.* to distress, to hurt, to torment, to torture, to trouble.

affliction ailment, blight, disease, disorder, illness, sickness. SEE ALSO **illness**.

affluent *They must be affluent to own a car like that.* prosperous, rich, wealthy, well-off, well-to-do.

afford *Can you afford a contribution to the*

famine appeal? to manage, to provide, to spare.

afloat adrift, floating.

afraid apprehensive, cowed, fearful, frightened, scared, terrified.

aft SEE **vessel**.

afternoon SEE **time**.

age 1 *the Victorian age.* era, period. SEE ALSO **time**. 2 *Dad's home-made wine won't taste so horrible if he leaves it to age.* to develop, to grow older, to mature, to ripen.

aged ancient, elderly, old.

aggravate 1 *If you scratch it will aggravate the soreness.* to make worse, to worsen. 2 (informal) *Don't aggravate mum by asking for more pocket-money.* to annoy, to bother, to exasperate, to irritate. ! Some people think this is a wrong use of *aggravate*.

aggressive *Most people think lions are aggressive animals.* attacking, belligerent, hostile, militant, pugnacious, warlike.

agile *Gymnasts need to be agile.* acrobatic, active, deft, graceful, lively, nimble, quick-moving, swift.

agitate *The thunder agitated the animals.* to disturb, to excite, to stir up.

agonizing *an agonizing wound.* excruciating, painful, unbearable.

agony anguish, pain, suffering, torment, torture.

agree 1 *Lucy agreed to pay for the broken window.* to consent, to undertake. 2 *Do you agree that I was right?* to accept, to acknowledge, to admit. 3 *We agreed that Logan would play in goal.* to choose, to decide, to establish, to fix, to settle. 4 *Unfortunately, Tony's story didn't agree with Lucy's.* to coincide, to correspond, to match.

agreeable *an agreeable companion, an agreeable occasion, etc.* amiable, decent, friendly, nice. SEE ALSO **kind, pleasant**.

agreement 1 *Lucy and Tony have quarrels, but they usually end in agreement.* accord, consent, concord, harmony. 2 *After a lot of arguing, they* *reached an agreement.* alliance, arrangement, bargain, contract, deal, pact, pledge, settlement, treaty, understanding.

agriculture farming.

aground stranded.

ahead forwards, onwards.

aid 1 *Even a small contribution will aid the starving.* to assist, to back, to help, to relieve, to support. **2** *They need our aid.* assistance, backing, co-operation, help, support.

ailment *No medicine will cure all ailments.* affliction, blight, complaint, disease, disorder, infection, infirmity, malady, sickness. SEE ALSO **illness**.

aim 1 *Aim the gun at the target.* to direct, to point. **2** *He is aiming to arrive for dinner.* to intend, to plan, to try. **3** *What's your aim in life?* ambition, cause, goal, intention, object, objective, plan, purpose, target.

air 1 *They fired into the air.* atmosphere, sky. **2** *to air a room.* to dry, to freshen, to ventilate. **3** *to air your opinions.* to display, to make known, to reveal, to show.

aircraft 1 KINDS OF AIRCRAFT ARE aeroplane, air-liner, airship, balloon, biplane, bomber, fighter, glider, hang-glider, helicopter, jet, jumbo jet, jump-jet, micro-light, plane, seaplane, supersonic aircraft. **2** PARTS OF AIRCRAFT ARE fin, fuselage, jet engine, joystick, propeller, rotor, rudder, tail, undercarriage, wing.

aircraft-carrier SEE **vessel**.

airfield aerodrome, airport, airstrip, landing-strip.

air force SEE **armed services**.

airgun SEE **weapon**.

air hostess SEE **job**.

air-liner SEE **aircraft**.

airport aerodrome, airfield, airstrip, landing-strip.

airship SEE **aircraft**.

airstrip SEE **airport**.

airy *an airy room.* breezy, draughty, fresh, ventilated.

aisle SEE **church**.

akin alike, related, similar.

alarm 1 *The thunder alarmed the animals.* to dismay, to disturb, to frighten, to scare, to shock, to startle, to surprise, to terrify, to upset. **2** *Alarm spread through the town when the volcano began to erupt.* consternation, dismay, fear, fright, panic, surprise. **3** *Move quickly into the playground when you hear the alarm.* bell, fire-alarm, gong, signal, siren, warning.

albatross SEE **bird**.

album 1 SEE **book**. **2** SEE **record**.

alcohol (informal) booze, liquor, spirits. SEE ALSO **drink**.

alcoholic 1 *alcoholic drink.* intoxicating. **2** *an alcoholic.* addict, drunkard.

ale beer. SEE ALSO **drink**.

alert 1 *You must stay alert if you play in goal.* attentive, awake, careful, lively, observant, vigilant, watchful. **2** *When the floods came, they rang the church bell to alert the villagers.* to caution, to warn.

algebra SEE **mathematics**.

alien *The green women in the spacecraft were obviously alien beings.* foreign, strange, unfamiliar.

alike akin, identical, similar.

alive *Is your pet hedgehog still alive?* existing, live, living.

alkali SEE **chemical**.

Allah SEE **Islam**.

allegiance *allegiance to the king.* duty, faithfulness, loyalty.

allergy SEE **illness**.

alley SEE **road**.

alliance *an alliance between two sides.* agreement, association, combination, league, pact, treaty, union.

alligator crocodile. SEE ALSO **reptile**.

allot *We allotted half our food to the visitors.* to allow, to deal out, to distribute, to divide, to give out, to ration, to share out.

allotment SEE **garden**.

allow 1 *They allowed us to use the first team's pitch.* to authorize, to approve,

to enable, to let, to license, to permit.
2 *We allowed £5 for spending money.* to allot, to give, to grant, to provide, to set aside.

alloy SEE **metal**.

all right 1 *Are you all right again after your illness?* fit, healthy, well. **2** *Is my work all right?* acceptable, adequate, passable, satisfactory, tolerable.

allude *Did mum allude to the spilt paint?* to mention, to refer to.

alluring *She wore an alluring dress.* attractive, bewitching, captivating, charming, enchanting, fascinating, fetching, glamorous. SEE ALSO **beautiful**.

ally collaborator, confederate, friend, partner.

almighty omnipotent.

almond SEE **nut**.

almost about, approximately, around, nearly, not quite, practically.

alone 1 *to be alone.* friendless, isolated, lonely, solitary. **2** *to perform alone.* solo.

alongside *Our friends parked their car alongside ours.* adjacent to, beside, next to.

aloud *to read aloud.* audibly, clearly, distinctly.

Alsatian SEE **dog**.

also additionally, besides, furthermore, moreover, too.

altar SEE **church**.

alter *Don't alter your story: it's excellent as it is.* to adapt, to adjust, to affect, to amend, to change, to convert, to edit, to modify, to transform, to vary.

alteration change, difference, modification.

alternative *The alternatives are beef or chicken.* choice, option, possibility.

altitude height.

altogether *We were not altogether satisfied.* absolutely, completely, entirely, quite, totally, utterly, wholly.

aluminium SEE **metal**.

always continually, continuously,

eternally, evermore, for ever, repeatedly, unceasingly.

amalgamate *Because they had so few players, the two teams amalgamated. They amalgamated the two teams.* to combine, to come together, to integrate, to join, to merge, to put together, to unite.

amateur *an amateur player.* unpaid.
! *Amateur is the opposite of professional.*

amaze 1 *His speed amazed us.* to astonish, to astound, to bewilder, to confuse, to shock, to stun, to surprise. **2** *amazed*: dazed, dumbfounded, nonplussed, thunderstruck. **3** *amazing*: exceptional, extraordinary, notable, phenomenal, remarkable, special, unusual.

ambassador consul, diplomat, representative.

amber 1 SEE **colour**. **2** SEE **jewellery**.

ambiguous *When you ride your bike, don't give ambiguous signals.* confusing, uncertain, unclear, vague.

ambition 1 *You need ambition to succeed in business.* drive, enterprise, enthusiasm. **2** *Lucy's ambition is to play for the county team.* aim, desire, goal, intention, objective, wish.

amble SEE **walk**.

ambulance SEE **vehicle**.

ambush *The outlaws ambushed the travellers in the mountains.* to attack, to ensnare, to intercept, to pounce on, to swoop on, to trap.

amend *Mr Brunswick amended the wording of his letter to the newspaper.* to adapt, to adjust, to alter, to change, to improve, to modify.

amiable *The crocodile seemed quite amiable.* agreeable, friendly, good-humoured, kind-hearted, nice, pleasant. SEE ALSO **kind**.

ammonia SEE **chemical**.

ammunition KINDS OF AMMUNITION ARE bullet, cannonball, cartridge, grenade, missile, round, shell, shrapnel. SEE ALSO **weapon**.

amnesia SEE **illness**.

amnesty pardon.

amount 1 *What did the collection amount to?* to add up to, to come to, to make, to total. **2** *Dad gave us a cheque for the full amount.* quantity, sum, total.

amphibious AMPHIBIOUS ANIMALS ARE frog, newt, toad. SEE ALSO **animal**.

ample *The spring provided an ample supply of water.* abundant, copious, generous, liberal, plentiful.

amplifier SEE **audio equipment**.

amplify *The head asked me to amplify my explanation.* to develop, to enlarge, to expand, to magnify.

amputate *to amputate a limb.* to cut off, to remove, to sever.

amuse 1 *A comedian's job is to amuse people.* to cheer up, to delight, to divert, to entertain. **2** *amusing:* SEE **funny**.

amusement *What's your favourite form of amusement?* diversion, enjoyment, fun, hobby, joke, laughter, merriment, pastime, play, pleasure, recreation. SEE ALSO **entertainment, game, sport**.

anaemia SEE **illness**.

anaesthetic SEE **medicine**.

analyse *Tomorrow we're going to analyse our traffic survey.* to examine, to study.

anarchy *There would be anarchy if we had no police.* chaos, confusion, disorder, lawlessness.

anatomy *A doctor has to know all about anatomy.* the body. SEE ALSO **body, science**.

ancestor *Mum's hobby is tracing her ancestors.* forefather, predecessor.

anchor 1 *to anchor a ship.* to berth, to moor, to tie up. **2** *to anchor something firmly.* SEE **fasten**.

anchorage harbour, haven, marina.

ancient aged, antiquated, antique, early, old, old-fashioned, prehistoric, primitive, venerable.

angel SEE **church**.

anger 1 *to be filled with anger.* exasperation, fury, rage, temper,

wrath. **2** *They angered the referee with their foul play.* to aggravate, to annoy, to enrage, to exasperate, to incense, to inflame, to infuriate, to madden, to provoke, to vex.

angle bend, corner.

angler fisherman.

angling fishing.

angry 1 bad-tempered, cross, enraged, fiery, fuming, furious, incensed, indignant, infuriated, irate, livid, mad, raging, raving, vexed, wild, wrathful. **2** *to be angry:* to be in a temper, to boil, to fume, to rage, to rave, to seethe. **3** *to make someone angry:* to enrage, to incense, to infuriate, to vex.

anguish agony, distress, pain, suffering, torment, torture.

animal 1 beast, brute, creature. **2** KINDS OF ANIMAL ARE amphibious animal, bird, carnivorous animal, fish, insect, mammal, marsupial, mollusc, pet, predator, quadruped, reptile, rodent, scavenger. **3** VARIOUS SPECIES ARE antelope, ape, ass, baboon, badger, bat, bear, beaver, bison, boar, buffalo, bull, bullock, camel, cat, cattle, cheetah, chimpanzee, cow, deer, dinosaur, dog, dolphin, donkey, dormouse, dromedary, elephant, elk, ferret, fox, gerbil, giraffe, goat, gorilla, grizzly bear, guinea-pig, hamster, hare, hedgehog, hippopotamus, horse, hyena, jackal, jaguar, kangaroo, koala, leopard, lion, llama, mammoth, mastodon, mink, mole, mongoose, monkey, moose, mouse, mule, octopus, otter, ox, panda, panther, pig, platypus, polar bear, porcupine, porpoise, rabbit, rat, reindeer, rhinoceros, seal, sea-lion, sheep, shrew, skunk, squirrel, stoat, tiger, tortoise, turtle, vole, wallaby, walrus, weasel, whale, wolf, zebra. **4** SEE ALSO **amphibious, bird, fish, insect, reptile, snake. 5** SEE ALSO **female, male, young**.

animated *an animated conversation.* boisterous, bright, brisk, cheerful, energetic, excited, exuberant, lively, quick, spirited, sprightly, vivacious.

ankle SEE **body, joint, leg**.

annexe *They built an annexe for the extra class.* extension, wing.

annihilate *Nuclear weapons can annihilate whole cities.* to destroy, to eliminate, to eradicate, to exterminate, (informal) to finish off, to kill, to slaughter, to wipe out.

anniversary birthday, jubilee.

announce 1 *The head announced that we would have an extra holiday.* to declare, to proclaim, to publish, to report, to state. **2** *Tony announced the items at the concert.* to introduce.

announcement *Watch out for a special announcement.* bulletin, communication, communiqué, declaration, message, notice, proclamation, report, statement.

annoy *Don't annoy the bull.* (informal) to aggravate, to bait, to bother, to cross, to displease, to exasperate, to irritate, to molest, to offend, to pester, to tease, to torment, to trouble, to try, to upset, to vex, to worry.

annual 1 *Sports day is an annual event.* yearly. **2** *I bought a football annual with my book token.* SEE **book**. **3** *Mrs Brunswick planted annuals in her garden.* SEE **plant**.

anonymous nameless, unidentified, unnamed.

anorak SEE **clothes**.

answer 1 *the answer to a question.* reaction, reply, response, retort. **2** *the answer to a problem.* explanation, solution, sum, total.

ant SEE **insect**.

antagonism *You could see the antagonism between the two fighters.* conflict, hostility, opposition.

Antarctic SEE **geography**.

antelope SEE **animal**.

anthem SEE **music**.

anthology SEE **book**.

anthracite SEE **fuel**.

antibiotic SEE **medicine**.

anticipate *In chess, you have to anticipate your opponent's next move.* to expect, to forecast, to foresee, to predict, to prevent. ! Some people think this is a wrong use of *anticipate*.

anticyclone SEE **weather**.

antidote SEE **medicine**.

antiquated *Do you remember that antiquated car of grandpa's?* aged, old, old-fashioned, out-of-date, quaint.

antique *antique furniture.* aged, ancient, old, old-fashioned.

antiseptic SEE **medicine**.

antisocial *an antisocial person.* disagreeable, nasty, obnoxious, offensive, rude, unfriendly.

anxiety care, concern, dismay, doubt, dread, fear, misgivings, strain, stress, tension, worry.

anxious 1 *Mum was anxious about travelling by air.* apprehensive, concerned, fearful, jittery, nervous, uneasy, worried. **2** *Tony is always anxious to do his best.* eager, keen.

apart divided, separate.

apartment flat.

ape SEE **animal**.

apex *The steeplejack climbed to the apex of the spire.* crown, head, peak, tip, top.

apiary hive.

apologetic *Mrs Brunswick was apologetic about the burnt cake.* penitent, regretful, remorseful, repentant, sorry.

apologize *I apologized for being rude.* to regret, to repent, to say sorry.

apostle disciple, follower.

apostrophe SEE **punctuation**.

appal 1 *The crowd's bad behaviour appalled us.* to alarm, to disgust, to dismay, to frighten, to horrify, to shock, to terrify. **2** *What an appalling piece of work!* SEE **bad**.

apparatus appliance, device, equipment, instrument, machinery, tool.

apparent *It was apparent that Logan was lying.* blatant, clear, evident, obvious, plain, self-explanatory.

apparition *Logan claims he saw an*

apparition in the haunted tower. ghost, hallucination, illusion, phantom, spirit, (informal) spook, vision.

appeal 1 *The stranded motorist appealed for help*. to ask, to beg, to entreat, to plead, to request. 2 *I bought the picture because it appealed to me*. to attract, to fascinate, to interest. 3 *appealing*: SEE **attractive**.

appear 1 *Our visitors appeared an hour late*. to arrive, to come, to turn up. 2 *Whenever we think we've finished, another difficulty appears*. to arise, to emerge, to loom, to materialize, to show. 3 *This appears to be the coat Lucy lost*. to look, to seem. 4 *Tony appeared as Joseph in the nativity play*. to act, to perform.

appease *They offered a sacrifice to appease the gods*. to calm, to pacify, to soothe.

appendicitis SEE **illness**.

appendix SEE **body**.

appetite *an appetite for food, an appetite for adventure, etc*. craving, desire, greed, hunger, longing, lust, passion, zest.

applaud *The audience applauded our performance*. to approve of, to cheer, to clap, to commend, to praise.

apple SEE **fruit**.

appliance apparatus, device, equipment, instrument, machinery.

applicant candidate, entrant, participant.

apply 1 *to apply for a job*. to ask. 2 *to apply ointment to a wound*. to administer, to spread. 3 *to apply your strength*. to employ, to use.

appoint *Who did they appoint as captain?* to choose, to elect, to name, to nominate, to select.

appointment *I've got an appointment with a friend after tea*. date, engagement, fixture, meeting, rendezvous.

appreciate 1 *Do you appreciate classical music?* to admire, to approve of, to enjoy, to like, to prize, to respect, to value. 2 *I appreciate that you must be*

tired. to know, to realize, to see, to understand.

apprehensive *Tony was apprehensive about his music exam*. afraid, anxious, concerned, fearful, frightened, nervous, uneasy, worried.

apprentice beginner, learner, novice.

approach 1 *The approach to the school is off Church Street*. access, entrance, entry, way in. 2 *The lion approached its prey stealthily*. to come near, to draw near, to move towards. 3 *approaching*: *approaching traffic*. advancing, oncoming.

appropriate *an appropriate punishment, appropriate clothes*. apt, becoming, deserved, due, fit, fitting, proper, right, suitable, timely.

approve 1 *Do you approve of what we did?* to admire, to applaud, to commend, to like, to love, to praise, to value. 2 *The council approved Mr Brunswick's application to build an extension*. to allow, to authorize, to permit, to tolerate.

approximately about, around, close to, nearly, roughly.

apricot SEE **fruit**.

apron SEE **clothes**.

apt 1 *an apt pupil*. clever, quick, skilful. 2 *an apt reply*. appropriate, deserved, fitting, proper, right, suitable.

aptitude *Lucy has considerable aptitude as a gymnast*. ability, gift, knack, skill, talent.

aqueduct SEE **bridge**.

arbitrary *an arbitrary decision*. unplanned, unreasonable.

arbitrate *When the captains quarrelled, the referee had to arbitrate*. to make peace, to negotiate.

arc curve.

arcade SEE **building**.

arch 1 SEE **building**. 2 *The cat arched its back*. to bend, to curve.

archaeology SEE **subject**.

archbishop SEE **church**.

archipelago SEE **geography**.

architect SEE **art, job**.

architecture SEE **art, subject**.

arctic 1 SEE **geography**. **2** *arctic weather*. bitter, bleak, freezing, frozen, (informal) perishing. SEE ALSO **cold**.

arduous *The mountaineers faced an arduous climb*. difficult, gruelling, hard, laborious, strenuous, tough.

area 1 *The Brunswicks like the area where they live*. district, locality, neighbourhood, region, sector, territory, vicinity, zone. **2** *a large area of ice*. expanse, sheet, surface. **3** SEE **measure**.

arena *a sports arena*. field, ground, pitch, stadium.

argue 1 *to argue about politics*. to debate, to discuss, to dispute, to quarrel. **2** *to argue about the price*. to bargain, to haggle. **3** *The lawyer argued that the man was guilty*. to contend, to reason.

argument 1 *We had an argument about what to watch on TV*. controversy, debate, disagreement, dispute, quarrel. **2** *The bloody knife was the biggest argument against him*. evidence, grounds, justification, proof, reason.

arid 1 *arid desert*. barren, dry, lifeless, parched, sterile. **2** *an arid subject*. boring, dull, uninteresting.

arise *We'll deal with any problems as they arise*. to appear, to begin, to come up, to crop up, to emerge, to occur, to result, to spring up.

aristocrat lord, noble, peer. SEE ALSO **title**.

arithmetic SEE **mathematics**.

arm 1 SEE **body**. **2** *an arm of a tree*. branch, limb. **3** *They armed themselves with sticks*. to provide, to supply.

armada *an armada of ships*. convoy, fleet, navy.

armaments SEE **weapon**.

armchair SEE **furniture**.

armed services GROUPS OF FIGHTING MEN ARE air force, army, battalion, brigade, cavalry, commandos, company, corps, garrison, fleet, foreign legion, infantry, marines, mercenaries, navy, paratroops, patrol, platoon, recruits, regiment, reinforcements, squad, squadron, task-force, troop. SEE ALSO **fighter**.

armistice *The armistice ended the fighting*. pact, peace, treaty, truce.

armour *Soldiers used to wear armour in battle*. mail, protection.

armoury arsenal, weapons.

army SEE **armed services**.

aroma fragrance, odour, perfume, scent, smell, whiff.

arouse 1 *The milkman aroused us by dropping four bottles*. to awaken, to call, to rouse, to wake up. **2** *The sound of music aroused our interest*. to excite, to incite, to inspire, to provoke, to stimulate, to stir.

arrange 1 *Tony is arranging books in the library*. to classify, to distribute, to group, to put in order, to set out, to sort. **2** *We arranged an outing for Saturday*. to fix, to organize, to plan, to prepare, to settle.

arrangement *We have an arrangement to buy eggs from a local farmer*. agreement, bargain, contract, deal, pact, settlement, understanding.

arrest 1 *The police arrested the suspect*. to capture, to catch, to detain, (informal) to nab, to seize, to take prisoner. **2** *A landslide arrested our progress*. to bar, to block, to check, to halt, to hinder, to stop.

arrive 1 *We arrived at our destination*. to come to, to reach. **2** *When will granny arrive?* to appear, to come, to turn up.

arrogant *an arrogant manner*. boastful, bumptious, (informal) cocky, conceited, disdainful, haughty, insolent, pompous, presumptuous, proud, scornful, self-important, snobbish, (informal) stuck-up, vain.

arrow SEE **weapon**.

arsenal armoury. SEE ALSO **weapon**.

arson SEE **crime**.

art 1 KINDS OF ART AND CRAFT ARE architecture, carpentry, cartoons, collage, crochet, drawing, embroidery, engraving, fashion design, graphics, illustrations, jewellery, knitting, metalwork, mobiles, modelling, mosaic, murals, needlework, origami, painting, patchwork, photography, portraits, pottery, prints, sculpture, sewing, sketching, spinning, stencils, weaving, wickerwork, woodwork. SEE ALSO **music, picture, theatre.** 2 VARIOUS ARTISTS AND CRAFTSMEN ARE architect, blacksmith, carpenter, engraver, goldsmith, painter, photographer, potter, printer, sculptor, weaver. FOR PERFORMING ARTISTS SEE **entertainment, music, theatre.** 3 *There's an art in lighting a bonfire.* craft, knack, skill, talent, technique, trick.

artery SEE **body.**

artful *People say that foxes are artful creatures.* astute, clever, crafty, cunning, ingenious, knowing, shrewd, skilful, sly, tricky, wily.

arthritis SEE **illness.**

article 1 *Have you any old articles for the jumble sale?* item, object, thing. 2 *Did you read Tony's article in the magazine?* SEE **writing.**

articulated lorry SEE **vehicle.**

artificial *an artificial beard.* bogus, faked, false, feigned, man-made, manufactured, (informal) phoney, pretended, synthetic, unnatural, unreal.

artillery SEE **weapon.**

artist SEE **art.**

artistic attractive, beautiful, creative, imaginative.

ascend 1 *We ascended the hill.* to climb, to go up, to mount, to scale. 2 *The road ascends to the church.* to rise, to slope up.

Ascension Day SEE **church.**

ash 1 *the ashes of a fire.* cinders, embers. 2 *an ash tree.* SEE **tree.**

ashamed *Logan never seems ashamed when Mrs Angel tells him off.* distressed, embarrassed, upset.

Ash Wednesday SEE **church.**

ask 1 *to ask a question, to ask for help, etc.* to beg, to demand, to enquire, to entreat, to implore, to inquire, to pose a question, to query, to question, to request. 2 *to ask someone to a party.* to invite.

asleep dormant, hibernating, inactive, resting, sleeping.

asparagus SEE **vegetable.**

aspect *There's one aspect of this affair we don't understand.* circumstance, detail, feature.

asphalt SEE **road.**

aspirin SEE **medicine.**

ass 1 SEE **animal.** 2 SEE **fool.**

assail *The defenders were assailed with missiles.* to assault, to attack, to bombard, to set on.

assassinate to murder. SEE ALSO **crime, kill.**

assault *They assaulted their victim without warning.* to assail, to attack, to bombard, to molest, to mug, to raid, to rape, to set on.

assemble 1 *A crowd assembled.* to accumulate, to collect, to come together, to congregate, to crowd together, to group, to herd, to meet, to muster, to swarm, to throng. 2 *We assembled our belongings.* to bring together, to gather, to get together, to pile up. 3 *These cars are assembled in Britain.* to build, to construct, to fit together, to make, to manufacture, to put together.

assembly *an assembly of Scouts.* conference, congress, council, gathering, meeting.

assert *He asserted that he was innocent.* to argue, to claim, to contend, to declare, to emphasize, to insist, to maintain, to proclaim, to state, to stress.

assess *The garage assessed the damage to the car.* to calculate, to estimate, to reckon, to value, to work out.

asset 1 *Good health is a great asset.* advantage, blessing, benefit. 2 *What assets have you got?* capital, funds, money, resources, savings, wealth.

assignment *Mrs Angel gave the class an assignment to be done by Monday.* job, project, task, work.

assist *Can you assist us?* to aid, to back, to help, to second, to serve, to support.

assistant accomplice, collaborator, deputy, helper, partner, second.

association *an association of youth clubs.* alliance, body, club, combination, company, group, league, organization, party, society, union.

assorted *assorted colours.* different, diverse, miscellaneous, mixed, varied, various.

assortment *Mum gave us an assortment of flowers to plant in the garden.* collection, mixture, variety.

assume *I assume you'd like some ice-cream?* to believe, to guess, to imagine, to presume, to suppose, to think.

assumed *an assumed name.* false, feigned, pretended.

assumption *My assumption is that you will be hungry.* guess, supposition, theory.

assurance *We had his assurance that the car worked properly.* guarantee, oath, pledge, promise, vow.

assure *He assured me the work would be done by Friday.* to promise, to tell, to vow.

assured *Although she was young, her manner was assured.* certain, confident, definite, positive, sure.

asteroid SEE **astronomy**.

asthma SEE **illness**.

astonish *The acrobats astonished the crowd.* to amaze, to astound, to dumbfound, to surprise.

astound *The news that the school might be closed astounded us.* to amaze, to astonish, to dumbfound, to shock, to stagger, to surprise.

astronaut cosmonaut, space-traveller.

astronomy 1 SEE **science**. **2** WORDS USED IN ASTRONOMY ARE asteroid, comet, constellation, cosmos, eclipse, galaxy, meteor, meteorite, moon, planet, satellite, shooting star, sun, universe, world.

astute *It was an astute move to bring on a* substitute *at that moment.* artful, clever, crafty, cunning, ingenious, observant, perceptive, shrewd.

asylum *The refugees hoped to find asylum in a neighbouring country.* haven, refuge, retreat, safety, sanctuary, shelter.

asymmetrical lop-sided, unbalanced, uneven.

athletics 1 VARIOUS EVENTS IN ATHLETICS ARE cross-country, decathlon, discus, high jump, hurdles, javelin, long jump, marathon, pentathlon, pole-vault, relay race, running, shot, sprinting, triple jump. **2** SEE **sport**.

atlas SEE **book**.

atmosphere 1 *a stuffy atmosphere.* air. **2** *There was a happy atmosphere at the party.* feeling, mood, tone.

atom 1 molecule, particle. **2** *an atom bomb.* SEE **weapon**.

atrocious *an atrocious terrorist attack.* barbaric, evil, hateful, wicked. SEE ALSO **cruel**.

atrocity crime, outrage.

attach 1 to anchor, to bind, to connect, to fasten, to fix, to join, to link, to secure, to tie, to unite. FOR WAYS OF ATTACHING THINGS SEE **fasten**. **2** *The twins are very attached.* close, fond, friendly, loving.

attack 1 *They launched an attack at dawn.* ambush, assault, blitz, charge, counter-attack, invasion, onslaught, raid. **2** *an attack of coughing.* bout, fit, outbreak, turn. **3** *Logan's gang attacked us for no reason.* to ambush, to assail, to assault, to bombard, to charge, to mug, to raid, to set on, to storm.

attainment achievement, success.

attempt *to attempt to break a record.* to endeavour, to exert yourself, to make an effort, to strive, to try.

attend 1 *Attend to your work.* to concentrate on, to observe, to think about, to watch. **2** *Who will attend to the goldfish while we are away?* to care for, to look after. **3** *Do you attend church?* to go to, to visit.

attention 1 *Give proper attention to your work.* care, concentration, diligence, heed, notice, regard. **2** *Thank you for your attention while I was ill.* consideration, kindness, politeness, thoughtfulness.

attentive *We were attentive because it was an interesting lesson.* alert, observant, thoughtful, vigilant, watchful.

attic loft. SEE ALSO **house**.

attire clothes, clothing, costume, dress, garments.

attitude 1 *Dad didn't like Logan's attitude when he refused to wash up.* behaviour, disposition, manner. **2** *What's your attitude towards smoking?* belief, feeling, opinion, standpoint, thought.

attract 1 *Magnets attract iron.* to draw, to pull. **2** *The old steam engines attracted Mr Brunswick.* to appeal to, to captivate, to entice, to fascinate, to lure.

attractive *an attractive person, an attractive picture, an attractive dress.* alluring, appealing, artistic, bewitching, captivating, charming, (informal) cute, endearing, enticing, fascinating, fetching, good-looking, glamorous, handsome, inviting, lovable, pleasing, pretty, quaint, seductive, tempting. SEE ALSO **beautiful**.

auburn SEE **hair**.

auction SEE **sale**.

audible *an audible voice.* clear, distinct.

audience crowd, spectators.

audio equipment KINDS OF AUDIO EQUIPMENT ARE amplifier, cassette recorder, compact disc player, earphones, gramophone, headphones, hi-fi, high-fidelity equipment, juke-box, loudspeaker, microphone, music centre, pick-up, radio, recorder, record-player, stereo, stylus, tape-recorder, tuner, turntable.

aunt SEE **family**.

au revoir farewell, goodbye.

austere 1 *Dad says his grandfather was*

an austere man. forbidding, hard, harsh, severe, stern, strict. **2** *an austere dress.* plain, simple.

authentic *an authentic antique.* actual, genuine, real, true.

author composer, creator, dramatist, novelist, playwright, poet, scriptwriter, writer. SEE ALSO **writer**.

authority 1 *We've got the head's authority to have a party.* approval, consent, permission. **2** *The police have the authority to stop the traffic.* control, influence, power, right. **3** *Mr Brunswick is an authority on steam trains.* expert, specialist.

authorize 1 *The head authorized the purchase of a new computer.* to agree to, to allow, to approve, to consent to, to permit. **2** *You aren't authorized to buy cigarettes for your dad.* to entitle, to license.

autobiography SEE **writing**.

autograph signature.

automatic 1 *Blinking is an automatic reaction.* impulsive, involuntary, spontaneous, unconscious, unthinking, unintentional. **2** *an automatic dishwasher.* mechanical, programmed. **3** *an automatic machine*: robot. **4** *an automatic weapon.* SEE **weapon**.

automobile car, motor car. SEE ALSO **vehicle**.

auxiliary *auxiliary engines.* additional, helping, supplementary, supporting.

available *There are plenty of books available in the library.* accessible, handy, obtainable, ready.

avalanche SEE **disaster**.

avenue SEE **road**.

average *It was an average sort of day.* common, mediocre, medium, middling, normal, typical, usual. SEE ALSO **ordinary**.

aversion *Tony has an aversion to spiders.* contempt, disgust, dislike, hatred, loathing, revulsion.

avid *Tony is an avid reader.* eager, enthusiastic, fervent, greedy, keen.

avoid *Mr Brunswick will do anything to*

avoid gardening! to dodge, to elude, to escape, to evade, to fend off, to shirk.

awake *A sentry must stay awake.* alert, attentive, conscious, lively, vigilant, watchful.

awaken *The alarm awakened us.* to arouse, to call, to rouse, to wake.

award 1 *They awarded first prize to Lucy.* to give, to hand over, to present. **2** VARIOUS AWARDS ARE badge, cup, decoration, medal, prize, reward, scholarship, trophy.

aware *When cycling, be aware of the traffic.* conscious, observant.

away *away from school.* absent, off.

awe *They watched the erupting volcano with awe.* admiration, fear, respect, reverence, wonder.

awful *Murder is an awful crime.* abominable, appalling, beastly, dreadful, hateful, horrible, nasty, shocking, terrible. SEE ALSO **bad, unpleasant**.

awkward 1 *an awkward machine.* cumbersome, inconvenient, unwieldy. **2** *Tony is awkward with tools.* blundering, clumsy, gawky, ungainly, unskilful. **3** *Are you trying to be awkward?* difficult, unco-operative.

axe chopper. SEE ALSO **tool**.

axle SEE **vehicle**.

azure blue. SEE ALSO **colour**.

B b

babble SEE **talk**.

baboon SEE **animal**.

baby child, infant, toddler. SEE ALSO **person**.

babyish childish, immature, infantile.

bachelor SEE **unmarried**.

back 1 *the back of the train.* end, rear, tail. **2** *the back of the envelope.* reverse. **3** *He backed away.* to move back, to retreat, to reverse, to withdraw. **4** *Will you back our plan?* to aid, to assist, to help, to promote, to second, to sponsor, to subsidize, to support.

backbone spine. SEE ALSO **body**.

backer *We've got a new backer for our team.* promoter, sponsor, supporter.

background *Tell me the background to this affair.* circumstances, setting.

backing *If we go ahead with the plan, will you give us your backing?* aid, assistance, help, sponsorship, subsidy, support.

backside behind, bottom, buttocks, rear, rump.

backstroke SEE **swim**.

backward handicapped, retarded, slow, underdeveloped, undeveloped. ! These words may sound insulting.

bacon gammon, ham, rashers. SEE ALSO **food, meat**.

bacteria (informal) bugs, germs, microbes, viruses.

bad 1 *a bad man, a bad deed, etc.* abhorrent, base, beastly, corrupt, criminal, cruel, deplorable, detestable, evil, immoral, infamous, malevolent, malicious, malignant, mean, naughty, offensive, regrettable, reprehensible, rotten, shameful, sinful, unworthy, vicious, vile, villainous, wicked, wrong. SEE ALSO **cruel**. **2** *a bad accident.* appalling, awful, calamitous, dire, dreadful, frightful, ghastly, hair-raising, hideous, horrible, nasty, serious, severe, shocking, terrible, unfortunate, unpleasant, violent. **3** *a bad performance, a bad piece of work, etc.* abominable, abysmal, appalling, awful, cheap, defective, deficient, dreadful, faulty, feeble, hopeless, imperfect, inadequate, incompetent, incorrect, ineffective, inefficient, inferior, (informal) lousy, pitiful, poor, unsound, useless, weak, worthless. **4** *bad food.* decayed, decomposing, diseased, foul, mildewed, mouldy, polluted, putrid, rotten, smelly, spoiled, tainted. **5** *a bad smell.* loathsome, nauseating, objectionable, obnoxious, odious, offensive, repellent, repulsive, revolting, sickening, vile. **6** *Smoking is bad for you.* damaging, dangerous, destructive, harmful, injurious, unhealthy. **7** *I feel bad today.* diseased, feeble, ill, indisposed, (informal) poorly, queer, sick, unwell. ! *Bad* has many shades of meaning, and these are only some of the other words you could use.

badge *the school badge.* crest, emblem, medal, rosette, sign, symbol.

badger SEE **animal**.

badminton SEE **sport**.

bad-tempered angry, cross, disgruntled, gruff, grumpy, irascible, irritable, moody, morose, peevish, petulant, rude, short-tempered, snappy, sulky, sullen, testy.

baffle 1 *The police were baffled by the strange crime.* to bewilder, to confuse, to frustrate, to perplex, to puzzle. **2** *baffling*: inexplicable, insoluble, mysterious.

bag basket, carrier-bag, case, handbag. SEE ALSO **container**.

baggage *We always have a lot of baggage when we go on holiday.* bags, cases, luggage, suitcases, trunks.

bagpipes SEE **music**.

bait *Logan is always baiting the younger children.* to annoy, to persecute, to pester, to tease, to torment, to worry.

bake 1 SEE **cook**. **2** to harden, to heat.

baker SEE **shop**.

balance 1 *He lost his balance and fell off.* equilibrium, stability, steadiness. **2** *Balance the boat so that it doesn't lean to one side.* to equalize, to even up, to make steady, to make symmetrical. **3** *The chemist weighed the pills on the balance.* scales, weighing-machine.

balcony SEE **building, theatre**.

bald bare, hairless.

balderdash (informal) *He talks a lot of balderdash!* (informal) bilge, drivel, gibberish, nonsense, rubbish, (informal) tripe, (informal) twaddle.

bale *a bale of straw.* bundle.

ball 1 *a glass ball.* globe, sphere. **2** *Cinderella went to a ball.* dance, disco, party, social.

ballad SEE **poem**.

ballerina ballet-dancer, dancer. SEE ALSO **entertainment, theatre**.

ballet SEE **entertainment, theatre**.

balloon SEE **aircraft**.

ballot *We held a ballot to choose the captain.* election, poll, vote.

ball-point pen. SEE ALSO **write**.

balmy *a balmy evening.* gentle, mild, peaceful, pleasant, soothing.

balsa SEE **wood**.

bamboo FOR OTHER PLANTS SEE **plant**.

ban *Some people would like to ban all smoking.* to bar, to forbid, to make illegal, to outlaw, to prevent, to prohibit, to veto.

band 1 *Our football shirts have a white band round the chest.* belt, hoop, line, loop, ribbon, ring, strip, stripe. **2** *a band of robbers.* company, crew, gang, group, horde, troop. **3** *a recorder band.* ensemble, group, orchestra. SEE ALSO **music**.

bandage dressing, lint, plaster. SEE ALSO **medicine**.

bandit brigand, buccaneer, highwayman, hijacker, outlaw, pirate, robber, thief.

bandy-legged SEE **leg**.

bang 1 *a bang on the head.* blow, hit, knock. SEE ALSO **hit**. **2** *a loud bang.* blast, boom, crash, explosion, report. SEE ALSO **sound**.

banger SEE **firework**.

bangle SEE **jewellery**.

banish *They used to banish criminals as a punishment.* to deport, to eject, to exile, to expel, to send away.

banisters SEE **building**.

banjo SEE **music, strings**.

bank 1 *We lay on a grassy bank.* embankment, mound, ridge, shore, slope. **2** *Mum'll give you the money when she's been to the bank.* SEE **shop**. **3** *The plane banked as it turned to land.* to heel, to incline, to lean, to list, to slant, to slope, to tilt.

banker SEE **job**.

banner *waving banners.* colours,

ensign, flag, standard, streamer.

banquet dinner, feast, meal, spread.

bantam SEE **farm, poultry**.

banter teasing.

baptize to christen. SEE ALSO
church.

bar 1 *a wooden bar*. beam, girder, rail,
rod. **2** *a refreshment bar*. café, counter,
pub, saloon. **3** *Logan was barred from
the club because he was too young*. to ban,
to exclude, to keep out, to prohibit.
4 *A fallen tree barred their way*. to
block, to deter, to hinder, to impede,
to obstruct, to prevent, to stop.

barbarian heathen, pagan, savage.
! It is insulting to use these words to
describe people of other nations.

barbaric *a barbaric attack*. atrocious,
cruel, fierce, savage, violent. SEE
ALSO **cruel**.

barbarous *a barbarous tribe*. savage,
uncivilized.

barbecue SEE **cook, meal, party**.

barber hairdresser. SEE ALSO **job,
shop**.

bard minstrel, poet, singer. SEE ALSO
writer.

bare 1 *bare legs, a bare patch*. bald,
naked, nude, unclothed, uncovered,
undressed. **2** *a bare hillside*. barren,
bleak, desolate, windswept. **3** *a bare
room*. empty, plain, unfurnished.
4 *He is not the sort of person to bare his
private thoughts*. to betray, to disclose,
to expose, to reveal, to uncover.

barely hardly, scarcely.

bargain 1 *After some arguing, they made
a bargain*. agreement, arrangement,
contract, deal, understanding. **2** *In
the market people bargain over the prices*.
to argue, to discuss terms, to haggle,
to negotiate.

barge SEE **vessel**.

bark SEE **sound**.

barley SEE **cereal**.

barmaid, barman waiter, waitress.
SEE ALSO **job**.

bar mitzvah SEE **Jew**.

barn SEE **building, farm**.

barnacle SEE **shellfish**.

barometer SEE **weather**.

baron, baroness SEE **title**.

barracks SEE **building**.

barrage 1 gunfire. **2** *a barrage across
the river*. barrier, dam.

barrel cask, tub. SEE ALSO **container**.

barrel-organ SEE **music**.

barren *barren desert*. arid, bare, lifeless,
sterile.

barricade *a barricade across a road*.
barrier, obstacle, obstruction.

barrier 1 *We built a barrier to keep the
spectators off the pitch*. barricade, fence,
hurdle, obstacle, railings, wall.
2 *They built a barrier across the river*.
barrage, dam.

barrister SEE **job, law**.

barrow cart, wheelbarrow.

base 1 *Dad made a concrete base for the
new shed*. basis, bottom, foot,
foundation, rest, stand, support.
2 *The climbers set up a base at the foot of
the mountain*. depot, headquarters.
3 *He based his argument on what he read
in the paper*. to establish, to found, to
set up. **4** *Stealing from old people is a
base crime*. contemptible, cowardly,
depraved, evil, immoral, low, mean,
wicked.

baseball SEE **sport**.

basement cellar, crypt, vault. SEE
ALSO **building**.

bash (informal) *He bashed his head
against a beam*. to bang, to batter, to
beat, to bump, (informal) to clout, to
dash, to hammer, to knock, to
smash, to strike, to thump, to
wallop, to whack. SEE ALSO **hit**.

bashful *There's no need to be so bashful
about getting first prize!* coy, demure,
faint-hearted, modest, reserved, self-
conscious, sheepish, shy, timid,
timorous.

basic *the basic facts*. chief, elementary,
essential, foremost, fundamental,
important, main, primary, principal.

basin bowl, dish. SEE ALSO
container.

basis *What was the basis of your story?*
base, foundation, starting-point.

basket bag. SEE ALSO container.

basketball SEE sport.

bass SEE sing.

bassoon SEE woodwind.

bastard illegitimate. ! Nowadays *bastard* is often insulting, while *illegitimate* is a polite word.

bat 1 *Bats usually fly at dusk.* SEE animal. **2** *You hit the ball with the bat.* club, racket. SEE ALSO sport.

batch *Is there anything good in the latest batch of records?* bunch, collection, consignment, group, set.

bath 1 *a bath of water.* SEE container. **2** *to have a bath.* sauna, shower, wash.

bathe 1 *Tony only bathes when it's really warm.* to go swimming, to swim, to take a dip. **2** *Bathe the wound in clean water.* to clean, to rinse, to swill, to wash.

bathroom 1 THINGS YOU FIND IN A BATHROOM ARE bath, bath mat, bath salts, comb, cosmetics, curlers, extractor fan, flannel, foam bath, hair-drier, medicine cabinet, mirror, nail-brush, nail-scissors, pumice-stone, razor, scales, shampoo, shaver, shower, soap, sponge, taps, tiles, toilet, toilet-roll, toothbrush, towel, towel rail, tweezers, ventilator, wash-basin. **2** SEE house.

baton *a policeman's baton.* cane, club, rod, stick.

battalion SEE armed services.

batter 1 *We battered on the door.* to bang, to bash, to beat, to hammer, to knock, to pound, to strike, to thump. SEE ALSO hit. **2** *fish cooked in batter.* SEE food.

battering-ram SEE weapon.

battery SEE electricity.

battle *Many died in the battle.* action, campaign, clash, combat, conflict, confrontation, encounter, engagement, struggle. SEE ALSO fight.

battle-axe SEE weapon.

battlements SEE building, castle.

battleship SEE vessel.

bawl *Stop bawling: I'm not deaf!* to bellow, to call, to cry, to roar, to scream, to shout, to shriek, to yell. SEE ALSO sound.

bay 1 *The ship sailed into a quiet bay.* cove, estuary, fiord, gulf, inlet. SEE ALSO geography. **2** *the baying of hounds.* SEE sound.

bayonet SEE weapon.

bay window SEE building.

bazaar *We held a bazaar to raise money for our camping trip.* auction, fair, jumble sale, market.

be 1 *Will I still be here in 50 years?* to continue, to exist, to live, to remain, to survive. **2** *When will the next eclipse be?* to happen, to occur, to take place.

beach *a sandy beach.* coast, sands, seaside, shore. SEE ALSO seaside.

beacon SEE warning.

bead 1 *She wore some pretty beads.* SEE jewellery. **2** *There were beads of sweat on her face.* blob, drip, drop.

beagle SEE dog.

beak SEE bird.

beaker *a beaker of water.* SEE container, drink.

beam 1 *That beam holds up the ceiling.* bar, girder, joist, rafter. **2** *a beam of light.* gleam, ray, shaft. **3** *He beamed at us happily.* to grin, to laugh, to smile.

bean SEE food, vegetable.

bear 1 *Will that pillar bear the weight?* to carry, to hold up, to prop up, to support. **2** *The angels bore good tidings.* to bring, to convey. **3** *Lucy's dog bore six puppies.* to give birth to, to produce. **4** *Mrs Brunswick cannot bear the smell of onions.* to abide, to cope with, to endure, to put up with, to stand, to suffer, to tolerate, to undergo. **5** SEE animal.

bearings *We lost our bearings in the fog.* course, direction, position, way.

beast *a wild beast.* animal, brute, creature, monster.

beastly 1 *beastly cruelty.* abominable, brutal, hateful, horrible. SEE ALSO cruel. **2** *beastly weather.* awful, nasty, terrible. SEE ALSO unpleasant.

beat 1 *They beat him mercilessly.* to batter, to cane, (informal) to clout, to flog, to knock about, to lash, to manhandle, to pound, to scourge, to strike, to thrash, to thump, to wallop, to whack, to whip. SEE ALSO **hit**. 2 *The cook beat the mixture until it was creamy.* to agitate, to mix, to stir, to whisk. 3 *Our opponents beat us easily.* to conquer, to crush, to defeat, (informal) to lick, to master, to outdo, to overcome, to overpower, to overthrow, to overwhelm, to rout, to subdue, (informal) to thrash, to vanquish. 4 *Our car could beat yours any day!* to exceed, to excel, to outdo, to surpass, to top, to win against. 5 *This music has a good beat.* pulse, rhythm, throb.

beautiful *a beautiful bride, beautiful embroidery, beautiful scenery, beautiful weather.* admirable, alluring, appealing, artistic, attractive, bewitching, brilliant, captivating, charming, dainty, elegant, exquisite, (old-fashioned) fair, fascinating, fetching, fine, good-looking, glamorous, glorious, gorgeous, graceful, handsome, imaginative, irresistible, lovely, magnificent, neat, picturesque, pleasing, pretty, quaint, radiant, scenic, seductive, spectacular, splendid, superb, tempting. ! The word *beautiful* has many shades of meaning. The words given here are only some of the other words you could use.

beaver SEE **animal**.

beckon SEE **gesture**.

become 1 *Remember that this little puppy will become a big dog!* to change into, to grow into, to turn into. 2 *That dress becomes you.* to be appropriate for, to fit, to suit.

becoming *a becoming dress.* appropriate, apt, attractive, decent, fitting, proper, suitable.

bed 1 bedstead, berth, bunk, divan, four-poster, hammock. SEE ALSO **bedclothes, furniture**. 2 *a flower bed.* border, patch, plot. SEE ALSO **garden**. 3 *the bed of a river.* bottom, course.

bedclothes, bedding THINGS YOU

USE TO MAKE A BED ARE bedspread, blanket, bolster, continental quilt, counterpane, coverlet, duvet, eiderdown, electric blanket, mattress, pillow, pillowcase, pillowslip, quilt, sheet, sleeping-bag.

bedlam *There was absolute bedlam in the classroom by the time Mrs Angel came back.* chaos, hubbub, pandemonium, riot, rumpus, turmoil, uproar. SEE ALSO **commotion**.

bedraggled *We came in from the rain very bedraggled.* dishevelled, scruffy, untidy, wet.

bedridden *The sick woman was bedridden.* infirm. SEE ALSO **ill**.

bedroom SEE **house**.

bedspread SEE **bedclothes**.

bedtime SEE **time**.

bee SEE **insect**.

beech SEE **tree**.

beef, beefburger SEE **meat**.

beefy *The wrestler looked a beefy character.* big, brawny, burly, hefty, muscular, strong, tough.

beer SEE **drink**.

beetle SEE **insect**.

beetroot SEE **salad, vegetable**.

befall *The travellers told us what had befallen them.* to come about, to happen, to occur, to take place.

before earlier, previously, sooner.

beg 1 *It was shameful to see the poor begging for food.* to cadge, to scrounge. 2 *Granny begged us to visit her soon.* to ask, to entreat, to implore, to plead, to request.

beggar *In many countries you see beggars in the street.* destitute person, homeless person, pauper, poor person, ragamuffin, tramp, vagrant.

begin 1 *Mrs Angel always stops trouble as soon as it begins.* to arise, to commence, to start. 2 *Mr Brunswick wants to begin a new business.* to create, to embark on, to found, to initiate, to introduce, to open, to originate, to set up.

beginner apprentice, learner, novice.

beginning 1 *the beginning of life on*

earth. birth, commencement, creation, origin, start. **2** *the beginning of a book*. introduction, opening, preface, prelude, prologue.

begrudge *You don't begrudge him his pocket-money, do you?* to be bitter about, to envy, to resent.

behave *I hope you'll behave well*. to act, to conduct yourself.

behaviour *Mrs Angel said their behaviour had been excellent*. attitude, conduct, manners.

behead to decapitate. SEE ALSO **execute, kill**.

behold (old-fashioned) *He beheld a vision of a golden city*. to discern, to look at, to make out, to see, to witness.

beige SEE **colour**.

being creature.

belated *It was two weeks before we sent belated thanks*. delayed, late.

belch *The factory chimneys belched out filthy smoke*. to discharge, to emit, to erupt, to fume, to send out, to smoke, to vomit.

belfry SEE **church**.

belief *religious beliefs*. attitude, conviction, creed, faith, opinion, religion, thought, trust, view.

believe 1 *You can't believe anything Logan says*. to accept, to have confidence in, to have faith in, to rely on, to trust. **2** *I believe he cheated*. to consider, to feel, to judge, to reckon, to think. **3** *I believe it was you who finished off the chocolates?* to assume, to presume, to suppose.

bell 1 *Didn't you hear the bell?* alarm, signal. **2** VARIOUS WAYS BELLS SOUND ARE to chime, to clang, to jangle, to jingle, to peal, to ping, to ring, to tinkle, to toll.

belligerent *Logan is a belligerent fighter*. aggressive, hostile, martial, militant, pugnacious, warlike.

bellow SEE **sound**.

bellows SEE **blacksmith**.

belly abdomen, stomach, (informal) tummy. SEE ALSO **body**.

belong 1 *This book belongs to me*. to be owned by. **2** *Do you belong to the youth club?* to be a member of.

belongings *Remember to take your belongings when you get off the train*. possessions, property, things.

beloved darling, dearest, loved.

belt 1 *She wore a belt round her waist*. girdle, loop, strap. **2** *The fox made for a belt of trees*. band, line, strip.

bench 1 *a park bench*. form, seat. **2** *a carpenter's bench*. table. SEE ALSO **furniture**.

bend 1 *The blacksmith bent an iron bar*. to arch, to buckle, to coil, to curl, to curve, to distort, to fold, to loop, to turn, to twist, to warp, to wind. **2** *We bent down to go under the low branch*. to bow, to crouch, to duck, to kneel, to stoop. **3** *a bend in the road*. angle, corner, curve, turn, twist.

benediction blessing. SEE ALSO **church**.

benefactor *The benefactor who paid for our new sports gear wants to remain anonymous*. donor, sponsor.

beneficial *They say that garlic is beneficial to your health*. advantageous, constructive, good, healthy, helpful, profitable, useful.

benefit *Clean air is one of the benefits of living in the country*. asset, advantage, blessing, gain, help, privilege, profit.

benevolent *a benevolent old gentleman*. considerate, good, helpful, humane, kindly, merciful, sympathetic, warm-hearted. SEE ALSO **kind**.

bent *a bent nail*. angled, crooked, curved, distorted, twisted, warped.

bequest *Mrs Brunswick received a small bequest from her grandmother's will*. inheritance, legacy.

bereavement *a bereavement in the family*. death, loss.

beret SEE **hat**.

berry SEE **fruit**.

berserk *The dog went berserk when the wasp stung him*. crazy, demented, frantic, frenzied, mad, violent, wild.

berth 1 *There were four berths in each cabin*. bed, bunk. **2** *The ship tied up at* *its berth.* anchorage, dock, landing-stage, moorings, pier, quay, wharf.

besides additionally, also, furthermore, moreover, too.

besiege *The Greeks besieged Troy for 10 long years.* to blockade, to cut off, to encircle, to surround.

bet 1 *People don't often gain anything by betting.* to gamble, to do the pools, to enter a lottery. 2 *How much was your bet?* stake, wager.

betray 1 *to betray someone who trusts you.* to cheat, to double-cross, to let down. 2 *to betray a secret.* to disclose, to divulge, to expose, to reveal.

betrayal disloyalty, treachery, treason.

betrothed engaged.

better *Are you better after your flu?* cured, healed, improved, recovering, recovered, well.

beverage drink. FOR VARIOUS DRINKS SEE **drink**.

bewilder 1 *The different lights bewildered the driver.* to baffle, to confuse, to distract, to muddle, to perplex, to puzzle. 2 *bewildered*: dazed, stunned.

bewitch 1 *The magical atmosphere bewitched us.* to captivate, to charm, to enchant, to fascinate. 2 *bewitched*: entranced, spellbound. 3 *bewitching*: SEE **attractive**.

biased *The referee was biased in favour of their team.* influenced, one-sided, prejudiced, unfair, unjust.

bib SEE **clothes**.

bicycle 1 (informal) bike, cycle, penny-farthing. SEE ALSO **cycle**. 2 PARTS OF A BICYCLE ARE brake, frame, gear, handlebar, pedal, saddle, spoke, wheel.

bid *What will you bid for this watch?* to offer, to propose.

bifocals glasses, spectacles.

big 1 *a big amount, a big person, a big shop, etc.* ample, bulky, colossal, considerable, enormous, extensive, fat, giant, gigantic, grand, great, hefty, high, huge, hulking, husky, immense, immeasurable, incalculable, infinite, large, lofty, mammoth, massive, mighty, monstrous, roomy, sizeable, spacious, substantial, tall, (informal) terrific, towering, tremendous, vast. 2 *a big decision, a big moment, etc.* grave, important, major, momentous, notable, serious, significant, weighty.

bike SEE **cycle**.

bikini SEE **clothes**.

bilge (informal) *Don't talk bilge!* (informal) balderdash, drivel, gibberish, nonsense, rubbish, (informal) tripe, (informal) twaddle.

bilious queasy, sick. SEE ALSO **illness**.

bill 1 *a bird's bill.* beak. SEE ALSO **bird**. 2 *Keep the bill to prove how much you paid.* account, receipt. 3 advertisement, notice, poster.

billiards SEE **game**.

billow *billowing waves.* to bulge, to rise, to swell.

billycan SEE **container, cook**.

billy-goat SEE **male**.

bin SEE **container**.

bind 1 *to bind things together.* to attach, to connect, to join, to secure, to tie. SEE ALSO **fasten**. 2 *to bind a wound.* to cover, to wrap.

bingo SEE **game**.

binoculars field-glasses. SEE ALSO **optical**.

biography SEE **writing**.

biology SEE **science**.

biplane SEE **aircraft**.

birch SEE **tree**.

bird 1 chick, cock, fledgeling, hen, nestling. 2 VARIOUS BIRDS ARE albatross, blackbird, budgerigar, bullfinch, buzzard, canary, chaffinch, chicken, coot, cormorant, crane, crow, cuckoo, curlew, dove, duck, eagle, emu, falcon, finch, flamingo, goldfinch, goose, grouse, gull, hawk, heron, jackdaw, jay, kingfisher, kiwi, lapwing, lark, magpie, nightingale, ostrich, owl, parrot, partridge, peacock, peewit, pelican, penguin, petrel, pheasant, pigeon, plover, puffin, quail, raven, robin, rook, seagull, skylark, sparrow, starling, stork, swallow, swan, swift, thrush, tit, turkey, vulture, wagtail, warbler, woodpecker, wren, yellowhammer. **3** VARIOUS PARTS OF A BIRD ARE beak, bill, claw, crest, down, feather, plumage, tail, talon, wing. **4** SEE **female, male, young**.

birth appearance, beginning, creation, origin, start. SEE ALSO **pregnant**.

biscuit cracker, wafer. FOR OTHER FOODS SEE ALSO **food**.

bishop SEE **church**.

bison SEE **animal**.

bit 1 *a bit of chocolate, a bit of stone, etc.* block, chip, chunk, crumb, dollop, fragment, grain, hunk, lump, morsel, particle, scrap, slab, speck. **2** *I don't need it all, just a bit of it.* division, fraction, helping, part, piece, portion, section, segment, share, slice.

bitch SEE **dog, female**.

bite 1 to chew, to gnaw, to munch, to nip, to snap, to sting. **2** *I'll just have a bite.* morsel, mouthful.

bitter 1 *a bitter smell.* acrid, harsh, sharp, unpleasant. SEE ALSO **taste**. **2** *a bitter experience.* distressing, painful, unhappy. **3** *bitter feelings.* cruel, embittered, envious, jealous, resentful, sour, spiteful. **4** *a bitter quarrel.* angry, vicious, violent. **5** *a bitter wind.* biting, cold, freezing, (informal) perishing, piercing, raw.

black 1 SEE **colour**. **2** *a black night.* dark, inky, pitch-black, sooty, starless, unlit. **3** *a black mood.* bad, depressing, evil, gloomy, sad, sombre, sinister.

black-beetle SEE **insect**.

blackberry bramble. SEE ALSO **fruit**.

blackbird SEE **bird**.

blacken *He blackened his face with soot.* to darken.

blackguard knave, rascal, rogue, scoundrel, villain.

blackmail SEE **crime**.

blacksmith 1 SEE **art, job**. **2** THINGS USED BY A BLACKSMITH ARE anvil, bellows, forge, hammer, tongs.

bladder SEE **body**.

blade *a sharp blade.* edge, knife, razor, sword.

blame 1 *They blamed me, but I didn't do it!* to accuse, to charge, to condemn, to criticize, to denounce, to incriminate, to rebuke, to reprimand, to scold. **2** *Tony admitted that the blame was his.* fault, guilt, responsibility.

blameless guiltless, innocent.

blancmange SEE **food**.

blank 1 *blank paper, a blank tape.* clean, empty, unmarked, unused. **2** *a blank look.* expressionless, vacant.

blanket SEE **bedclothes**.

blare *The trumpets blared.* to bray, to roar, to shriek. SEE ALSO **sound**.

blasphemous *It would be blasphemous to tear up a Bible.* irreverent, sacrilegious, sinful, wicked.

blast 1 *a blast of air.* gale, wind. **2** *a bomb blast.* bang, boom, explosion, noise, report.

blatant *a blatant mistake.* conspicuous, evident, obvious, open, unconcealed, undisguised, unmistakable.

blaze 1 *The fire blazed up.* to burn, to flame, to flare. **2** *The firemen couldn't control the blaze.* conflagration, fire, inferno.

blazer SEE **clothes**.

bleach *The sun bleached our curtains.* to discolour, to fade, to whiten.

bleak *a bleak moor.* bare, barren, cold, desolate, dismal, windswept.

bleat, bleep SEE **sound**.

blemish *There wasn't a blemish in Lucy's work.* blot, defect, fault, flaw, imperfection, mark, spot, stain.

blend *Tony blended the ingredients for his cake.* to combine, to mingle, to mix. SEE ALSO **cook**.

blessed hallowed, holy, sacred.

blessing 1 *The vicar said the blessing.* benediction, grace, prayer. **2** *The fine weather this year is a great blessing to the farmers.* advantage, asset, benefit, comfort, help.

blight affliction, ailment, disease, illness, sickness.

blind 1 sightless, unseeing. SEE ALSO **handicap. 2** *Please close the blind.* curtain, screen, shade, shutters.

blink *blinking lights.* to flicker, to wink.

bliss *It's bliss to have a nice hot bath!* delight, ecstasy, happiness, joy, pleasure, rapture.

blister SEE **illness**.

blitz attack, onslaught, raid.

blizzard SEE **weather**.

bloated *The pictures of starving children with bloated stomachs horrified us.* distended, swollen.

blob *a blob of paint.* bead, drop, spot.

block 1 *a block of ice-cream.* brick, chunk, hunk, lump, slab. **2** *The drain was blocked with leaves.* to bung up, to clog, to fill, to jam, to stop up. **3** *An overturned lorry blocked our way.* to bar, to barricade, to deter, to hamper, to hinder, to hold back, to impede, to obstruct, to prevent, to prohibit.

blockade siege.

blockage *a blockage in a drain.* block, hindrance, impediment, obstacle, obstruction.

blockhead ass, dope, dunce, half-wit, idiot, ignoramus, imbecile, moron, nit, nitwit, twerp. | These words are insulting.

bloke (informal) fellow, guy, man.

blond, blonde *blond hair.* fair, light. SEE ALSO **hair**. | A man is *blond*; a woman is *blonde*.

blood SEE **body**.

bloodhound SEE **dog**.

bloodshed carnage, killing, massacre, murder, slaughter.

bloodthirsty brutal, ferocious, fierce, inhuman, murderous, pitiless, ruthless, savage, vicious, violent. SEE ALSO **cruel**.

bloody blood-stained, gory.

bloom *Most flowers bloom in summer.* to blossom, to flourish, to flower.

blossom to bloom, to flower.

blot 1 *a blot of ink.* blotch, spot, stain. **2** *a blot on the landscape.* blemish,

eyesore. **3** *Look out, you've made me blot the page!* to mar, to mark, to smudge, to spoil, to stain. **4** *The fog blotted out the view.* to conceal, to cover, to erase, to hide, to mask, to rub out, to wipe out.

blow 1 *The wind blew.* to puff, to whistle. **2** *The tyres need blowing up.* to inflate. **3** *The bomb blew up.* to burst, to detonate, to explode, to go off. **4** *The falling branch gave him a nasty blow on the head.* bang, bump, hit, knock. **5** *It was a terrible blow when s lost her purse.* bombshell, jolt, shock, surprise.

blubber *Stop blubbering and help me clea up!* to cry, to snivel, to sob, to wail, to weep.

blue 1 SEE **colour**. **2** *I'm feeling blue today.* dejected, depressed, gloomy, melancholy, unhappy.

bluebell SEE **flower**.

bluebottle SEE **insect**.

blues SEE **music**.

bluff *Don't believe Logan: he's only bluffing.* to deceive, to fool, to hoax, to hoodwink, (informal) to kid, to lie, to mislead, to pretend, to take in, to trick.

blunder 1 *to blunder about.* to stagger, to stumble. **2** *to make a blunder.* (informal) clanger, error, (informal) howler, mistake, (informal) slip-up. **3** *blundering:* awkward, bungling, clumsy, gawky, lumbering, ungainly.

blunderbuss SEE **weapon**.

blunt 1 *a blunt knife.* dull, unsharpened, worn. **2** *a blunt reply.* abrupt, candid, curt, direct, frank, honest, impolite, outspoken, plain, rude, straight, straightforward.

blurred *a blurred photograph.* cloudy, confused, dim, faint, fuzzy, hazy, indistinct, misty, unclear.

blurt SEE **talk**.

blush to colour, to flush, to glow, to redden.

blustery *blustery weather.* gusty, squally, windy. SEE ALSO **weather**.

boa-constrictor SEE **snake**.

boar SEE **animal, male**.

board 1 *wooden boards.* plank, timber.
2 *to board a ship.* to embark. **3** *He boards in a hotel.* to live, to lodge.

boarder guest, lodger, resident, tenant.

boast *People who boast are usually unpopular.* to brag, to crow, to gloat, to show off, to swank.

boastful arrogant, conceited, haughty, proud, (informal) stuck-up.

boat craft, ship. SEE ALSO **vessel**.

boat-house SEE **building**.

bobsleigh SEE **sport**.

bodice SEE **clothes**.

body 1 *Doctors have to know about the body.* anatomy. **2** *The body of the dead animal was burned.* carcass, corpse, remains. **3** *The boxer aimed blows at his opponent's body.* trunk. **4** PARTS OF YOUR BODY ARE abdomen, adenoids, ankle, appendix, arm, artery, backbone, belly, bladder, blood, bone, bowels, brain, breast, buttocks, calf, cheek, chest, chin, ear, elbow, eye, finger, foot, forehead, funny-bone, gland, gullet, gums, guts, hand, head, heart, heel, hip, intestines, jaw, kidney, knee, knee-cap, knuckle, leg, limb, lip, liver, lung, marrow, mouth, muscle, navel, neck, nerve, nipple, nose, nostril, pores, rib, saliva, scalp, shin, shoulder, shoulder-blade, skeleton, skin, skull, spine, stomach, thigh, throat, thumb, toe, tongue, tonsils, tooth, trunk, vein, vertebra, waist, windpipe, womb, wrist.

bodyguard *The President always has a bodyguard.* guard, protector.

bog *Don't get stuck in the bog.* fen, marsh, quagmire, quicksands, swamp.

bogie SEE **railway**.

bogus *a bogus £5 note.* counterfeit, faked, false, feigned, (informal) phoney, pretended.

boil 1 *It's uncomfortable to have a boil on your bottom.* abscess, inflammation, sore. SEE ALSO **illness**. **2** *Are the*

potatoes boiling yet? to bubble, to seethe, to simmer, to stew. SEE ALSO **cook**.

boisterous *boisterous behaviour.* animated, disorderly, irrepressible, lively, noisy, obstreperous, rough, rowdy, unruly, wild.

bold 1 *a bold adventure, a bold explorer.* adventurous, brave, courageous, daring, enterprising, fearless, heroic, intrepid, self-confident, valiant. **2** *It was a bit bold to ask for a day off school.* brazen, cheeky, forward, impertinent, impudent, insolent, presumptuous, rude, shameless. **3** *bold writing.* big, clear, large.

bolster cushion, pillow. SEE ALSO **bedclothes**.

bolt 1 *Dad fixed a bolt on the door.* bar, catch, latch, lock. **2** *We bolt the door when we go out.* to close, to fasten, to lock, to secure. **3** *The animals have bolted!* to escape, to flee, to run away. **4** *Don't bolt your food.* to gobble, to gulp. SEE ALSO **eat**.

bomb SEE **weapon**.

bombard *They bombarded us with missiles.* to assail, to assault, to attack, to fire at, to pelt, to shell, to shoot at.

bomber SEE **aircraft**.

bombshell *The £100 prize came as a complete bombshell!* shock, surprise.

bond 1 *The prisoner couldn't undo his bonds.* chain, cord, fetters, handcuffs, rope, shackles. **2** *There is usually a strong bond between twins.* connection, link, relationship.

bondage slavery.

bone SEE **body**.

bonnet 1 *the bonnet of a car.* SEE **vehicle**. **2** *a woolly bonnet.* cap, hat. SEE ALSO **hat**.

bonus *At Christmas mum gives us a bonus on top of our normal pocket-money.* addition, extra, supplement.

boo to hoot, to jeer. SEE ALSO **sound**.

booby trap ambush, snare, trap.

book 1 publication, volume. **2** KINDS OF BOOK ARE album, annual, anthology, atlas, booklet, diary, dictionary, encyclopaedia, fiction, hardback, hymn-book, manual, manuscript, omnibus, paperback, reference book, scrap-book, scroll, textbook. SEE ALSO **magazine, writing**. 3 PARTS OF A BOOK ARE chapter, epilogue, index, introduction, preface, prologue, title. 4 *Have you booked tickets for the pantomime?* to order, to reserve.

bookcase SEE **furniture**.

booklet book, brochure, leaflet, pamphlet.

bookmaker SEE **job**.

boom bang, blast, crash, explosion. SEE ALSO **sound**.

boomerang SEE **weapon**.

boost *Winning a race boosts your morale.* to encourage, to help, to improve, to increase, to raise.

boot, bootee SEE **shoe**.

booth *a telephone booth, a voting booth.* compartment, cubicle, kiosk, stall, stand.

booty *The thieves dropped their booty as they escaped.* contraband, loot, plunder, (informal) swag, takings, trophies.

booze SEE **alcohol**.

border 1 *We showed our passports at the border.* boundary, frontier. 2 *We put a colourful border round the edge.* edging, frame, frieze, frill, fringe, hem, margin, verge. 3 *a flower border.* bed. SEE ALSO **garden**.

bore 1 *to bore a hole.* to drill, to penetrate, to perforate, to pierce. 2 *The long speech bored most of the audience.* to tire, to weary.

boring *a boring book, boring work, etc.* arid, commonplace, dreary, dry, dull, flat, long-winded, monotonous, tedious, unexciting, uninteresting, wordy.

borrow *Can I borrow your pen?* to be lent, to use.

Borstal SEE **punishment**.

bosom breast, chest, heart.

boss *Who's the boss here?* chief, controller, director, employer, foreman, governor, head, leader, manager, master, proprietor, ruler, superintendent, supervisor.

bossy *You may be captain, but don't get bossy!* dictatorial, domineering, masterful, tyrannical.

botany SEE **science**.

bother 1 *There was some bother in the playground at dinner time.* ado, commotion, disorder, disturbance, fuss, to-do. SEE ALSO **commotion**. 2 *Is the dog a bother to you?* inconvenience, nuisance, trouble, worry. 3 *Are the wasps bothering you?* to annoy, to disturb, to exasperate, to irritate, to molest, to pester, to plague, to trouble, to upset, to vex, to worry. 4 *Don't bother to wash up.* to care, to mind.

bottle SEE **container**.

bottom 1 *the bottom of a wall.* base, foot, foundation. 2 *The wasp stung me on the bottom.* backside, behind, buttocks, rear, rump. 3 *the bottom of the sea.* bed, depths.

bough *a bough of a tree.* branch, limb.

boulder *The beach was strewn with large boulders.* rock, stone.

bounce *The ball bounced over the fence.* to bound, to jump, to rebound, to recoil, to ricochet, to spring.

bound 1 *Grandpa is bound to be here soon.* certain, compelled, obliged, required, sure. 2 *The rocket was bound for the moon.* aimed at, destined for, directed towards. 3 *He bounded over the fence.* to bounce, to hop, to jump, to leap, to skip, to spring, to vault.

boundary *A fence marked the boundary.* border, circumference, edge, frontier, limit, margin, perimeter.

boundless *Lucy has boundless energy.* endless, everlasting, limitless, unlimited, unrestricted.

bounty *Millionaires are not always known for their bounty.* charity, generosity.

bouquet *a bouquet of flowers.* arrangement, bunch, posy, spray, wreath.

bout 1 *a boxing bout.* combat, contest,

fight, match, round. 2 *a bout of coughing.* attack, fit, turn.

boutique SEE **shop.**

bow 1 *bows and arrows.* SEE **weapon.** 2 *Tie it in a bow.* SEE **knot.** 3 *the bow of a ship.* SEE **vessel.** 4 *They bowed before the queen.* to bend, to curtsy, to stoop.

bowels SEE **body.**

bowl 1 *a bowl of soup.* basin. SEE ALSO. **container.** 2 *He bowled a faster ball.* to fling, to hurl, to lob, to pitch, to throw, to toss.

bow-legged SEE **leg.**

bowler 1 SEE **cricket.** 2 SEE **hat.**

bowls SEE **game.**

box 1 carton, case, chest, crate. SEE ALSO **container.** 2 *boxing:* SEE **fight, sport.**

box-office SEE **theatre.**

boy (insulting) brat, lad, (insulting) urchin, youngster, youth. SEE ALSO **person.**

bra SEE **underclothes.**

brace couple, pair.

bracelet SEE **jewellery.**

braces SEE **clothes.**

bracket SEE **punctuation.**

brag *Even if you did win, don't brag about it.* to boast, to crow, to gloat, to show off, to swank.

braid *She decorated the hem of her skirt with red braid.* band, ribbon.

brain 1 SEE **body.** 2 *Use your brains!* intellect, intelligence, reason, sense, understanding, wisdom, wit.

brainwash *People can be brainwashed by advertising.* to indoctrinate.

brainwave (informal) SEE **idea.**

brainy *Tony is the brainy one in the family.* academic, bright, clever, intellectual, intelligent.

brake SEE **vehicle.**

bramble blackberry.

bran SEE **food.**

branch 1 *the branch of a tree.* arm, bough, limb. 2 *a branch of the bank.* department, part, office, section. 3 *The road branches a short distance from here.* to divide, to fork.

brand 1 *What brand of margarine do you buy?* kind, make, trademark. 2 *The farmer brands his cattle with a hot iron.* to mark, to stamp.

brandish *He brandished his umbrella to catch our attention.* to flourish, to shake, to twirl, to wave.

brandy SEE **drink.**

brass 1 *a brass door-knob.* SEE **metal.** 2 BRASS INSTRUMENTS ARE bugle, cornet, horn, trombone, trumpet, tuba. SEE ALSO **music.**

brat SEE **child.**

brave *She was brave to go back into the burning house.* adventurous, bold, courageous, daring, fearless, gallant, heroic, intrepid, noble, plucky, spirited, undaunted, valiant.

bravery *Everyone praised her bravery.* courage, daring, determination, fortitude, (informal) grit, (informal) guts, heroism, nerve, pluck, prowess, spirit, valour.

brawl *There was a brawl outside the football ground.* clash, confrontation, fight, quarrel, row, scrap, scuffle, squabble, struggle, tussle.

brawny *That weight-lifter looks a brawny fellow.* beefy, burly, muscular, strong, tough.

bray SEE **sound.**

brazen *It was brazen to march up to the prince and ask for a kiss!* bold, cheeky, forward, impertinent, impudent, insolent, rude, shameless.

breach *a breach in the sea wall.* break, crack, gap, hole, opening, space, split.

bread loaf, roll. SEE ALSO **food.**

break 1 *to break an egg, to break a leg, to break down a wall.* to burst, to chip, to crack, to crumple, to crush, to damage, to demolish, to destroy, to fracture, to knock down, to ruin, to shatter, to smash, to splinter, to split, to squash, to wreck. 2 *The sandcastle broke up.* to collapse, to crumble, to decay, to deteriorate, to disintegrate, to fall apart, to tumble down. 3 *Did he break the law?* to disobey, to disregard, to infringe, to violate. **4** *There was a break in the pipe.* breach, chink, crack, cut, gap, gash, hole, leak, opening, rift, slit, split, tear. **5** *We ran home in a break between the showers.* interlude, interval, lapse, lull, pause, respite, rest.

breaker *The breakers crashed on the shore.* surf, waves.

breakfast SEE **meal**.

breakneck *breakneck speed.* dangerous, hasty, headlong, suicidal.

breast bosom. SEE ALSO **body**.

breast-stroke SEE **swim**.

breathless *Lucy was breathless after her race.* exhausted, gasping, panting, tired out.

breathe *Don't breathe the fumes.* to inhale.

breech *the breech of a gun.* SEE **gun**.

breeches SEE **clothes**.

breed **1** *Lucy's mice bred rapidly.* to increase, to multiply, to produce young, to reproduce. **2** *What breed of dog is that?* kind, species, variety.

breeze *a cool breeze.* air, draught, wind.

breezy airy, draughty, fresh, windy.

brew SEE **cook**.

brewer SEE **job**.

bribe *You mustn't try to bribe the judge.* to corrupt, to entice, to influence, to pervert, to tempt.

brick block. SEE ALSO **building**.

bricklayer SEE **job**.

bride, bridegroom, bridesmaid SEE **wedding**.

bridge **1** KINDS OF BRIDGE ARE aqueduct, fly-over, suspension bridge, viaduct. **2** *the bridge of a ship.* SEE **vessel**. **3** *Can you play bridge?* SEE **cards**.

bridle SEE **horse**.

brief **1** *We paid a brief visit to granny.* little, momentary, passing, short, temporary, transient. **2** *He gave me a brief summary of the story.* abbreviated, abridged, compact, concise, condensed, terse.

briefs knickers, panties, pants, shorts,

trunks, underpants. SEE ALSO **underclothes**.

brigade SEE **armed services**.

brigand bandit, buccaneer, desperado, gangster, highwayman, outlaw, pirate, robber, thief.

bright **1** *bright colours, bright lights, a bright day, etc.* brilliant, clear, flashy, gaudy, gleaming, radiant, resplendent, shining, shiny, showy, sparkling, sunny, vivid. SEE ALSO **light**. **2** *a bright manner, a bright voice.* animated, cheerful, happy, lively. **3** *a bright idea, a bright pupil.* brainy, clever, ingenious, intelligent, quick, shrewd, (informal) smart.

brighten *We need to brighten this gloomy place up.* to cheer up, to illuminate, to lighten, to light up.

brilliant **1** *brilliant lights.* bright, dazzling, gleaming, glittering, resplendent, shining, sparkling. SEE ALSO **light**. **2** *a brilliant scientist.* brainy, clever, gifted, intelligent, marvellous, outstanding, talented, wonderful. **3** (informal) *Their playing was brilliant today.* SEE **excellent**.

brim *The reservoir was full to the brim.* brink, edge, rim, top.

brimming full, overflowing.

bring **1** *Mrs Brunswick asked Tony to bring the shopping.* to carry, to fetch, to take. **2** *A change in the wind will bring snow.* to cause, to create, to generate, to give rise to, to induce, to lead to, to provoke. **3** *We are planning to bring out a new magazine.* to introduce, to issue, to produce, to publish, to release, to start. **4** *Parents have to bring up their children.* to care for, to educate, to look after, to raise, to rear, to train.

brink *He stood on the brink of the pool.* brim, edge, rim.

brisk *You need some brisk exercise.* animated, energetic, fast, lively, quick, rapid, speedy, sprightly.

bristle hair.

brittle *Eggshell is extremely brittle.* breakable, crisp, fragile, frail.

broad 1 *a broad path.* wide. **2** *a broad plain.* expansive, extensive, large. **3** *a broad outline of a story.* general, imprecise, indefinite, vague.

broadcast 1 *to broadcast a concert.* to relay, to send out, to transmit, to televise. **2** *broadcasting*: SEE **communication**.

brochure *We got a brochure from the travel agent.* booklet, catalogue, leaflet, pamphlet, prospectus.

brogue 1 SEE **shoe**. **2** *an Irish brogue.* accent, dialect, language.

bronchitis SEE **illness**.

bronze SEE **metal**.

brooch clasp. SEE ALSO **jewellery**.

brood 1 *a brood of chicks.* family, litter. SEE ALSO **group**. **2** *It's no use brooding about past mistakes.* to meditate, to mope, to ponder, to reflect, to sulk, to think.

brook burn, stream.

broom 1 brush. **2** SEE **shrub**.

broth SEE **food**.

brother SEE **family**.

brown SEE **colour**.

brownie SEE **legend**.

bruise to damage, to injure. SEE ALSO **wound**.

brunette SEE **hair**.

brush 1 broom. FOR OTHER HOUSEHOLD TOOLS SEE **house**. **2** *Brush out the garage when you have finished your woodwork.* to clean, to sweep.

Brussels sprouts SEE **vegetable**.

brutal *a brutal murder.* atrocious, beastly, bloodthirsty, ferocious, inhuman, murderous, pitiless, ruthless, savage, vicious, violent. SEE ALSO **cruel**.

brute animal, beast, creature.

bubble 1 *soap bubbles.* foam, froth, lather, suds. **2** *The water was bubbling.* to boil, to fizz, to fizzle, to foam, to froth, to seethe.

bubbly *bubbly drinks.* effervescent, fizzy, foaming, sparkling.

buccaneer bandit, brigand, highwayman, marauder, outlaw, pirate, robber.

buck 1 *a buck rabbit.* SEE **male**. **2** (informal) *Buck up!* SEE **hurry**.

bucket pail. SEE ALSO **container**.

buckle 1 *the buckle of a belt.* clasp, fastener, fastening. **2** *The framework buckled under the heavy weight.* to bend, to collapse, to crumple, to curve, to dent, to distort, to twist, to warp.

bud SEE **plant**.

Buddhist SEE **religion**.

budge *The stubborn donkey wouldn't budge.* to move, to shift.

budgerigar SEE **bird, pet**.

buffalo SEE **animal**.

buffer SEE **railway**.

buffet 1 *We went to the buffet for a snack.* bar, café, cafeteria, snack-bar. **2** *Mrs Brunswick made a buffet for Lucy's party.* SEE **meal**.

bug (informal) **1** *There are bugs on these roses.* insect. **2** *Tony has a bug which makes him feel poorly.* SEE **bacteria, illness**. **3** *a bug in a computer program.* error, fault, mistake.

bugle SEE **brass**.

build 1 *Tony builds models.* to assemble, to construct, to erect, to make, to put together, to put up. **2** *Mr Brunswick is beginning to build up his business.* to develop, to enlarge, to expand, to increase, to strengthen.

builder SEE **job**.

building 1 construction, edifice, structure. **2** KINDS OF BUILDING ARE abbey, arcade, art gallery, barn, barracks, boat-house, bungalow, cabin, castle, cathedral, chapel, château, church, cinema, complex, cottage, crematorium, dovecote, factory, farmhouse, filling station, flats, garage, granary, gymnasium, hall, hotel, house, inn, library, lighthouse, mansion, mill, minaret, monastery, mosque, museum, observatory, orphanage, outhouse, pagoda, palace, pavilion, pier, pigsty, police station, post office, power-station, prison, pub, public house, restaurant, shed, shop, silo, skyscraper, slaughterhouse, stable, studio, synagogue, temple, theatre, tower, villa, warehouse, waterworks, windmill, woodshed. SEE ALSO **house, shop. 3** PARTS OF BUILDINGS ARE arch, balcony, banisters, basement, battlements, bay window, belfry, bow window, brickwork, buttress, ceiling, cellar, chimney, cloisters, courtyard, crypt, dome, drawbridge, dungeon, eaves, floor, foundations, foyer, gable, gallery, gateway, gutter, joist, keep, lobby, masonry, parapet, porch, portcullis, quadrangle, rafter, rampart, roof, room, sill, spire, staircase, steeple, tower, turret, vault, veranda, wall, window, window-sill. **4** MATERIALS USED IN BUILDING ARE asbestos, asphalt, brick, cement, concrete, fibreglass, glass, hardboard, metal, mortar, plaster, plastic, plywood, slate, stone, tile, timber, wood.

bulb 1 *an electric bulb.* lamp, light. **2** FLOWERS THAT GROW FROM BULBS ARE bluebell, crocus, daffodil, hyacinth, lily, snowdrop, tulip. SEE ALSO **flower, plant.**

bulge 1 *What's that bulge in the middle of the new carpet?* bump, hump, knob, lump, swelling. **2** *The shopping bag was bulging with interesting shapes.* to billow, to protrude, to stick out, to swell.

bulk *The bulk of the airship amazed us.* largeness, magnitude, size, volume.

bull SEE **cattle, farm, male.**

bulldog SEE **dog.**

bulldozer SEE **vehicle.**

bullet SEE **ammunition.**

bulletin *a news bulletin.* announcement, communiqué, dispatch, notice, proclamation, report, statement.

bullfight 1 *bullfighting:* SEE **sport. 2** *a bullfighter:* matador, toreador.

bullfinch SEE **bird.**

bullock SEE **cattle, young.**

bull's-eye 1 *to hit the bull's-eye.* centre, target. **2** SEE **sweet.**

bully *Logan sometimes bullies younger children.* to frighten, to intimidate, to

persecute, to terrorize, to threaten, to torment.

bumble-bee SEE **insect.**

bump 1 *Mr Brunswick had a bump in the car.* blow, collision, crash, hit, knock. **2** *How did you get that bump on the head?* bulge, hump, lump, swelling. **3** *He bumped us deliberately.* to bang, to collide with, to crash into, to jolt, to knock, to ram, to strike, to thump, to wallop. SEE ALSO **hit.**

bumper SEE **vehicle.**

bumptious *The man next door has got bumptious since he was promoted.* arrogant, boastful, cocky, conceited, officious, self-important.

bumpy *a bumpy road.* irregular, rough, uneven.

bun SEE **cake.**

bunch 1 *a bunch of carrots, a bunch of friends.* batch, bundle, clump, cluster, collection, crowd, gathering, group, pack, set. **2** *a bunch of flowers.* bouquet, posy, spray.

bundle *a bundle of waste paper.* bale, bunch, collection, package, parcel, sheaf.

bung *Who took the bung out of the barrel?* cork, plug, stopper.

bungalow SEE **building, house.**

bungle *Trust Logan to bungle the job!* to mess up, to spoil.

bunk bed, berth. SEE ALSO **furniture.**

burden 1 *to carry a burden.* load, weight. **2** *It may help to share your burdens.* problem, trouble, worry.

bureau 1 desk. SEE ALSO **furniture.** **2** *an information bureau.* office.

burglar intruder, robber, thief. SEE ALSO **criminal.**

burial SEE **funeral.**

burly *a burly figure.* beefy, big, brawny, hefty, husky, muscular, strong, tough.

burn 1 VARIOUS WAYS THINGS BURN ARE to blaze, to flame, to flare, to smoulder. **2** WAYS TO BURN THINGS ARE to char, to cremate, to ignite, to kindle, to light, to scald, to scorch, to set fire to, to singe. **3** SEE ALSO **fire.** **4** *a Scottish burn.* brook, stream.

burnished *burnished brass.* polished, shiny.

burrow 1 *a rabbit's burrow.* hole, tunnel, warren. 2 *The rabbits burrowed under the fence.* to dig, to excavate, to tunnel.

burst *The tyre burst. They burst open the door. They burst into laughter.* to blow out, to break, to erupt, to explode, to force open.

bury to conceal, to cover, to hide.

bus SEE **vehicle**.

bush SEE **shrub**.

business 1 *The new shop is doing a lot of business.* buying and selling, commerce, industry, trade. 2 *What sort of business do you want to go into?* calling, career, employment, job, occupation, profession, trade, work. 3 *Mr Brunswick worked for a sports equipment business.* company, concern, corporation, establishment, firm, organization. 4 *It's none of your business.* affair, concern, matter.

busy 1 *Mum is busy in the garden.* active, diligent, employed, engaged, industrious, involved, occupied. 2 *It's busy in town on Saturdays.* bustling, frantic, hectic, lively.

busybody *to be a busybody:* SEE **interfere**.

butane SEE **fuel**.

butcher SEE **shop**.

butler SEE **servant**.

butt 1 *a rifle butt.* SEE **gun**. 2 *a water butt.* SEE **container**. 3 *The goat butted her.* to bump, to knock, to strike, to thump. SEE ALSO **hit**. 4 *Please don't butt in.* to interfere, to interrupt, to intervene, to intrude, to meddle.

butter SEE **fat**.

buttercup SEE **flower**.

butterfingers SEE **clumsy**.

butterfly SEE **insect**.

butterscotch SEE **sweet**.

buttocks backside, behind, bottom, rear, rump.

button *Button your coat!* SEE **fasten**.

buttress SEE **building**.

buy to acquire, to gain, to get, to get on hire purchase, to obtain, to pay for, to procure, to purchase.

buzz SEE **sound**.

buzzard SEE **bird**.

by-law SEE **regulation**.

bypass SEE **road**.

bystander *The police asked the bystanders to describe the accident.* eyewitness, observer, onlooker, passer-by, spectator, witness.

C c

cab taxi. SEE ALSO **vehicle**.

cabaret SEE **entertainment**.

cabbage SEE **vegetable**.

cabin SEE **building**.

cabinet 1 *a china cabinet.* SEE **furniture**. 2 SEE **government**.

cable 1 *an anchor cable.* chain, cord, hawser, line, rope. 2 *an electric cable.* flex, lead, wire. 3 *They sent a cable to say they'd arrive tomorrow.* telegram, wire.

cable television SEE **communication**.

cache *a cache of arms.* depot, dump, hoard, stores.

cackle SEE **sound**.

cactus SEE **plant**.

cadge *The cat from next door always cadges food from us.* to beg, to scrounge.

café bar, buffet, cafeteria, canteen, restaurant, snack-bar.

cage *an animal's cage.* coop, enclosure, hutch, pen.

cagoule SEE **clothes**.

cake 1 KINDS OF CAKES ARE bun, doughnut, éclair, flan, fruit cake, gingerbread, meringue, scone, shortbread, sponge, tart. 2 SEE ALSO **food**.

caked *caked with mud.* dirty, muddy.

calamitous *Setting sail today was a calamitous mistake.* dire, disastrous, dreadful, serious, terrible, tragic, unfortunate, unlucky.

calamity *The hotel fire was a terrible calamity.* accident, catastrophe, disaster, misadventure, misfortune, mishap, tragedy.

calculate *Calculate how many sandwiches we need for the party.* to add up, to assess, to compute, to estimate, to figure out, to reckon, to total, to work out.

calendar FOR SPECIAL TIMES OF THE YEAR SEE **time**.

calf 1 *a new-born calf.* SEE **cattle, young**. 2 *My calves ache after that running.* SEE **body, leg**.

call 1 *Did you hear someone call?* to cry out, to exclaim, to shout, to yell. 2 *The head called Lucy to his office.* to summon. 3 *I couldn't call because the phone was out of order.* to dial, to phone, to ring, to telephone. 4 *When did granny call?* to drop in, to visit. 5 *On Saturdays mum calls us at nine o'clock.* to arouse, to awaken, to rouse, to wake up. 6 *What did they call the baby?* to baptize, to christen, to name. 7 *What will you call your story?* to entitle.

calling *What was grandpa's calling in life?* business, career, employment, job, occupation, profession, trade.

callous *a callous murder.* cold-blooded, hard-hearted, heartless, insensitive, merciless, pitiless, ruthless, unfeeling. SEE ALSO **cruel**.

calm 1 *calm water.* even, flat, motionless, placid, smooth, still. 2 *a calm mood.* peaceful, quiet, sedate, serene, tranquil, untroubled. 3 *Keep calm!* cool, level-headed, patient, sensible. 4 *He was upset and it took ages to calm him.* to appease, to lull, to pacify, to quieten, to soothe.

calypso SEE **music**.

camel dromedary. SEE ALSO **animal**.

camera SEE **photography**.

camouflage *We camouflaged our hide-out.* to conceal, to cover up, to disguise, to hide, to mask, to screen.

camp SEE **holiday**.

campaign *We fought a campaign to save our playing-fields.* action, battle, crusade, fight, operation, struggle, war.

campus *the school campus.* grounds, site.

can 1 *a can of beans.* tin. 2 *They can most of the peas they grow at the farm.* SEE **preserve**.

canal channel, waterway.

canary SEE **bird, pet**.

cancel 1 *We cancelled the game because of the snow.* to abandon, to give up, to postpone, to scrap. 2 *They cancelled our order.* to cross out, to delete, to erase, to wipe out.

cancer SEE **illness**.

candid *Give me a candid answer.* direct, frank, honest, open, outspoken, plain, straightforward.

candidate *a candidate for an exam.* applicant, competitor, entrant.

candle SEE **light**.

candy SEE **sweet**.

cane 1 *Mrs Brunswick put up some canes for her runner beans.* rod, stick. 2 *to give someone the cane.* SEE **punishment**.

canister SEE **container**.

cannon SEE **weapon**.

canoe SEE **vessel**.

canteen *Let's have a snack in the canteen.* buffet, café, cafeteria, restaurant, snack-bar.

canter SEE **horse, move**.

canvas SEE **cloth**.

canyon *a deep canyon.* defile, gorge, pass, ravine, valley. SEE ALSO **geography**.

cap 1 *Boys don't usually wear caps these days.* SEE **hat**. 2 *Where's the cap off the ketchup bottle?* cover, covering, lid, top.

capable *Lucy is a capable organizer.* able, accomplished, clever, competent, efficient, gifted, handy, practical, proficient, skilful, skilled, talented.

capacity 1 *the capacity of a container.* size, volume. 2 *It isn't within my capacity to run one hundred metres in ten seconds.* ability, capability, competence, skill, talent.

cape SEE **clothes**.

caper *The lambs capered about the field.* to dance, to frisk, to jump, to leap, to play, to prance, to romp, to skip.

capital 1 *Paris is the capital of France.* SEE **geography**. **2** *Mr Brunswick needs more capital to start his new business.* funds, money, property, riches, savings, wealth.

capitulate *The town capitulated after a long siege.* to give in, to submit, to surrender, to yield.

capsize *The boat capsized.* to overturn, to tip over, to turn over, to turn turtle.

capsule 1 *The doctor gave her some capsules for her rheumatism.* pill, tablet. SEE ALSO **medicine**. **2** *a space capsule.* SEE **space**.

captain *the captain of a ship.* commander, master, skipper. SEE ALSO **chief**.

caption *Write a caption under your picture.* heading, headline, title.

captivate 1 *The kittens captivated us.* to attract, to bewitch, to charm, to delight, to enchant, to entrance, to fascinate. **2** *captivating*: SEE **attractive**.

captive *They guarded their captives closely.* convict, hostage, prisoner.

capture *Did they capture the thief?* to arrest, to catch, to corner, (informal) to nab, to seize, to take.

car automobile, motor car. SEE ALSO **vehicle**.

caravan SEE **vehicle**.

carbon SEE **chemical**.

carburettor SEE **vehicle**.

carcass *the carcass of an animal.* body, corpse, remains.

card 1 cardboard. SEE ALSO **paper**. **2** *a game of cards.* SEE **cards**.

cardigan SEE **clothes**.

cardinal SEE **church**.

cards 1 playing-cards. **2** CARD GAMES ARE bridge, patience, pontoon, rummy, snap, whist. **3** SUITS ARE club, diamond, heart, spade. **4** VALUES ARE ace, jack, joker, king, knave, number 2 to 10, queen. **5** SEE ALSO **game**.

care 1 *We should care about the starving.* to bother, to concern yourself, to mind, to trouble, to worry. **2** *He cares for his dog.* to attend to, to cherish, to guard, to keep, to look after, to mind, to mother, to protect, to tend, to watch over. **3** *Work with care.* attention, carefulness, caution, concentration, diligence, exactness, heed, pains, thoroughness. **4** *He doesn't have a care in the world!* anxiety, concern, trouble, worry. **5** *She left the baby in Lucy's care.* charge, custody, keeping, protection, safe-keeping.

career 1 *She's training for a career in industry.* business, calling, employment, job, occupation, profession, trade, work. **2** *They careered along.* to dash, to hurtle, to race, to rush, to speed, to tear, (informal) to zoom. SEE ALSO **move**.

carefree *Our dog lives a carefree life.* contented, easy, easygoing, happy, light-hearted, untroubled.

careful 1 *Be careful when you are on your bike.* alert, attentive, cautious, diligent, observant, prudent, vigilant, wary, watchful. **2** *Tony's work is always careful.* conscientious, deliberate, exhaustive, methodical, meticulous, neat, orderly, organized, painstaking, precise, scrupulous, systematic, thorough.

careless 1 *careless driving.* inattentive, inconsiderate, irresponsible, negligent, rash, reckless, uncaring. **2** *careless work.* confused, disorganized, hasty, jumbled, messy, scatter-brained, shoddy, slapdash, sloppy, slovenly, thoughtless, untidy.

caress *She caressed the baby's skin.* to fondle, to kiss, to pat, to pet, to stroke. SEE ALSO **touch**.

caretaker SEE **job**.

cargo *to transport cargo.* freight, goods, load, merchandise.

carnage *a terrible scene of carnage.* bloodshed, killing, slaughter. SEE ALSO **kill**.

carnation SEE **flower**.

carnival *We want good weather for our carnival.* celebration, fair, festival, fête, gala, jamboree, show.

carnivorous SEE **animal**.

carol SEE **music, sing**.

carp SEE **fish**.

carpenter joiner. SEE ALSO **art, job**.

carpentry woodwork.

carpet SEE **floor**.

carriage SEE **vehicle**.

carrot SEE **vegetable**.

carry 1 *Can we carry this wardrobe up the stairs?* to bring, to lift, to manhandle, to move, to remove, to take, to transfer. **2** *Aircraft carry passengers and goods.* to convey, to ferry, to ship, to transport. **3** *The foundations carry the weight of the building.* to bear, to hold up, to support. **4** *Have you carried out my orders?* to accomplish, to achieve, to complete, to do, to enforce, to execute, to finish, to perform. **5** *Shall we carry on?* to continue, to go on, to keep on, to last, to persevere, to persist, to remain, to stay, to survive.

cart barrow. SEE ALSO **vehicle**.

cart-horse SEE **horse**.

carton box, case. SEE ALSO **container**.

cartoon SEE **film, picture**.

cartridge SEE **container**.

carve SEE **cut**.

case 1 box, carton, crate. SEE ALSO **container**. **2** *It was an obvious case of favouritism.* example, illustration, instance. **3** *The detective said he'd never known a case like this one.* inquiry, investigation.

cash change, coins, money, notes.

cashier SEE **job**.

cask barrel, tub. SEE ALSO **container**.

casket SEE **container**.

casserole SEE **cook**.

cassette SEE **record**.

cassock SEE **clothes**.

cast 1 *We cast a coin into the well.* to bowl, (informal) to chuck, to fling, to hurl, to lob, to pitch, to sling, to throw, to toss. **2** *The sculptor cast his*

statue in bronze. to form, to mould, to shape.

castanets SEE **percussion**.

castaway SEE **maroon**.

castle 1 château, citadel, fort, fortress, palace. SEE ALSO **building**. **2** PARTS OF A CASTLE ARE battlements, buttress, courtyard, drawbridge, dungeon, gate, keep, magazine, moat, parapet, portcullis, rampart, tower, turret, wall.

casual 1 *a casual meeting.* accidental, chance, unexpected, unintentional, unplanned. **2** *casual clothes, a casual manner.* careless, easygoing, informal, relaxed.

casualty *Although it looked a bad accident, there were no casualties.* dead person, fatality, injured person, victim, wounded person.

cat kitten, (informal) pussy, tabby, tomcat. SEE ALSO **animal, pet**.

catalogue *a shopping catalogue, a library catalogue.* brochure, directory, index, list, register.

catamaran SEE **vessel**.

catapult SEE **weapon**.

cataract 1 *There are many cataracts along the river.* rapids, torrent, waterfall. **2** *a cataract in the eye.* SEE **illness**.

catarrh SEE **illness**.

catastrophe *The plane crash was a terrible catastrophe.* accident, calamity, disaster, misfortune, mishap, tragedy.

catch 1 *to catch a ball.* to clutch, to grab, to grasp, to hang on to, to hold, to seize, to snatch, to take. **2** *to catch a rabbit, to catch a fish.* to ensnare, to hook, to net, to trap. **3** *to catch a thief.* to arrest, to corner, to capture, (informal) to nab, to stop. **4** *to catch an illness.* to be infected by, to contract, to get. **5** *a catch on a door.* bolt, latch, lock.

catching *a catching disease.* contagious, infectious.

catchy *a catchy tune.* attractive, memorable, tuneful.

category *The cars were in categories*

depending on the size of the engine. class, group, kind, set, sort.

cater *We catered for twelve people at Christmas.* to cook, to provide.

caterer SEE **job**.

caterpillar grub, larva, maggot.

cathedral SEE **church**.

Catherine wheel SEE **firework**.

catkin SEE **flower**.

cattle bullocks, bulls, calves, cows, heifers, oxen, steers. SEE ALSO **animal, farm**.

catty *Lucy was hurt by her friend's catty remarks.* malevolent, malicious, nasty, sly, spiteful, vicious.

cauldron pot, saucepan. SEE ALSO **container, cook**.

cauliflower SEE **vegetable**.

cause 1 *What was the cause of the trouble?* grounds, occasion, origin, reason, source. **2** *We are collecting for a good cause.* aim, object, purpose. **3** *It'll cause trouble if we don't share the sweets fairly.* to bring about, to give rise to, to induce, to lead to, to provoke, to result in.

causeway SEE **road**.

caution 1 *Proceed with caution.* attentiveness, care, heed, vigilance, wariness. **2** *The police let him off with a caution.* reprimand, warning. **3** *They cautioned us about the danger of falling rocks.* to alert, to warn.

cautious *Mrs Brunswick is a cautious driver.* attentive, careful, deliberate, vigilant, wary, watchful.

cavalcade parade, procession.

cavalry SEE **armed services**.

cave cavern, cavity, grotto, hole, pothole.

caviare SEE **food**.

cavity cave, hole, hollow.

CB SEE **communication**.

cease *Cease work!* to break off, to cut off, to discontinue, to end, to finish, to stop, to terminate.

ceaseless *Logan's ceaseless chatter annoys Mrs Angel.* chronic, constant, continual, continuous, incessant, interminable, non-stop, permanent, persistent, relentless, unending.

cedar SEE **tree**.

ceiling SEE **building**.

celebrate 1 *Let's celebrate!* to be happy, to rejoice, to revel. **2** *How shall we celebrate granny's seventieth birthday?* to keep, to observe, to remember.

celebrated *a celebrated actor.* distinguished, eminent, famous, noted, popular, renowned, well-known.

celebration KINDS OF CELEBRATION ARE anniversary, banquet, birthday, carnival, feast, festival, festivity, jamboree, jubilee, party, wedding.

celery SEE **salad, vegetable**.

celestial *celestial music.* blissful, divine, heavenly.

cell 1 *a monk's cell, a prison cell.* den, prison, room. **2** *an electric cell.* battery.

cellar basement, crypt, vault.

cello SEE **music, strings**.

Celsius SEE **temperature**.

cement SEE **building**.

cemetery burial-ground, churchyard, graveyard. SEE ALSO **funeral**.

censor *They censored the violent film.* to ban, to cut, to forbid, to prohibit.

censure 1 *He deserved the referee's censure for that foul.* condemnation, criticism, disapproval, rebuke, reprimand. **2** *The referee censured him.* to reproach, to scold, (informal) to tick off.

centigrade SEE **temperature**.

centimetre SEE **measure**.

centipede SEE **insect**. ! *Centipedes* are not proper insects.

central heating SEE **fire, house**.

centre *the centre of the earth, the centre of town.* core, focus, heart, hub, inside, middle, nucleus.

century SEE **time**.

cereal 1 corn, grain. **2** CEREALS GROWN BY FARMERS ARE barley, maize, oats, rice, rye, sweetcorn, wheat. **3** *breakfast cereal.* cornflakes.

ceremony 1 *They held a ceremony to*

open the sports centre. event, function, occasion. **2** *The wedding was conducted with great ceremony.* formality, grandeur, pageantry, pomp, ritual, spectacle.

certain 1 *When the brakes failed, disaster seemed certain.* destined, fated, inescapable, inevitable, sure, unavoidable. **2** *If your watch doesn't go, the shop is certain to refund your money.* bound, compelled, obliged, required, sure. **3** *Are you certain it will rain?* assured, confident, definite, positive, sure.

certificate *a certificate for swimming.* award, degree, diploma, document. SEE ALSO **qualification**.

chaffinch SEE **bird**.

chain 1 *The prisoners were in chains.* bonds, fetters. **2** *Form a chain.* column, cordon, line, row, sequence, series. **3** *The slaves were chained together.* to link, to tie. SEE ALSO **fasten**.

chair armchair, seat. SEE ALSO **furniture**.

chalet SEE **house**.

chalk SEE **rock**.

challenge 1 *The sentry challenged the intruder.* to confront. **2** *He challenged his rival to fight a duel.* to dare, to defy.

chamber room.

chamber music SEE **music**.

champagne SEE **drink**.

champion hero, victor, winner.

championship *a snooker championship.* competition, contest, tournament.

chance 1 *It happened by chance.* accident, coincidence, destiny, fate, fluke, fortune, luck, misfortune. **2** *There's a chance of rain.* danger, possibility, risk. **3** *Now it's your chance to try.* opportunity, turn. **4** *a chance meeting.* accidental, casual, lucky, unexpected, unintentional, unplanned.

chancel SEE **church**.

chancellor SEE **government**.

chancy *It's chancy driving on icy roads.* dangerous, hazardous, risky.

chandelier SEE **light**.

change 1 *to change your mind, to change the rules, etc.* to adapt, to adjust, to affect, to alter, to amend, to convert, to influence, to modify, to process, to reform, to transform, to vary. **2** *to change clothes, to change places, etc.* to exchange, to replace, to substitute, to switch, to swop. **3** *The pumpkin changed into a coach.* to become, to turn into. **4** *Have you any change?* cash, coins, money, notes.

changeable *The weather in Britain is very changeable.* erratic, fickle, inconsistent, temperamental, unpredictable, unreliable, variable.

channel 1 *We dug a channel to take away the water.* canal, dike, ditch, gully, gutter, waterway. **2** *Which channel is your programme on?* station, wavelength.

chant SEE **music, sing**.

chaos *It was chaos when Logan let off the fire-extinguisher.* anarchy, bedlam, confusion, lawlessness, shambles.

chaotic *a chaotic mess.* confused, disorderly, disorganized, haphazard, higgledy-piggledy, incoherent, jumbled, mixed up, muddled, topsy-turvy.

chapel, chaplain SEE **church**.

chapter SEE **book**.

char *charred remains.* to blacken, to burn, to scorch, to singe.

character 1 *Logan's grandfather is an interesting character.* human being, individual, person. **2** *Who was your favourite character in the pantomime?* part, role. **3** *This brand of tea has a character of its own.* characteristic, flavour, quality, taste. **4** *Tony has a nice character.* attitude, disposition, manner, nature, personality, temperament. **5** *the characters of the alphabet.* letter, sign, symbol.

characteristic *A red breast is the characteristic feature of the robin.* distinctive, essential, individual, particular, recognizable, special, unique.

charade SEE **game**.

charcoal SEE **fuel**.

charge 1 *Their charges are reasonable.* cost, fare, fee, payment, price, rate, terms, toll, value. **2** *They left the dog in my charge.* care, command, control, custody, keeping, protection, safe-keeping. **3** *Did the police charge him?* to accuse, to blame, to prosecute. **4** *The cavalry charged.* to attack, to assault, to storm.

chariot SEE **vehicle**.

charity 1 *The animals' hospital depends on your charity.* generosity, kindness, love. **2** *We collected for a charity.* good cause.

charm 1 *People used to believe in the power of charms.* enchantment, magic, sorcery, spell, witchcraft, wizardry. **2** *He charmed us with his music.* to attract, to bewitch, to captivate, to enchant, to entrance, to fascinate, to spellbind. **3** *charming:* SEE **attractive**.

chart 1 map, plan. **2** diagram, graph.

charter *We chartered a bus for our trip to the zoo.* to hire, to rent.

chase *Our dog chased that rabbit for miles.* to follow, to hound, to hunt, to pursue, to track, to trail.

chasm *We nearly fell into the chasm.* abyss, crater, hole, pit.

chaste *Holy people are expected to be chaste.* decent, good, innocent, modest, pure, virgin, virtuous.

chat SEE **talk**.

château castle, mansion, stately home. SEE ALSO **building**.

chatter to gossip, to prattle. SEE ALSO **talk**.

chatterbox SEE **talkative**.

chauffeur driver. SEE ALSO **servant**.

cheap 1 *You can find cheap clothes in the sales.* cut-price, economical, inexpensive, reasonable. **2** *It was cheap stuff which didn't last.* inferior, poor, shoddy, tawdry, tinny.

cheat 1 to deceive, to defraud, to dupe, to fool, to hoax, to hoodwink, to outwit, to swindle, to take in. SEE ALSO **trick**. **2** *to cheat in an examination.* to crib.

check 1 *Mrs Angel checked our answers.* to compare, to examine, to test. **2** *A fallen tree checked our progress.* to arrest, to bar, to block, to curb, to delay, to foil, to halt, to hamper, to hinder, to impede, to stop. **3** *Mr Brunswick took the car to the garage for a check.* examination, investigation, test.

checkmate SEE **chess**.

cheek 1 SEE **body, head**. **2** (informal) *She's got a cheek!* nerve.

cheeky *a cheeky manner, a cheeky remark.* arrogant, bold, discourteous, disrespectful, forward, impertinent, impolite, impudent, insolent, insulting, presumptuous, rude, saucy, shameless.

cheer 1 *The audience cheered.* to applaud, to clap, to shout. **2** *The clowns cheered us up.* to amuse, to brighten, to divert, to entertain.

cheerful *a cheerful mood.* animated, bright, delighted, elated, festive, gay, glad, gleeful, good-humoured, happy, jolly, jovial, joyful, laughing, light-hearted, lively, merry, optimistic, pleased, rapturous, spirited, warm-hearted.

cheese SEE **food**.

cheetah SEE **animal**.

chef cook. SEE ALSO **job**.

chemical VARIOUS CHEMICALS ARE acid, alcohol, alkali, ammonia, arsenic, carbon, chlorine, fluoride, litmus, sulphur.

chemist SEE **job, shop**.

chemistry SEE **science**.

cheque SEE **money**.

cherish *I shall cherish the lovely present you gave me.* to care for, to look after, to love, to prize, to protect, to treasure, to value.

cherry SEE **fruit**.

chess 1 PIECES USED IN CHESS ARE bishop, castle or rook, king, knight, pawn, queen. **2** TERMS USED IN CHESS ARE checkmate, mate, stalemate. **3** SEE **game**.

chest 1 SEE **body**. **2** *a chest full of treasure.* box, case, crate, trunk. SEE ALSO **container**. **3** *a chest of drawers.* SEE **furniture**.

chestnut SEE **tree**.

chew to bite, to crunch, to eat, to gnaw, to munch, to nibble. SEE ALSO **eat**.

chewing-gum SEE **sweet**.

chick SEE **bird, young**.

chicken cockerel, fowl, hen, rooster. SEE **bird, meat, poultry**.

chicken-pox SEE **illness**.

chief 1 *What was the chief lesson you learned?* basic, dominant, essential, fundamental, greatest, important, leading, main, major, outstanding, primary, prime, principal, supreme. **2** *the chief cook.* head, leading, senior. **3** *Who's the chief around here?* boss, captain, chieftain, commander, director, employer, governor, head, leader, manager, master, president, principal, ruler.

chiefly generally, mainly, mostly, predominantly, primarily, usually.

chilblain SEE **illness**.

child baby, boy, (insulting) brat, girl, infant, (informal) kid, (informal) nipper, offspring, toddler, (insulting) urchin, youngster, youth.

childish *Mrs Angel says it's childish to make rude noises.* babyish, immature, infantile, juvenile.

chill 1 *Lucy caught a chill.* SEE **illness**. **2** *to chill food.* to freeze, to refrigerate.

chilly *a chilly evening.* cold, cool, frosty, icy, (informal) nippy, raw, wintry.

chime SEE **bell, sound**.

chimney SEE **building**.

chimney-sweep SEE **job**.

chimpanzee SEE **animal**.

chin SEE **body, head**.

china earthenware, porcelain, pottery. SEE ALSO **crockery**.

chink *a chink in the curtains.* crack, gap, opening, slit, split.

chip 1 *I knocked a chip off the plate.* bit, flake, fragment, piece, scrap, slice, splinter. **2** *fish and chips.* SEE **food**. **3** *a silicon chip.* SEE **computer**. **4** *Who chipped this cup?* to break, to crack, to damage, to splinter.

chirp SEE **sound**.

chisel SEE **cut, tool**.

chivalrous *a chivalrous knight.* courteous, gallant, gentlemanly, heroic, noble, polite.

chlorine SEE **chemical**.

chocolate SEE **sweet**.

choice *Can we have a choice?* alternative, option, pick, selection.

choir chorus. SEE ALSO **music**.

choke 1 *The smoke choked us. This collar is choking me.* to smother, to stifle, to strangle, to suffocate, to throttle. **2** *The firemen choked in the smoke.* to gasp, to suffocate. **3** *The car won't start without the choke.* SEE **vehicle**.

cholera SEE **illness**.

choose *We chose a captain.* to appoint, to decide on, to draw lots, to elect, to name, to nominate, to opt for, to pick, to prefer, to select, to settle on, to vote for.

chop 1 *to chop wood.* to hack, to hew, to slash, to split. SEE ALSO **cut**. **2** *lamb chops.* SEE **meat**.

chopper axe. SEE ALSO **tool**.

chop-suey SEE **food**.

chord SEE **music**.

chores *We help with chores around the house.* drudgery, errands, jobs, tasks, work.

chorus 1 choir. SEE ALSO **music**. **2** *We joined in the chorus.* refrain.

christen *Tony was christened Antony.* to baptize, to name.

Christianity FOR WORDS TO DO WITH THE CHRISTIAN CHURCH SEE **church**.

Christmas yule, yuletide. SEE ALSO **church, time**.

chromatic scale SEE **music**.

chromium SEE **metal**.

chronic *a chronic illness.* ceaseless, constant, continual, continuous, everlasting, incessant, lifelong, permanent, persistent, unending.

chrysalis SEE **insect**.

chrysanthemum SEE **flower**.

chub SEE **fish**.

chubby *a chubby figure.* dumpy, fat, plump, podgy, portly.

chuck (informal) *Stop chucking things*

into the water. to fling, to hurl, to lob, to sling, to throw, to toss.

chuckle to giggle, to titter. SEE ALSO **laugh**.

chum companion, friend, mate.

chunk *a chunk of cheese, a chunk of wood.* bar, block, brick, dollop, hunk, lump, mass, piece, slab.

church 1 CHURCH BUILDINGS ARE abbey, cathedral, chapel, convent, monastery, parish church, priory. **2** PARTS OF A CHURCH ARE aisle, altar, belfry, buttress, chancel, chapel, cloisters, crypt, dome, gargoyle, porch, precinct, spire, steeple, tower, vestry. **3** THINGS YOU FIND IN A CHURCH ARE Bible, candle, crucifix, font, hymn-book, lectern, memorial tablet, pews, prayer book, pulpit. **4** WORDS TO DO WITH CHURCH ARE Advent, angel, Ascension Day, Ash Wednesday, baptism, benediction, christening, Christmas, communion, confirmation, Easter, Good Friday, gospel, hymn, incense, Lent, martyr, mass, Nativity, New Testament, Old Testament, Palm Sunday, patron saint, Pentecost, prayer, preaching, psalm, requiem, Resurrection, sabbath, sacrament, saint, scripture, sermon, service, Shrove Tuesday, Whitsun, worship. **5** PEOPLE CONNECTED WITH CHURCH ARE archbishop, bishop, cardinal, chaplain, choir, clergyman, congregation, curate, deacon, deaconess, dean, evangelist, friar, minister, missionary, monk, nun, parson, pastor, Pope, preacher, priest, rector, verger, vicar.

churchyard burial-ground, cemetery, graveyard.

churn SEE **container**.

chutney SEE **food**.

cider SEE **drink**.

cigar, cigarette SEE **smoke**.

cinders *the cinders of a fire.* ashes, embers.

cine-camera SEE **photography**.

cinema SEE **building, entertainment**.

circle 1 disc, hoop, ring. SEE ALSO **shape**. **2** *The plane circled before landing.* to go round, to turn, to wheel. **3** *The police circled the hide-out.* to encircle, to enclose, to ring.

circuit 1 *a racing circuit.* race-course. **2** *I completed one circuit.* circle, lap, orbit, revolution.

circulate *We circulated a notice about our sale.* to distribute, to issue, to send round.

circumference *It's a mile round the circumference of our playing-field.* boundary, edge, limit, perimeter.

circumstances *Don't jump to conclusions before you know the circumstances.* background, conditions, details, facts, position, situation.

circus WORDS TO DO WITH A CIRCUS ARE acrobat, clown, contortionist, juggler, lion-tamer, ring, tight-rope, trapeze. SEE ALSO **entertainment**.

cistern *a water cistern.* tank. SEE ALSO **container**.

citadel castle, fort, fortress, garrison.

citizen *the citizens of a town.* inhabitant, native, resident.

citrus fruit CITRUS FRUITS ARE grapefruit, lemon, lime, orange, tangerine. SEE ALSO **fruit**.

city *London is a huge city.* conurbation, town. SEE ALSO **geography**.

civil *I know you're angry, but try to be civil.* considerate, courteous, polite, respectful, well-mannered.

civilized *a civilized nation.* cultured, orderly, organized.

claim 1 *I didn't claim my pocket-money last week.* to ask for, to demand, to request, to require. **2** *Logan claims that he's stronger than Tony.* to assert, to declare, to insist, to maintain, to pretend, to state.

clam SEE **shellfish**.

clamber *We clambered up the rocks.* to climb, to crawl, to scramble.

clammy *His hands were clammy.* damp, dank, humid, moist.

clamour *The starlings always make a*

clamour. commotion, din, hubbub, noise, racket, row, screeching, shouting, uproar.

clamp SEE **fasten**.

clan family, group, tribe.

clang, clank SEE **sound**.

clap *The audience clapped*. to applaud, to cheer, to praise.

clarify *We asked Mrs Angel to clarify what she wanted us to do*. to define, to explain, to make clear.

clarinet SEE **woodwind**.

clash 1 *the clash of cymbals*. SEE **sound**. **2** *a clash between two gangs*. battle, collision, combat, conflict, confrontation, contest, fight, struggle.

clasp 1 *She wore a gold clasp*. brooch, buckle, fastener, fastening. **2** *She clasped the child in her arms*. to cling to, to embrace, to grasp, to grip, to hold, to hug, to squeeze. **3** *He clasped his hands*. to hold together, to wring.

class 1 *Whose class are you in?* form, group, set. **2** *In gymnastics Lucy's in a class of her own*. category, classification, grade, group, kind, set, sort, species, type.

classic *This book is a classic!* masterpiece.

classical *classical music*. highbrow.

classify *We classified the petals according to shape*. to arrange, to group, to put into sets, to sort.

classroom SEE **school**.

claustrophobia SEE **illness**.

claw 1 *a bird's claws*. nail, talon. **2** *The animal clawed at its attacker*. to scratch, to tear.

clay SEE **rock**.

clean 1 *a clean floor*. hygienic, spotless, washed. **2** *clean water*. clear, fresh, pure. **3** *clean paper*. blank, unmarked, untouched, unused. **4** *to clean the house, to clean yourself, etc*. to bathe, to brush, to dust, to hoover, to mop up, to rinse, to sponge down, to sweep out, to swill, to wash, to wipe.

cleaner SEE **job**.

clear 1 *clear water*. clean, colourless, pure, transparent. **2** *a clear case of*

cheating. apparent, blatant, evident, obvious, plain. **3** *clear handwriting*. bold, definite, legible, plain, simple. **4** *a clear sound*. audible, distinct. **5** *a clear picture*. focused, visible, well-defined. **6** *a clear explanation*. coherent, comprehensible, intelligible, lucid, understandable, unambiguous. **7** *a clear sky*. bright, cloudless, starlit, sunny, unclouded. **8** *a clear road*. free, open, passable, uncluttered, vacant. **9** *The fog cleared*. to disappear, to evaporate, to fade, to melt away, to vanish. **10** *Wait for the water to clear*. to become transparent, to clarify. **11** *When the alarm went, we cleared the building*. to empty, to evacuate. **12** *The horse cleared the fence*. to bound over, to jump, to leap over, to spring over, to vault. **13** *We asked Mrs Angel to clear up one point*. to clarify, to explain, to make clear.

clearing *a clearing in the forest*. gap, space.

clef SEE **music**.

clench *to clench your teeth*. to clamp up, to close, to grit.

clergyman SEE **church, preacher**.

clerk office worker, secretary, typist. SEE ALSO **job**.

clever *a clever child, a clever idea, etc*. able, academic, accomplished, apt, artful, artistic, astute, brainy, bright, brilliant, crafty, cunning, cute, deft, expert, gifted, handy, imaginative, ingenious, intellectual, intelligent, quick, quick-witted, sharp, shrewd, skilful, skilled, slick, smart, talented, wily, wise.

click SEE **sound**.

client *a client of the bank*. customer.

cliff SEE **seaside**.

climate SEE **geography, weather**.

climax *The music built up to a climax*. crisis, highlight, peak.

climb *to climb a ladder*. to ascend, to clamber up, to go up, to mount, to scale.

climber CLIMBING PLANTS ARE honeysuckle, hops, ivy, vine.

cling 1 *Ivy clings to the wall.* to adhere, to stick. 2 *The baby clung to its mother.* to clutch, to clasp, to grasp, to hug.

clinic health centre, infirmary. SEE ALSO **medicine**.

clink SEE **sound**.

clip 1 *a paper-clip.* fastener. SEE ALSO **fasten**. 2 *a clip from a film.* excerpt, extract. 3 *to clip a hedge.* to crop, to shear, to snip, to trim. SEE ALSO **cut**.

clipper SEE **vessel**.

cloak SEE **clothes**.

cloakroom SEE **house**.

clock KINDS OF CLOCK ARE alarm clock, digital clock, grandfather clock, hour- glass, pendulum clock, stop-watch, sundial, watch.

clog 1 SEE **shoe**. 2 *Don't clog the drain with all that paper.* to block, to bung up, to jam, to obstruct, to stop up.

cloisters SEE **building, church**.

close 1 *Close the door.* to bolt, to fasten, to lock, to seal, to secure, to shut. 2 *They closed the road.* to bar, to barricade, to block, to stop up. 3 *We closed the concert with a song.* to conclude, to end, to finish, to stop, to terminate. 4 *Our house is close to the park.* adjacent, near, neighbouring. 5 *The twins are close to each other.* affectionate, attached, familiar, fond, friendly, intimate, loving. 6 *It's close in here: open a window.* airless, humid, muggy, oppressive, stifling, stuffy, sultry, warm. 7 *He's close with his money.* mean, mingy, miserly, stingy.

clot *a clot of blood.* lump.

cloth 1 *Mrs Brunswick bought some cloth to make curtains.* fabric, material, stuff, textile. 2 KINDS OF CLOTH ARE canvas, corduroy, cotton, denim, elastic, felt, flannel, gauze, lace, linen, muslin, nylon, patchwork, polyester, rayon, sacking, satin, silk, taffeta, tapestry, tartan, tweed, velvet, wool, worsted.

clothes 1 attire, costume, dress, garments, outfit. 2 VARIOUS GARMENTS ARE anorak, apron, bib, bikini, blazer, blouse, bra, braces, breeches, briefs, cagoule, cape, cardigan, cassock, cloak, coat, corset, drawers, dress, dressing-gown, duffle coat, dungarees, frock, garter, gauntlet, girdle, glove, gown, jacket, jeans, jersey, jodhpurs, jumper, kilt, knickers, leg-warmers, leotard, lingerie, livery, mackintosh, miniskirt, mitten, muffler, night-dress, oilskins, overalls, overcoat, panties, pants, panty-hose, parka, petticoat, pinafore, poncho, pullover, pyjamas, raincoat, rompers, sari, scarf, shawl, shirt, shorts, singlet, skirt, slacks, slip, smock, sock, sou'wester, stockings, suit, surplice, sweater, tie, tights, trunks, T-shirt, tunic, underpants, uniform, vest, waistcoat, wet-suit, wind-cheater, yashmak. SEE ALSO **hat, shoe**. 3 PARTS OF A GARMENT ARE bodice, button, button-hole, collar, cuff, hem, lapel, pocket, sleeve.

cloud SEE **weather**.

cloudless *a cloudless sky.* bright, clear, starlit, sunny, unclouded.

cloudy 1 *a cloudy sky.* dull, gloomy, grey, overcast. 2 *The windows are cloudy.* blurred, dim, milky, misty, murky, opaque, steamy, unclear.

clout (informal) *She clouted her brother with the newspaper.* to bang, (informal) to bash, to drive, to hammer, to knock, to punch, to slam, to slog, to smash, to strike, to swipe, to thump, to wallop, to whack. SEE ALSO **hit**.

clown 1 fool, jester. 2 SEE ALSO **circus, entertainment**.

club 1 *to hit someone with a club.* baton, cudgel, stick. 2 *to hit a ball with a club.* bat. 3 *a football club, a book club.* association, league, organization, party, society, union. 4 *the ace of clubs.* SEE **cards**.

cluck SEE **sound**.

clue *Give me a clue what I'm getting for Christmas.* hint, indication, inkling, key, sign, suggestion.

clump *Look at that clump of daffodils.* bunch, cluster, collection, group, tuft. SEE ALSO **group**.

clumsy 1 awkward, blundering, fumbling, gawky, hulking, lumbering, ungainly, unskilful. **2** *to be clumsy*: to be a butterfingers.

cluster *a cluster of trees, people, etc.* bunch, clump, collection, crowd, gathering, group. SEE ALSO **group**.

clutch 1 *He clutched the rope.* to clasp, to cling to, to grab, to grasp, to grip, to hold on to, to seize, to snatch. **2** *The driver had his foot on the clutch.* SEE **vehicle**. **3** *a clutch of eggs.* SEE **group**.

clutter *Please get rid of the clutter in your bedroom.* confusion, jumble, junk, litter, mess, muddle.

coach 1 *We travelled by coach.* SEE **vehicle**. **2** *to coach a football team.* to instruct, to teach, to train.

coal SEE **fuel**.

coarse 1 *coarse cloth.* hairy, harsh, rough, scratchy. **2** *coarse language.* blasphemous, common, crude, foul, impolite, improper, indecent, offensive, rude, uncouth, vulgar.

coast 1 *In summer we sometimes go to the coast.* beach, sea-shore, seaside, shore. **2** *Lucy coasted down the hill on her bike.* to drift, to free-wheel, to glide.

coat 1 SEE **clothes**. **2** *a coat of paint.* coating, cover, covering, film.

coax *We coaxed the animal back into its cage.* to entice, to induce, to persuade, to tempt.

cobble 1 pebble, stone. **2** FOR OTHER SURFACES SEE **road**.

cobbler shoemaker. SEE ALSO **job**.

cobra SEE **snake**.

cock SEE **bird, male**.

cockerel SEE **chicken, poultry**.

cockle SEE **shellfish**.

cockroach SEE **insect**.

cocktail SEE **drink**.

cocky (informal) *Don't get cocky just because she said your work was the best.* arrogant, boastful, bumptious, cheeky, conceited, impudent, insolent, rude, self-satisfied.

cocoa SEE **drink**.

coconut SEE **nut**.

cod SEE **fish**.

code 1 *The Highway Code.* laws, regulations, rules. **2** *A message in code was sent to the government spy.* language, signs, signals.

coeducational SEE **school**.

coffee SEE **drink**.

coffin SEE **funeral**.

coherent *a coherent argument, a coherent story.* clear, convincing, logical, reasonable, sound.

coil *to coil a rope.* to bend, to curl, to entwine, to loop, to turn, to twist, to wind.

coin cash, change, money.

coincide *Fortunately, our opinions about holidays coincide.* to agree, to correspond, to match.

coincidence *We met by coincidence.* accident, chance, luck.

coke SEE **fuel**.

cold 1 *cold weather, cold hands, etc.* Arctic, biting, bitter, bleak, chill, chilly, cool, freezing, frosty, frozen, icy, (informal) nippy, (informal) perishing, raw, shivery, wintry. **2** *cold feelings, a cold heart.* callous, cold-blooded, cool, cruel, half-hearted, hard, hard-hearted, heartless, indifferent, insensitive, uncaring, unconcerned, unfeeling, unfriendly, unkind. **3** *to have a cold*: to cough, to sneeze. SEE ALSO **illness**.

cold-blooded *a cold-blooded killing.* callous, cruel, hard-hearted, heartless, insensitive, merciless, pitiless, ruthless, unfeeling.

colic SEE **illness**.

collaborate *We were allowed to collaborate on the project.* to co-operate, to work together.

collaborator accomplice, ally, assistant, partner.

collage SEE **picture**.

collapse 1 *Several people collapsed in the heat.* to drop, to faint, to fall down. **2** *The building collapsed in the earth-quake.* to buckle, to fall in, to fold up, to tumble down. **3** *The earthquake caused the collapse of many old buildings.* destruction, downfall, end, fall, ruin.

collapsible *a collapsible chair.* folding.

collar SEE **clothes**.

collect 1 *Squirrels collect nuts. A crowd collected to watch the fire.* to accumulate, to assemble, to bring together, to cluster, to come together, to crowd, to gather, to group, to hoard, to muster, to pile up, to store. **2** *Please collect the bread from the baker's.* to bring, to fetch, to get, to obtain.

collection *a collection of stamps.* accumulation, assortment, batch, crowd, gathering, hoard, mass, pile, set, stack. SEE ALSO **group**.

college polytechnic, university. SEE ALSO **educate**.

collide *The car collided with the gatepost.* to bump into, to crash into, to knock, to run into, to slam into, to smash into, to strike. SEE ALSO **hit** .

collie SEE **dog**.

collision *There was a collision at the end of the road.* accident, bump, crash, impact, knock, smash.

colon SEE **punctuation**.

colonel SEE **rank**.

colony 1 settlement. **2** *a colony of ants.* SEE **group**.

colossal *A colossal statue towered above us.* enormous, giant, gigantic, huge, immense, mammoth, massive, mighty, monstrous, towering, vast. SEE ALSO **big**.

colour 1 dye, hue, shade, tinge, tint, tone. **2** VARIOUS COLOURS ARE amber, azure, beige, black, blue, bronze, brown, cream, crimson, fawn, gilt, gold, golden, green, grey, indigo, ivory, jet-black, khaki, lavender, maroon, mauve, navy blue, orange, pink, purple, red, rosy, sandy, scarlet, tan, tawny, turquoise, vermilion, violet, white, yellow. **3** *I'm colouring a picture.* to dye, to paint, to stain, to tinge, to tint. **4** *Tony's fair skin colours easily.* to blush, to flush, to redden, to tan. **5** *The regiment was carrying its colours.* banner, ensign, flag, standard.

colourful *colourful flowers.* bright, brilliant, flashy, gaudy, showy, vivid.

colourless *a colourless scene.* dingy, dismal, dowdy, drab, dreary, dull, grey, shabby.

colt SEE **horse**.

column 1 pile, pillar, pole, post, prop, shaft, support. **2** *a column of soldiers.* file, line, procession, queue, rank, row.

coma SEE **illness**.

comb *I've combed the house and still can't find my pen.* to ransack, to rummage through, to scour, to search.

combat *a fierce combat.* action, battle, bout, conflict, contest, duel, fight, struggle.

combination alliance, blend, compound, mixture, union.

combine 1 *We'll have enough players if we combine the first and second teams.* to add together, to amalgamate, to couple, to join, to merge, to put together, to unite. **2** *Combine the ingredients in a bowl.* to blend, to integrate, to mingle, to mix.

combine harvester SEE **farm**.

come 1 *Our visitors have come.* to appear, to arrive. **2** *Tell me when we come to my station.* to arrive at, to get to, to reach. **3** *There are some dark clouds coming.* to advance, to approach, to draw near. **4** FOR OTHER WORDS WHICH YOU CAN USE SEE **move**.

comedian, comedy SEE **entertainment**.

comet SEE **astronomy**.

comfort 1 *to live in comfort.* ease, luxury, relaxation. **2** *His dog died yesterday, so try to give him some comfort.* consolation, relief, sympathy. **3** *He was upset, so we tried to comfort him.* to calm, to console, to ease, to relieve, to soothe, to sympathize with.

comfortable *a comfortable chair.* cosy, easy, luxurious, relaxing, restful, snug, soft.

comic 1 absurd, amusing, comical, facetious, farcical, funny, humorous, hysterical, laughable, ludicrous, (informal) priceless, ridiculous, silly, uproarious, witty. **2** *A comic sang some songs and made us laugh.* comedian, fool, jester, wit. **3** *Tony bought a comic to read on the train.* SEE **magazine**.

comma SEE **punctuation**.

command 1 *The general issued a command that all fighting should stop.* decree, instruction, order. **2** *He commanded that all fighting should stop.* to decree, to demand, to direct, to instruct, to order, to require, to rule. **3** *A captain commands his ship.* to administer, to be in charge of, to control, to direct, to govern, to head, to lead, to manage, to rule, to supervise.

commander captain, head, leader. SEE ALSO **chief**.

commando SEE **armed services, soldier**.

commence *We're ready to commence.* to begin, to embark on, to initiate, to open, to start, to take the initiative.

commend *The head commended our efforts.* to applaud, to approve of, to praise, to recommend.

comment 1 *Did mum make any comment about your dirty clothes?* mention, observation, opinion, reference, remark, statement. **2** *He commented that the weather had been bad.* to explain, to mention, to observe, to remark, to say.

commentary *They broadcast a commentary on the big match.* account, description, report.

commentator SEE **job**.

commerce *A country depends on commerce to keep going.* business, buying and selling, trade, traffic.

commercial 1 *commercial affairs.* business, economic, financial. **2** *a TV commercial.* advertisement, (informal) plug.

commit *to commit a crime.* to carry out, to do, to perform.

committee *a school committee.* council.

common 1 *The school committee discusses our common problems.* communal, general, joint, mutual, shared. **2** *It's common to have turkey at Christmas. Our car is a common make.* commonplace, conventional, customary, everyday, familiar, frequent, habitual, normal, ordinary, prevalent, regular, typical, usual, well-known, widespread. **3** *Don't use common language!* coarse, crude, rude, vulgar. **4** *We play football on the common.* heath, park.

commonplace *a commonplace event.* boring, common, everyday, indifferent, mediocre, normal, ordinary, unexciting, usual.

commotion *There was a commotion when a dog attacked the sheep.* ado, bedlam, bother, chaos, clamour, confusion, din, disorder, disturbance, fuss, hubbub, hullabaloo, noise, pandemonium, racket, riot, row, rumpus, tumult, turbulence, turmoil, unrest, upheaval, uproar.

communal *Most schools have communal washing facilities.* common, joint, mutual, shared.

communicate 1 *to communicate with other people.* to contact, to correspond with, to get in touch with, to speak to, to talk to. **2** *to communicate our thoughts.* to convey, to express, to indicate, to say, to show, to speak, to write.

communication 1 *to send a communication.* announcement, information, message, report, statement. **2** KINDS OF COMMUNICATION ARE advertising, broadcasting, cable, cable television, CB, correspondence, intercom, letter, the media, newspaper, note, the press, radar, radio, telecommunications, telegram, telephone, television, walkie-talkie, wire, wireless. **3** SEE **language**.

communicative *a communicative person.* chatty, talkative.

communion SEE **church**.

communiqué announcement, bulletin, dispatch, message, report, statement.

Communist SEE **politics**.

community nation, public, society.

compact 1 *a compact set of instructions.* brief, compressed, concise, condensed, short. **2** *a compact typewriter.* neat, portable, small.

compact disc SEE **record**.

companion *Who was your companion this morning?* chum, comrade, escort, friend, mate, partner.

company 1 *We enjoy other people's company.* companionship, fellowship, friendship, society. **2** *a company of rebels.* band, crew, gang, troop. SEE ALSO **armed services**. **3** *a theatrical company.* association, club, group, society. **4** *a shipping company.* business, concern, firm, organization, union.

compare 1 *Compare your answers with your neighbour's.* to check against, to contrast with, to set against. **2** *Their team cannot compare with ours.* to compete with, to match, to rival.

comparison *Look at the comparison between your work and Tony's.* contrast, difference, similarity.

compartment 1 *The box has compartments for nails of different sizes.* division, section. **2** *At the baths there are compartments where you can change.* booth, cubicle.

compass SEE **mathematics, navigate**.

compassion *The muggers showed no compassion for their victim.* feeling, mercy, pity, sympathy.

compel 1 *You can't compel me to play for your side.* to drive, to force, to oblige, to order, to press, to require, to urge. **2** *compelled: They'll be compelled to use the motorway if they want to get here for tea.* bound, certain, obliged, sure.

compensate *Will the insurance compensate us for what we lost in the fire?* to make up, to recompense, to repay.

compère SEE **entertainment**.

compete 1 *We competed against a good side in the final.* to conflict, to contend, to contest, to oppose, to rival, to struggle. **2** *How many runners are competing in this race?* to enter, to participate, to take part.

competent *Mr Brunswick needs a competent bricklayer to build his extension.* able, capable, effective, efficient, experienced, handy, practical, proficient, qualified, skilful, skilled, trained.

competition 1 *a darts competition.* championship, contest, event, game, match, tournament. **2** *The competition between the teams was intense.* competitiveness, rivalry. **3** SEE **game, sport**.

competitor *competitors in a quiz.* candidate, contestant, entrant, opponent, participant, rival.

compile *We compiled a magazine.* to arrange, to compose, to edit, to put together.

complacent *Lucy knew she mustn't be complacent after winning the gold cup.* self-righteous, self-satisfied, smug.

complain *We complained about the awful food.* to grouse, to grumble, to moan, to object, to protest.

complaint 1 *We had a complaint about the food.* grievance, objection, protest. **2** *Flu is a common complaint in winter.* affliction, ailment, disease, disorder, infection, malady, sickness. SEE ALSO **illness**.

complete 1 *When will you complete the work?* to accomplish, to achieve, to carry out, to conclude, to do, to end, to finish, to fulfil, to perform, to round off. **2** *We've got the complete story on video.* entire, full, intact, total, unabridged, whole. **3** *His story was complete rubbish.* absolute, perfect, pure, sheer, total, utter.

complex *A computer is a complex machine.* complicated, elaborate, intricate, involved, sophisticated.

complexion 1 *The colour of your dress suits your complexion.* colour, skin, texture. **2** WORDS USED TO DESCRIBE PEOPLE'S COMPLEXION ARE black, brown, dark, fair, freckled, pasty, ruddy, swarthy, tanned, white.

complicated *The instructions were too*

complicated *to understand.* complex, difficult, elaborate, hard, intricate, involved, sophisticated.

complication *We thought we had no problems, but then we discovered a complication.* difficulty, problem, setback, snag.

compliment *It's nice to get compliments.* appreciation, congratulations, flattery, praise, tribute.

complimentary *People made complimentary remarks about Lucy's gymnastics.* admiring, appreciative, approving, flattering.

component *The garage got the components needed to mend the car.* bit, element, part, unit.

compose 1 *The team is composed of good players.* to compile, to constitute, to make up, to put together. 2 *to compose music.* to create, to write.

composer, composition SEE **music.**

compost SEE **garden.**

compound 1 *The chemist made up a nasty-looking compound.* blend, combination, mixture. 2 *The animals were kept in a compound overnight.* enclosure, pen, run.

comprehend *I can't comprehend how terrible it must be to experience an earthquake.* to appreciate, to follow, to grasp, to know, to realize, to see, to understand.

comprehensive SEE **school.**

compress 1 *to compress something into a small space.* to crush, to press, to squash, to squeeze. 2 *compressed:* compact, concise, condensed.

comprise *This album comprises the best hits of the year.* to consist of, to contain, to include.

compulsion *Taking drugs can become a compulsion.* addiction, habit.

compulsory *At our school it's compulsory to have a shower after games.* necessary, required, unavoidable.

compute *It would be interesting to compute how many hours Lucy trains in a year.* to add up, to calculate, to count, to reckon, to total, to work out.

computer WORDS TO DO WITH COMPUTING ARE chip, cursor, data, disc, disc drive, floppy disc, hardware, interface, joystick, keyboard, micro, microchip, microcomputer, micro-processor, monitor, printer, print-out, program, software, terminal, VDU, word-processor.

comrade chum, companion, friend, mate, partner.

conceal *to conceal a mistake, to conceal the truth, etc.* to blot out, to bury, to camouflage, to cover up, to disguise, to envelop, to hide, to hush up, to keep quiet, to mask.

conceited *Logan was so conceited when his poem went in the magazine!* arrogant, boastful, bumptious, (informal) cocky, proud, self-important, (informal) stuck-up.

conceive 1 *to conceive a baby.* SEE **pregnant.** 2 *to conceive an idea.* to create, to imagine, to invent, to plan, to think up.

concentrate 1 *Concentrate on your work.* to attend to, to think about. 2 *Their supporters concentrated on the far side of the field.* to accumulate, to collect, to gather, to mass. 3 *to concentrate a liquid.* to condense, to reduce, to thicken.

concept *When dad was a boy, space travel was a strange concept.* belief, idea, notion, thought.

concern 1 *Some people don't show any concern for the starving.* care, interest, responsibility. 2 *They think it's no concern of theirs.* affair, business, matter. 3 *Uncle Graham has a job with a business concern.* company, firm, organization. 4 *Paying her gas bill is a great concern to granny.* anxiety, cause of distress, fear, worry. 5 *Road safety concerns us all.* to affect, to be important to, to interest, to involve, to matter to. 6 *concerned:* anxious, bothered, caring, distressed, fearful, troubled, worried. 7 *concerning:* about, involving, regarding, relating to.

concert SEE **entertainment.**

concerto SEE **music.**

concise *a concise dictionary, a concise account, etc.* brief, compact, condensed, short, small, terse.

conclude 1 *We concluded the concert with a song.* to close, to complete, to end, to finish, to round off, to stop, to terminate. **2** *When you didn't arrive, we concluded that the car had broken down.* to decide, to gather, to judge.

conclusion 1 *We were tired at the conclusion of the journey.* close, end, finish. **2** *You have heard the evidence, so what is your conclusion?* decision, judgement, opinion.

concoct *Logan concocts all sorts of excuses.* to counterfeit, to devise, to feign, to invent, to make up, to put together, to think up.

concord *It would be nice if everyone lived in concord.* agreement, harmony, peace.

concrete SEE **building**.

concussion SEE **illness**.

condemn 1 *The head condemned the vandals who broke the windows.* to blame, to denounce, to disapprove of, to rebuke. **2** *The judge condemned the muggers to a spell in prison.* to convict, to punish, to sentence.

condense 1 *to condense a book.* to abbreviate, to abridge, to compress, to shorten. **2** *to condense a liquid.* to concentrate, to reduce, to thicken.

condition 1 *The lavatories were in a bad condition.* order, situation, state. **2** *An athlete has to keep in condition.* fitness, health.

conduct 1 *We were praised for our good conduct.* attitude, behaviour, manners. **2** *The curator conducted us round the museum.* to escort, to guide, to lead, to pilot. **3** *Mrs Angel conducts the school choir.* to be in charge of, to direct, to lead. **4** *Everyone conducted themselves well.* to act, to behave.

conductor 1 *a bus conductor.* SEE **job**. **2** *the conductor of an orchestra.* SEE **music**.

cone SEE **shape**.

conference *Mrs Angel went to a teachers' conference.* assembly, committee, congress, debate, gathering, meeting.

confess *Logan confessed that he broke the window.* to acknowledge, to admit, to own up.

confetti SEE **wedding**.

confide *to confide in:* to tell secrets to, to trust.

confidence *We have confidence in our goalie.* belief, faith, hope, trust.

confident 1 *I'm confident that you'll succeed.* certain, hopeful, optimistic, positive, sure. **2** *a confident person.* assertive, assured, definite.

confidential *Mrs Brunswick keeps her confidential papers locked in a box.* intimate, personal, private, secret.

confine *Battery hens are confined in a very small space.* to cramp, to curb, to detain, to enclose, to gaol, to imprison, to intern, to limit, to restrict, to shut in.

confirm *Our experiments confirmed that plants need light to grow.* to demonstrate, to establish, to prove, to show, to verify.

confirmation SEE **church**.

confiscate *Mrs Angel confiscated my catapult.* to seize, to take away.

conflagration *Three fire-engines came to deal with the conflagration.* blaze, fire, inferno.

conflict 1 *an angry conflict.* antagonism, confrontation, discord, hostility, opposition. **2** *Many men died in the conflict.* action, battle, clash, combat, encounter, fight, struggle, war, warfare. **3** *The twins' views seldom conflict.* to clash, to compete, to contend, to oppose each other.

conform *Conform to the rules.* to abide by, to keep to, to fit in with, to obey.

confront 1 *Even Logan won't confront the headmaster.* to argue with, to attack, to challenge, to defy, to face up to, to resist, to stand up to. **2** *We went the wrong way and suddenly confronted a 'no entry' sign.* to encounter, to face, to meet.

confuse 1 *The complicated rules confused us.* to baffle, to bewilder, to distract,

to mislead, to perplex, to puzzle.
2 *Don't confuse those two packs of cards.*
to jumble, to mix up, to muddle.
3 *confused:* chaotic, disjointed,
disorganized, flustered, fuddled,
garbled, higgledy-piggledy,
incoherent, jumbled, mixed up,
muddled, rambling, topsy-turvy,
unclear.

confusion *There was terrible confusion
when the animals escaped.* ado, anarchy,
bedlam, bother, chaos, clutter,
commotion, confusion, din, disorder,
disturbance, fuss, hubbub,
hullabaloo, jumble, mess, muddle,
pandemonium, racket, riot, rumpus,
shambles, tumult, turbulence,
turmoil, uproar.

congested *The roads are congested at
rush hour.* blocked, full, jammed,
overcrowded.

congratulate *Everyone congratulated
Lucy when she won the gold cup.* to
applaud, to commend, to praise.

congregate *On summer evenings, we
congregate outside the sweet shop.* to
assemble, to come together, to
cluster, to collect, to crowd, to
gather, to get together, to group, to
mass, to meet, to muster, to swarm,
to throng.

congregation SEE **church**.

congress assembly, conference,
gathering, meeting.

conifer SEE **tree**.

conjunction SEE **language**.

conjurer SEE **entertainment**.

conjuring *The magician did some
conjuring.* illusions, magic, tricks.

connect *Connect these two bits of rope.* to
attach, to fasten, to fix, to join, to
link, to relate, to tie.

connection bond, link, relationship.

conquer to beat, to crush, to defeat,
(informal) to lick, to master, to
overcome, to overpower, to
overthrow, to overwhelm, to rout, to
subdue, to succeed against, to
suppress, (informal) to thrash, to
vanquish.

conquest capture, occupation,
victory, win.

conscientious *a conscientious worker.*
careful, diligent, dutiful, hard-
working, honest, scrupulous, serious,
thorough.

conscious 1 *In spite of the knock on the
head, he remained conscious.* alert,
awake, aware. **2** *It was a conscious foul.*
deliberate, intended, intentional,
premeditated.

consecrated *The churchyard is
consecrated ground.* blessed, hallowed,
holy, religious, sacred.

consent *We wondered if mum and dad
would consent to a party.* to agree to, to
allow, to approve of, to authorize, to
permit.

consequence *The floods were a
consequence of all that snow.* effect, end,
issue, outcome, result, sequel.

conservation *the conservation of the
countryside.* preservation.

Conservative SEE **politics**.

conservatory SEE **house**.

consider 1 *He considered the problem for
a long time.* to contemplate, to
discuss, to meditate on, to ponder, to
reflect on, to study, to think about.
2 *Do you consider he was telling the truth?*
to believe, to judge, to reckon.

considerable *a considerable amount of
rain.* big, biggish, noticeable,
significant, sizeable, substantial,
worthwhile.

considerate *It was considerate of you to
lend granny your umbrella.* attentive,
friendly, helpful, kind, kind-hearted,
obliging, polite, sympathetic,
thoughtful, unselfish.

consignment *a fresh consignment of
strawberries.* batch, delivery.

consist *What does this fruit salad consist
of?* to be composed of, to contain, to
include.

consistent 1 *Tony is a very consistent
chess-player.* dependable, faithful,
regular, reliable, steady. **2** *That is not
consistent with what you said yesterday.*
compatible with, in accordance with.

console *to console someone who is*

unhappy. to comfort, to ease, to soothe, to sympathize with.

consort SEE **royal**.

conspicuous *a conspicuous landmark, a conspicuous case of cheating.* blatant, impressive, notable, noticeable, obvious, prominent, pronounced, showy, striking, unconcealed, unmistakable, visible.

conspiracy *a conspiracy against the government.* intrigue, plot, scheme.

constable (informal) cop or copper, officer, policeman, policewoman.

constant 1 *a constant cough, a constant rhythm.* ceaseless, chronic, continual, everlasting, incessant, invariable, non-stop, permanent, persistent, repeated, unending. **2** *a constant friend.* dedicated, dependable, devoted, faithful, firm, loyal, reliable, steady, trustworthy, unchanging.

constellation SEE **astronomy**.

constipation SEE **illness**.

constituency SEE **government**.

constitute *In soccer, eleven players constitute a team.* to compose, to form, to make up.

constitution SEE **government**.

construct *We constructed a den out of old planks.* to assemble, to build, to erect, to fit together, to make, to put together.

constructive *a constructive suggestion.* beneficial, co-operative, helpful, positive, useful.

consul ambassador, diplomat, representative.

consult *I consulted the doctor about my cough.* to discuss with, to refer to.

consume 1 *We consumed an enormous amount of food.* to devour, to digest, to eat, to gobble up, to swallow. **2** *If we buy a video, it'll consume all our savings.* to exhaust, to use up.

contact 1 *Mrs Brunswick contacted the police about her lost brooch.* to communicate with, to correspond with, to get in touch with, to speak to, to talk to. **2** *The wires must contact each other before the electric current will flow.* to connect with, to touch.

contagious *a contagious disease.* catching, infectious.

contain 1 *What does this cake contain?* to be composed of, to consist of, to incorporate. **2** *What does this box contain?* to hold, to include.

container 1 receptacle. **2** VARIOUS CONTAINERS ARE bag, barrel, basin, basket, bath, beaker, billycan, bin, bottle, box, bucket, butt, can, canister, carton, cartridge, case, cask, casket, casserole, cauldron, chest, churn, cistern, coffin, cup, dish, drum, dustbin, envelope, flask, glass, goblet, hamper, handbag, haversack, hold-all, holster, jar, jug, keg, kettle, knapsack, money-box, mould, mug, pail, pan, pannier, pitcher, pot, pouch, purse, rucksack, sack, satchel, saucepan, suitcase, tank, tankard, teapot, test tube, Thermos, tin, trough, trunk, tub, tumbler, urn, vacuum-flask, vase, vat, wallet, watering-can, wineglass.

contaminate *The fish died because the water was contaminated by chemicals.* to defile, to infect, to poison, to pollute, to soil.

contemplate 1 *We contemplated the lovely view.* to eye, to gaze at, to look at, to observe, to regard, to stare at, to view, to watch. **2** *We contemplated what to do next.* to consider, to meditate, to plan, to ponder, to reflect on, to study, to think about.

contemporary 1 *contemporary events.* current, simultaneous, topical. **2** *contemporary music.* fashionable, modern, newest, (informal) trendy, up-to-date.

contempt disgust, dislike, disrespect, loathing, scorn.

contemptible *The judge said that the muggers were contemptible.* despicable, detestable, hateful, pitiful, worthless.

contemptuous *Don't be contemptuous: we did our best.* disdainful, scornful, sneering.

contend 1 *We contended against strong*

opposition. to compete, to contest, to dispute, to fight, to oppose, to rival, to struggle. **2** *Tony contended that he put the oven on at the right time.* to argue, to assert, to claim, to declare, to maintain.

content *The cat looks content after his dinner.* carefree, comfortable, happy, relaxed, satisfied.

contest 1 *to contest a title.* to compete for, to contend for, to fight for, to struggle for. **2** *to contest a decision.* to argue against, to challenge, to oppose, to resist. **3** *a sporting contest.* bout, championship, combat, competition, conflict, duel, fight, game, match, struggle.

contestant competitor, participant.

continent SEE **geography**.

continental quilt SEE **bedclothes**.

continual *Stop your continual chattering!* ceaseless, chronic, constant, continuous, endless, eternal, everlasting, frequent, incessant, interminable, lasting, limitless, non-stop, permanent, perpetual, persistent, recurrent, relentless, repeated, unending, uninterrupted.

continue 1 *How long will the fine weather continue?* to carry on, to endure, to go on, to keep on, to last, to linger, to live on, to persist, to remain, to stay, to survive. **2** *Please continue with your work.* to carry on, to persevere, to proceed, to resume.

continuous SEE **continual**.

contortionist SEE **circus, entertainment**.

contour SEE **geography**.

contraband *The smugglers hid their contraband.* booty, loot.

contract 1 *Our team has signed a contract with a new goalkeeper.* agreement, bargain, deal, pact, settlement, treaty. **2** *Most substances contract as they get colder.* to decrease, to diminish, to dwindle, to lessen, to reduce, to shrink.

contradict *Are you contradicting me?* to oppose, to speak against.

contradictory *We heard contradictory*

reports about the match. conflicting, incompatible, inconsistent, opposite.

contralto SEE **sing**.

contraption *What do you use that contraption for?* contrivance, device, gadget, invention, machine.

contrary 1 *In our debate, Tony spoke for the proposal, and Lucy put the contrary view.* opposite, reverse. **2** *contrary winds.* adverse, hostile, opposing, unfavourable. **3** *a contrary child.* defiant, disobedient, obstinate, perverse, rebellious, stubborn.

contrast 1 *Mrs Angel contrasted Logan's work with Tony's.* to compare, to set against. **2** *The colours of the two dresses contrasted.* to differ. **3** *There was an obvious contrast between them.* comparison, difference, distinction.

contribute *Everyone contributed something to eat.* to donate, to give, to provide, to supply.

contribution *Please make a contribution to the school fund.* fee, gift, offering, payment, subscription.

contrivance *I invented a contrivance for sweeping the snow away.* contraption, device, gadget, invention.

control 1 *Mrs Angel controls the class well.* to administer, to command, to cope with, to deal with, to direct, to dominate, to govern, to handle, to look after, to manage, to manipulate, to master, to regulate, to rule, to supervise. **2** *They built a dam to control the floods.* to check, to curb, to hold back, to restrain. **3** *Who is in control here?* charge, command, management, rule. **4** *Mrs Angel has good control over the class.* authority, discipline, influence, power.

controversy *There is a controversy about whether they should build a bypass.* argument, debate, disagreement, dispute, issue, quarrel.

conundrum riddle.

conurbation SEE **geography**.

convalescent *Granny is convalescent in hospital after her operation.* getting better, improving, recovering, recuperating.

convector SEE **fire**.

convenient *There's a convenient shop round the corner.* accessible, available, handy, suitable, useful.

convent SEE **church**.

convention *It's a convention to give presents at Christmas.* custom, formality, rule, tradition.

conventional *'How are you?' is a conventional way to greet people.* accustomed, common, commonplace, customary, everyday, habitual, normal, ordinary, orthodox, regular, traditional, usual.

converge *The motorways converge in a mile.* to come together, to intersect, to join, to meet, to merge.

conversation chat, chatter, dialogue, discussion, talk.

convert *We converted the attic into a games room.* to adapt, to alter, to amend, to change, to modify, to process, to transform, to turn.

convey 1 *Please convey our best wishes to your father.* to bear, to carry, to deliver, to send, to take. **2** *Lorries convey goods all over the country.* to carry, to take, to transfer, to transport. **3** *Does that signal convey anything to you?* to communicate, to indicate, to mean.

convict 1 *The convicts were forced to work hard all day.* captive, criminal, prisoner. **2** *He was convicted for murder.* to condemn, to sentence.

conviction *religious convictions.* belief, creed, faith, opinion, view.

convince *He tried to convince the jury that he was innocent.* to persuade, to win over.

convoy *a convoy of ships.* armada, fleet. SEE ALSO **group**.

convulsion fit, seizure, spasm. SEE ALSO **illness**.

coo SEE **sound**.

cook 1 WAYS TO COOK ARE to bake, to barbecue, to boil, to brew, to fry, to grill, to pickle, to poach, to roast, to simmer, to steam, to stew, to toast. **2** OTHER THINGS YOU DO IN COOKING ARE to blend, to chop, to grate, to freeze, to knead, to mix, to peel, to sieve, to sift, to stir, to whisk. **3** CONTAINERS USED TO COOK IN ARE basin, billycan, casserole, cauldron, dish, frying-pan, kettle, pan, percolator, pot, saucepan. **4** SEE ALSO **kitchen**. **5** *Would you like to be a cook?* SEE **job**.

cool 1 *cool weather.* chilly, cold. **2** *Keep cool!* calm, level-headed, sensible, unflustered. **3** *When he asked her to go out with him, she was rather cool.* distant, half-hearted, indifferent, reserved, unconcerned, unenthusiastic, unfriendly. **4** *to cool food.* to chill, to freeze, to refrigerate.

coop *a chicken coop.* cage, enclosure, pen.

co-operate *Logan wouldn't co-operate with Tony.* to aid, to assist, to collaborate with, to help, to support, to work together with.

co-operative *The dealer was co-operative when the TV went wrong.* accommodating, constructive, helpful, willing.

coot SEE **bird**.

cop SEE **police**.

cope *Can you cope with the housework?* to control, to deal with, to endure, to handle, to look after, to manage, to suffer, to tolerate, to withstand.

copious *copious supplies of food.* abundant, ample, generous, lavish, liberal, plentiful, profuse.

copper SEE **metal**.

coppice, copse *a coppice of birch trees.* grove, thicket, wood.

copulate *Animals copulate when the time is right for them to have young ones.* to couple, to have sexual intercourse, to mate.

copy 1 *a copy of a painting, a copy of Stevenson's Rocket, etc.* double, duplicate, fake, forgery, imitation, likeness, model, photocopy, print, replica, reproduction, twin. **2** *to copy a picture, to copy someone's work, etc.* to counterfeit, to crib, to duplicate, to forge, to imitate, to photocopy, to print, to reproduce. **3** *to copy someone's* *voice.* to imitate, to impersonate, to mimic.

coral SEE **jewellery**.

cord *a length of cord.* cable, lace, line, rope, string, twine.

cordial 1 *a cordial welcome.* friendly, genial, kind, warm, warm-hearted. **2** *lime cordial.* SEE **drink**.

cordon *a cordon of policemen.* chain, line, row.

corduroy SEE **cloth**.

core *the core of an apple, the core of the earth, etc.* centre, heart, inside, middle, nucleus.

cork *Put the cork back in the bottle.* bung, plug, stopper.

corkscrew SEE **kitchen**.

cormorant SEE **bird**.

corn 1 cereal, grain. SEE ALSO **cereal**. **2** *corns on your feet.* SEE **illness**.

corner 1 *the corner of the room.* angle, nook. **2** *the corner of the road.* bend, crossroads, intersection, junction, turn. **3** *After a chase, they cornered him.* to capture, to catch, to trap.

cornet SEE **brass**.

cornflakes SEE **cereal, food**.

cornflour SEE **food**.

cornflower SEE **flower**.

coronation crowning. SEE ALSO **royal**.

coroner SEE **law**.

coronet crown, diadem. SEE ALSO **hat**.

corporal SEE **rank**.

corporal punishment SEE **punishment**.

corporation 1 *the town corporation.* council. **2** *a business corporation.* organization.

corps SEE **armed services**.

corpse body, carcass, remains.

correct 1 *Can the garage correct the fault in the car?* to cure, to put right, to rectify, to remedy, to repair. **2** *Mrs Angel corrected our maths.* to assess, to mark. **3** *Is that the correct time?* accurate, exact, faultless, precise, right, true.

correspond 1 *Tony corresponds with a girl in Paris.* to communicate with, to send letters to, to write to. **2** *Tony's answer doesn't correspond with Logan's.* to agree with, to coincide with, to match.

correspondent *a newspaper correspondent.* journalist, reporter. SEE ALSO **writer**.

corridor hall, passage. SEE ALSO **house**.

corrode *Chemicals corroded the metal.* to eat away, to erode, to rot, to rust.

corrupt 1 *You don't expect a judge to be corrupt.* criminal, crooked, depraved, dishonest, evil, immoral, low, untrustworthy, wicked. **2** *You'd get into serious trouble if you tried to corrupt a judge.* to bribe, to influence, to pervert, to tempt.

corset SEE **underclothes**.

cosmetics 1 make-up. **2** VARIOUS COSMETICS ARE cream, deodorant, eye-shadow, lipstick, lotion, nail varnish, perfume, scent, talcum powder.

cosmonaut astronaut, space-traveller.

cosmos universe.

cost *What's the cost of a return ticket?* charge, expense, fare, payment, price, value.

costly *costly jewels.* dear, exorbitant, expensive, precious, priceless, (informal) pricey, valuable.

costume *The actors wore weird costumes.* attire, clothing, dress, garments, outfit. SEE ALSO **clothes**.

cosy *a cosy room, a cosy atmosphere, etc.* comfortable, relaxing, restful, secure, snug, soft, warm.

cot cradle. SEE ALSO **furniture**.

cottage SEE **house**.

cotton 1 SEE **cloth**. **2** *If you find some cotton, I'll sew your button on.* thread.

couch SEE **furniture**.

cough SEE **illness**.

council 1 *We held a council to decide what to do.* assembly, committee, conference. **2** *the town council.* corporation.

council-house SEE **house**.

count 1 *It's amazing how quickly the bank clerk counts the money.* to add up, to calculate, to compute, to figure out, to number, to reckon, to total, to work out. **2** *You can count on Tony to do his best.* to bank on, to depend on, to rely on, to trust.

count, countess SEE **title**.

countenance *His countenance shows that he's had bad news.* appearance, expression, face, features, look.

counter 1 *You play ludo with counters.* disc, token. **2** *You can buy a drink at the counter.* bar, table.

counterfeit 1 *They were put in prison for counterfeiting £5 notes.* to copy, to fake, to forge, to imitate. **2** *They weren't really ill, only counterfeiting.* to pretend, to sham.

counterpane SEE **bedclothes**.

countless *There are countless stars in the sky.* frequent, innumerable, many, numberless, numerous, untold.

country 1 *the countries of the world.* land, nation, state. **2** KINDS OF COUNTRY ARE democracy, dictatorship, kingdom, monarchy, realm, republic. **3** *There's some lovely country near here.* countryside, landscape, rural surroundings, scenery. **4** SEE **geography**.

county SEE **geography**.

couple 1 *a couple of rabbits.* brace, pair. **2** *They coupled the wagons to the locomotive.* to combine, to join, to link, to unite.

coupon *If you save ten coupons you get a free mug.* ticket, token, voucher.

courage *We admired the firemen's courage.* bravery, daring, determination, fortitude, (informal) grit, (informal) guts, heroism, nerve, (informal) pluck, prowess, spirit, valour.

courageous bold, brave, daring, determined, fearless, heroic, intrepid, plucky, valiant.

courier SEE **job**.

course 1 *The pilot checked the air-liner's course.* bearings, direction, route, way. **2** *a course of driving lessons.* series.

3 *a race-course.* SEE **sport**. **4** *We had beef for the main course.* SEE **meal**.

court 1 *The court decided that he was guilty.* court martial, lawcourt. SEE ALSO **law**. **2** *a tennis court.* SEE **sport**. **3** *to court someone.* to go out with, to make love to, to woo.

courteous *Granny says that her paper-boy is a courteous young man.* chivalrous, civil, considerate, gallant, gracious, polite, respectful, well-mannered.

courtesy good manners, politeness.

courtyard enclosure, quadrangle, yard. SEE ALSO **building**.

cousin SEE **family**.

cove *a sandy cove.* bay, inlet.

cover 1 *Fog covered the town.* to blot out, to bury, to camouflage, to clothe, to conceal, to enclose, to envelop, to hide, to mask, to obscure, to plaster, to protect, to shroud. **2** *An encyclopaedia covers many subjects.* to deal with, to include, to incorporate. **3** *a jam-pot cover, a cover to keep the rain off, etc.* cap, coat, covering, envelope, folder, lid, protection, roof, top, wrapper. **4** *The animals searched for cover in the bad weather.* hiding-place, protection, refuge, shelter.

covering *a light covering of snow.* cap, coating, layer, skin.

coverlet SEE **bedclothes**.

cow SEE **animal, farm, female**.

cowardly *a cowardly person, a cowardly action.* base, faint-hearted, fearful, spineless, timid, unheroic, (informal) yellow.

cowed *Logan seemed cowed in front of our famous visitor.* afraid, fearful, frightened, scared, terrified.

cower *The terrified dog cowered in a corner.* to cringe, to crouch, to grovel, to hide, to quail, to shrink.

cowslip SEE **flower**.

cox SEE **sailor**.

coy *Don't be coy: come and be introduced.* bashful, modest, self-conscious, sheepish, shy, timid.

crab SEE **shellfish**.

crab-apple SEE **fruit**.

crack 1 *a crack in the wall.* break, chink, cranny, crevice, flaw, fracture, gap, opening, rift, split. **2** *He cracked a bone in his leg.* to break, to chip, to fracture, to snap, to splinter, to split. **3** *the crack of a rifle.* SEE **sound**.

cracker 1 SEE **firework**. **2** biscuit. SEE ALSO **food**.

crackle SEE **sound**.

cradle cot. SEE ALSO **furniture**.

craft 1 *Few people know the craft of thatching.* handicraft, skill, technique, trade. FOR VARIOUS CRAFTS SEE **art**. **2** *There were many kinds of craft in the harbour.* boat, ship. SEE ALSO **vessel**.

craftsman SEE **art**.

crafty *They say the fox is a crafty creature.* artful, astute, clever, cunning, deceitful, ingenious, knowing, skilful, sly, sneaky, tricky, wily.

crag *The climb up the crag was dangerous.* cliff, precipice, rock.

cram 1 *The room was crammed with people.* to crowd, to fill, to jam, to pack. **2** *Don't cram any more in your mouth!* to squeeze, to stuff.

cramp 1 *cramp in the leg.* SEE **illness**. **2** clamp. SEE ALSO **tool**. **3** *I'm sorry you are so cramped in this little room.* to confine, to enclose, to restrict.

crane 1 SEE **bird**. **2** derrick.

crane-fly SEE **insect**.

cranky (informal) *It seems a bit cranky to have jam with scrambled egg.* eccentric, odd, unconventional, weird, zany.

cranny *a cranny in a rock.* crack, gap, split.

crash 1 *The car crashed into the wall.* to bump, to collide, to knock, to smash. SEE ALSO **hit**. **2** *We heard a crash.* SEE **sound**. **3** *Did you see the crash?* accident, bump, collision, derailment, impact, knock, smash.

crash-helmet SEE **hat**.

crate box, carton, case. SEE ALSO **container**.

crater *The explosion left a deep crater.* abyss, chasm, hole, pit.

crawl 1 *He crawled along a narrow ledge.* to clamber, to creep, to edge, to worm. **2** SEE **swim**.

crayon SEE **write**.

craze *the latest craze.* diversion, enthusiasm, fashion, mania, pastime.

crazy 1 *The dog went crazy when it was stung by a wasp.* berserk, delirious, demented, deranged, frantic, frenzied, hysterical, insane, lunatic, mad, (informal) potty, unhinged, wild. **2** *a crazy comedy.* absurd, farcical, illogical, irrational, ludicrous, preposterous, ridiculous, silly, stupid, unreasonable, zany.

creak SEE **sound**.

cream SEE **colour, food**.

crease *to crease a piece of paper.* to crinkle, to crumple, to fold, to furrow, to pleat, to wrinkle.

create *to create something beautiful, to create trouble, etc.* to begin, to breed, to bring about, to compose, to conceive, to construct, to establish, to form, to found, to generate, to initiate, to invent, to make, to originate, to produce, to think up.

creation *the creation of the world.* beginning, birth, construction, invention, origin.

creative *Artists are creative people.* artistic, imaginative, inventive, original, resourceful.

creator author, discoverer, inventor, maker, painter.

creature being. SEE ALSO **animal, bird, fish, insect, reptile, snake**.

crèche nursery.

credible *No one thought the story about Martians was credible.* believable, plausible, reasonable.

credit *Lucy's win brought credit to the school.* honour, merit, reputation.

creditable *Tony gave a creditable performance in the swimming gala.* admirable, commendable, honourable, praiseworthy, respectable, worthy.

credit card SEE **money**.

creed *a religious creed.* belief, conviction, faith.

creek inlet. SEE ALSO **geography**.

creep *to creep along the ground.* to crawl, to edge, to slink, to slither, to worm. SEE ALSO **move**.

creepy *I don't like creepy noises in the dark.* eerie, frightening, ghostly, scary, spooky, uncanny, weird.

cremate SEE **burn**.

cremation SEE **funeral**.

crescent *a crescent moon.* curved.

cress SEE **salad**.

crest *the school crest.* badge, emblem, seal, sign, symbol.

crestfallen *Logan was crestfallen when he didn't win.* dejected, disappointed, discouraged, downcast, down-hearted, forlorn, glum, miserable, wretched. SEE ALSO **sad**.

crevice *a crevice in the rock.* crack, cranny, gap, split.

crew *a ship's crew.* company, team. SEE ALSO **group**.

crib *to crib in a test.* to cheat, to copy.

cricket 1 WORDS TO DO WITH CRICKET ARE batsman, boundary, bowler, fielder, innings, lbw, maiden over, over, pads, slips, stumps, test match, wicket, wicket-keeper. 2 SEE **sport**. 3 *A cricket chirped in the grass.* SEE **insect**.

crime 1 dishonesty, misdeed, offence, racket, sin, wrongdoing. 2 VARIOUS CRIMES ARE abduction, arson, assassination, assault, blackmail, burglary, hijacking, hold-up, kidnapping, manslaughter, mugging, murder, pilfering, poaching, rape, robbery, shoplifting, smuggling, stealing, theft.

criminal 1 convict, crook, culprit, delinquent, hooligan, malefactor, offender, outlaw, thug, wrongdoer. SEE ALSO **rogue, ruffian**.
2 VARIOUS KINDS OF CRIMINAL ARE assassin, bandit, blackmailer, brigand, buccaneer, burglar, desperado, gangster, gunman, highwayman, hijacker, kidnapper, mugger, murderer, outlaw, pickpocket, pirate, poacher, robber,

shop-lifter, smuggler, terrorist, thief, vandal.

crimson SEE **colour**.

cringe *The frightened dog cringed in his kennel.* to cower, to crouch, to flinch, to grovel, to quail, to wince.

crippled 1 *a crippled person.* disabled, handicapped, hurt, injured, lame, maimed, mutilated. 2 *a crippled vehicle.* damaged, immobilized.

crisis *We had a crisis when we found a gas leak.* danger, emergency.

crisp 1 *crisp biscuits.* brittle, crackly, fragile, hard and dry. 2 *potato crisps.* SEE **food**.

criticism *The head's criticism of our behaviour was unfair.* censure, disapproval, reprimand, reproach.

criticize *Mrs Angel criticized us for being noisy.* to find fault with, to judge, to rebuke, to scold.

croak SEE **sound**.

crochet SEE **art**.

crockery 1 china, earthenware, porcelain, pottery. 2 VARIOUS ITEMS OF CROCKERY ARE basin, bowl, cup, dish, jug, plate, pot, saucer, teapot.

crocodile alligator. SEE ALSO **reptile**.

crocus SEE **bulb, flower**.

croft farm. SEE ALSO **building**.

crook delinquent, gangster, offender, wrongdoer. SEE ALSO **criminal**.

crooked 1 *a crooked road.* angled, bent, twisted, twisty, zigzag. 2 *a crooked salesman.* corrupt, criminal, dishonest, untrustworthy.

croon SEE **sing**.

crop 1 *to crop the grass.* to clip, to shear, to trim. SEE ALSO **cut**. 2 *A difficulty has cropped up.* to arise, to come up, to emerge, to occur, to spring up, to turn up. 3 *The corn crop is good this year.* harvest, produce, yield. 4 *He hit the horse with his crop.* lash, whip.

croquet SEE **sport**.

cross 1 *The road crosses the river.* to go across, to intersect with, to pass over, to span. 2 *The trains crossed at high speed.* to pass. 3 *They crossed out my name.* to cancel, to delete, to erase, to wipe out. **4** *Mrs Brunswick was cross when Lucy trod on her plants.* angry, annoyed, bad-tempered, grumpy, indignant, irate, irritated, short-tempered, upset, vexed.

crossbow SEE **weapon**.

cross-country SEE **athletics**.

cross-examine *to cross-examine a witness.* to examine, to question.

cross-eyed squinting.

crossroads interchange, intersection, junction.

crossword SEE **game**.

crotchet SEE **music**.

crouch *They crouched in the low tunnel.* to bend, to bow, to cower, to duck, to kneel, to stoop.

crow 1 SEE **bird**. **2** *The cock crows every morning.* SEE **sound**. **3** *Logan was crowing about the goal he scored.* to boast, to brag, to show off, (informal) to swank.

crowbar SEE **tool**.

crowd 1 *There was a crowd round the ambulance.* bunch, cluster, collection, crush, gathering, horde, host, mob, multitude, pack, rabble, swarm, throng. SEE ALSO **group**. **2** *The crowd cheered.* audience, spectators. **3** *We crowded round when we heard there was free food.* to assemble, to congregate, to flock, to gather, to herd, to swarm, to throng. **4** *They crowded us into a small room.* to cram, to crush, to huddle, to overcrowd, to pack, to press, to push, to shove, to squeeze.

crown 1 coronet, diadem. SEE ALSO **hat, royal**. **2** *the crown of a hill.* apex, head, top.

crow's nest SEE **vessel**.

crucifix SEE **church**.

crucify SEE **execute**.

crude 1 *crude oil.* natural, raw, unprocessed, unrefined. **2** *We made a crude table out of planks.* clumsy, primitive, rough, unskilful. **3** *crude language.* coarse, common, improper, indecent, rude, vulgar.

cruel *a cruel action, a cruel person.* atrocious, barbaric, beastly, blood-thirsty, bloody, brutal, callous, cold-blooded, ferocious, fierce, hard, hard-hearted, harsh, heartless, inhuman, merciless, murderous, pitiless, relentless, ruthless, sadistic, savage, severe, stern, tyrannical, unfeeling, unjust, unkind, vicious, violent.

cruise *to go on a cruise.* holiday, journey, sail, voyage. SEE ALSO **travel**.

cruiser SEE **vessel**.

crumb *a crumb of bread.* bit, fragment, particle, scrap, speck.

crumble *The road surface is crumbling.* to break up, to disintegrate.

crumple *Don't crumple the clothes I've just ironed!* to crease, to crush, to dent, to fold, to wrinkle.

crunch 1 *The monster crunched his victim in his massive jaws.* to break, to chew, to crush, to munch, to smash, to squash. **2** *We heard the crunch of their feet on the gravel.* SEE **sound**.

crusade *a crusade against drinking and driving.* campaign, struggle, war.

crush 1 *He crushed his finger in the door.* to break, to crumple, to crunch, to grind, to jam, to mangle, to mash, to pound, to press, to pulp, to smash, to squash, to squeeze. **2** *We crushed their best team.* to conquer, to defeat, to overcome, to overpower, to overthrow, to overwhelm, to rout, to subdue, (informal) to thrash.

crust *the crust of a loaf, the crust of the earth.* outside, rind, skin.

crutch *The lame man needed a crutch.* prop, support.

cry 1 *Baby cries when she's tired.* to blubber, to grizzle, to shed tears, to snivel, to sob, to wail, to weep. **2** *Who cried out?* to bawl, to call, to exclaim, to scream, to shout, to yell.

crypt *the church crypt.* basement, cellar, vault. SEE ALSO **church**.

crystal *a crystal ball.* glass.

cub SEE **young**.

cube SEE **shape**.

cubicle *Do you know if there are any changing cubicles at the swimming-baths?* booth, compartment, kiosk.

cuckoo SEE **bird**.

cucumber SEE **salad, vegetable**.

cuddle *Baby loves to cuddle her mother.* to caress, to embrace, to fondle, to huddle against, to hug, to kiss, to nestle against, to snuggle against.

cudgel *The bandits were armed with cudgels.* baton, cane, club, stick.

cue *In our nativity play, Logan missed the cue for him to come on.* reminder, sign, signal.

cuff 1 (informal) to clout, to knock, to slap, to smack, to swipe. SEE ALSO **hit**. **2** *the cuffs of a shirt.* SEE **clothes**.

cul-de-sac SEE **road**.

culprit *Have they caught the culprit yet?* offender, trouble-maker, wrongdoer. SEE ALSO **criminal**.

cultivate *to cultivate the land, to cultivate crops.* to farm, to grow, to produce, to raise.

cultivated *a cultivated person.* courteous, cultured, educated, well-bred. SEE ALSO **polite**.

cultivation agriculture, farming, gardening.

cultural *cultural pursuits.* civilizing, educational, high-brow, improving, intellectual.

culture *a nation's culture.* art, background, education, learning.

cultured *a cultured person.* civilized, cultivated, educated, well-bred.

cumbersome *a cumbersome machine.* awkward, heavy, unwieldy.

cunning *a cunning trick.* artful, astute, clever, crafty, ingenious, knowing, skilful, sly, tricky, wily.

cup 1 SEE **drink**. **2** *Lucy won a cup on sports day.* award, prize, trophy.

cupboard SEE **furniture**.

cup-tie SEE **sport**.

cur dog, mongrel.

curate SEE **church**.

curator SEE **job**.

curb *I don't want to curb your enthusiasm, but please be a little quieter.* to check, to control, to hamper, to hinder, to hold back, to limit, to restrain.

curdle *curdled milk.* to clot, to go sour.

cure 1 *Can they cure arthritis?* to heal, to remedy. **2** *Dad cured that nasty noise in the car.* to correct, to put right, to rectify. **3** *Is there a cure for the common cold?* medicine, remedy, therapy, treatment. **4** SEE **medicine**.

curious 1 *Our cat was curious about the puppy.* inquisitive, interested, nosey, prying. **2** *There's a curious smell in here.* abnormal, odd, peculiar, queer, strange, unusual.

curl to bend, to coil, to loop, to turn, to twist, to wind.

curlew SEE **bird**.

currant SEE **fruit**.

currency SEE **money**.

current 1 *Beware of currents in the water.* flow, stream, tide, undertow. **2** *What do you think of current fashions?* contemporary, fashionable, modern, present, prevailing, up-to-date.

curry SEE **food**.

curse 1 *He let out a curse.* exclamation, oath, swear-word. **2** *Logan's dad cursed us for waking him.* to damn, to swear at.

cursor SEE **computer**.

cursory *The mechanic only gave the car a cursory inspection.* hasty, hurried, quick.

curt *His curt answer showed he was in a bad mood.* abrupt, rude, short.

curtail *They had to curtail their holiday when Mrs Brunswick was ill.* to break off, to cut, to shorten.

curtain *Close the curtains.* blind, drape, screen.

curtsy *She curtsied to acknowledge the applause.* to bend, to bow.

curve 1 arc, arch, bend, curl, loop, turn, twist. **2** *curved:* arched, bowed, crescent, curled, looped, twisted.

cushion bolster, pillow. SEE ALSO **furniture**.

custard SEE **food**.

custodian *the custodian of the museum.* guardian, keeper, warder.

custom *It's our custom to take flowers when we visit friends.* convention, habit, institution, practice, routine, tradition.

customary *Every Friday, the Brunswicks have their customary fish and chips.* accustomed, common, conventional, habitual, normal, ordinary, regular, traditional.

customer buyer, client.

customs *customs duty.* duty, tax.

cut 1 VARIOUS WAYS TO CUT THINGS ARE to amputate, to carve, to chisel, to chop, to clip, to crop, to gash, to grate, to guillotine, to hack, to hew, to lop, to mince, to mow, to nick, to prune, to saw, to scalp, to sever, to shave, to shear, to shred, to slash, to slice, to slit, to snip, to split, to stab, to trim. **2** *Mrs Angel cut the story as it was too long.* to abbreviate, to abridge, to censor, to shorten. **3** *I was talking to granny on the phone, but we were cut off.* to interrupt, to stop, to terminate. **4** *a cut on the finger.* gash, injury, nick, notch, slash, slit, tear, wound.

cute SEE **attractive, clever.**

cutlass SEE **weapon.**

cutlery 1 ITEMS OF CUTLERY ARE bread-knife, carving knife, dessert-spoon, fork, knife, ladle, spoon, tablespoon, teaspoon. **2** SEE **kitchen.**

cutlet SEE **meat.**

cut-price cheap, inexpensive.

cutter SEE **vessel.**

cutting 1 *a railway cutting.* SEE **railway. 2** *plant cuttings.* SEE **plant.**

cycle 1 KINDS OF CYCLE ARE bicycle, (informal) bike, moped, (informal) motor bike, motor cycle, penny-farthing, scooter, tandem, tricycle. SEE ALSO **travel, vehicle. 2** *a cycle of events.* sequence, series.

cyclone hurricane, storm, tempest, tornado, typhoon. SEE ALSO **weather.**

cygnet SEE **young.**

cylinder SEE **shape.**

cymbal SEE **percussion.**

cypress SEE **tree.**

D d

dab SEE **touch.**

dachshund SEE **dog.**

daddy-long-legs SEE **insect.**

daffodil SEE **bulb, flower.**

dagger SEE **weapon.**

dainty *dainty embroidery.* delicate, exquisite, fine, neat, pretty.

dairy SEE **shop.**

daisy SEE **flower.**

dale *Yorkshire Dales.* glen, valley.

dally *Don't dally: we must move on.* to dawdle, to hang about, to linger, to loaf, to loiter.

Dalmatian SEE **dog.**

dam *They built a dam across the stream.* bank, barrage, barrier, dike, embankment, wall, weir.

damage 1 *Did it cause any damage?* destruction, devastation, havoc, injury, sabotage. **2** *Did the accident damage the car?* to break, to chip, to cripple, to dent, to destroy, to harm, to hurt, to immobilize, to injure, to mar, to scratch, to spoil, to strain, to wound.

dame 1 SEE **woman. 2** SEE **title.**

damn to condemn, to curse.

damp *The spare room feels damp.* clammy, dank, humid, moist.

dampen to moisten.

damson SEE **fruit.**

dance 1 *We danced for joy.* to caper, to jig about, to jump about, to leap, to prance, to skip. **2** KINDS OF DANCING ARE disco dancing, hornpipe, jig, limbo dancing, minuet, reel, tap-dancing, waltz. **3** *Lucy went to a dance.* ball, disco, party, social.

dancer SEE **entertainment.**

dandelion SEE **flower.**

dandruff SEE **illness.**

danger 1 *There's a danger of catching cold in this weather.* chance, possibility, risk, threat. **2** *Astronauts are always facing danger.* crisis, distress, hazard, peril, pitfall, trouble.

dangerous 1 *a dangerous journey.* chancy, hazardous, perilous, precarious, risky, unsafe. 2 *a dangerous lion.* destructive, harmful, treacherous. 3 *a dangerous criminal.* desperate, violent.

dangle *The rope dangled just above his head.* to be suspended, to droop, to hang, to sway, to swing.

dank clammy, damp, moist.

dare 1 *Would you dare to jump off that rock?* to risk, to venture. 2 *Logan dared Tony to eat four ice-creams.* to challenge, to defy.

daring *a daring explorer, a daring feat, etc.* adventurous, bold, brave, fearless, intrepid.

dark 1 *a dark place, a dark sky, etc.* black, dim, gloomy, murky, shadowy, shady, sombre, starless, sunless, unlit. 2 *dark hair.* black, brown, brunette. 3 *a dark complexion.* swarthy, tanned.

darken *The sky darkened.* to blacken.

darling beloved, dear, love, sweetheart.

darn *Tony darned the hole in his jumper.* to mend, to patch, to repair, to sew, to stitch.

dart 1 *to play darts.* SEE **game**. 2 *to dart about.* SEE **move**.

dash 1 *He dashed his foot against a rock.* to beat, to smash, to strike. SEE ALSO **hit**. 2 *Lucy dashed home.* to hasten, to hurry, to run, to rush, to speed, (informal) to zoom. SEE ALSO **move**.

data *Feed the data into the computer.* evidence, facts, information, statistics.

date 1 SEE **time**. 2 *Lucy has a date with a friend.* appointment, engagement, fixture, meeting, rendezvous. 3 *Do you like dates?* SEE **fruit**.

daughter SEE **family**.

daunt *The steepness of the climb daunted us.* to discourage, to dishearten, to dismay, to frighten, to intimidate, to put off.

dawdle *Don't dawdle: we haven't got all day.* to be slow, to dally, to hang about, to lag behind, to linger, to straggle.

dawn day-break, sunrise.

day SEE **time**.

day-break dawn, sunrise.

day-dream dream, fantasy, illusion, reverie.

daylight SEE **light**.

dazed *The blow dazed him.* amazed, bewildered, confused, shocked, stunned.

dazzle SEE **light**.

deacon, deaconess SEE **church**.

dead 1 *the dead king.* deceased, late. 2 *Is that fish dead?* killed, lifeless. 3 *It's so cold my fingers are dead.* deadened, numb, paralysed.

deaden *The silencer deadens the noise of the engine.* to muffle, to quieten, to soften, to stifle, to suppress.

deadly *a deadly illness.* fatal, lethal, mortal, terminal.

deaf SEE **handicap**.

deafening *a deafening roar.* loud, noisy.

deal 1 *Deal the cards.* to allot, to distribute, to divide, to give out, to share out. 2 *Mrs Angel dealt with the problem.* to attend to, to control, to cope with, to grapple with, to handle, to look after, to manage, to sort out, to tackle. 3 *I want a book that deals with insects.* to be concerned with, to cover. 4 *Dad made a deal with the garage about his new car.* agreement, bargain, contract, pact, settlement, understanding. 5 *They went to a great deal of trouble.* amount, quantity, volume.

dealer *If you have a complaint, take the goods back to your dealer.* merchant, retailer, shopkeeper, stockist, supplier, trader.

dean SEE **church**.

dear 1 *dear friends.* beloved, darling, loved. 2 *dear goods.* costly, expensive, (informal) pricey.

death decease, end, passing. SEE ALSO **funeral**, **kill**.

debate 1 *We debated whether to go to the*

pictures. to argue, to discuss, to dispute. 2 *We had a debate about cruelty to animals.* argument, conference, controversy, discussion, dispute.

debris *The debris of the aircraft was scattered over a wide area.* fragments, remains, rubble, ruins, wreckage.

decade SEE **time.**

decapitate to behead. SEE ALSO **kill.**

decathlon SEE **athletics.**

decay *Meat decays quickly in warm weather.* to decompose, to deteriorate, to disintegrate, to go bad, to perish, to rot, to spoil.

deceased *the deceased king.* dead, late.

deceit *We saw through his deceit.* deception, dishonesty, fraud, hoax, pretence, ruse, trickery, untruthfulness.

deceitful *a deceitful person.* dishonest, false, furtive, lying, secretive, shifty, sneaky, treacherous, unfaithful, untrustworthy.

deceive *He tried to deceive us, but we discovered the truth.* to be an impostor, to bluff, to cheat, to defraud, to dupe, to fool, to hoax, to hoodwink, to kid, to lie, to mislead, to outwit, to pretend, to swindle, to take in, to trick.

decent 1 *decent behaviour.* becoming, chaste, good, honourable, law-abiding, modest, proper, respectable. 2 *a decent meal.* agreeable, nice, pleasant, satisfactory.

deception *We soon discovered the deception.* deceit, dishonesty, fraud, hoax, pretence, ruse, trickery.

deceptive *When you look into the pool, you get a deceptive impression of the depth.* deceiving, false, misleading, unreliable.

decide 1 *Have you decided what to say?* to conclude, to fix on, to resolve, to settle. 2 *We decided on fish and chips.* to choose, to elect, to opt for, to pick, to select.

decided *He is very decided in his opinions.* adamant, determined, firm, resolute.

deciduous SEE **tree.**

decimal *decimal scales.* metric.

decipher *I can't decipher his writing.* to decode, to interpret, to make out, to read, to understand.

decision *After all that talking, what was your decision?* conclusion, judgement, outcome, result.

deck *the deck of a ship.* floor, level. SEE ALSO **vessel.**

declare *He declared that he would never play again.* to announce, to assert, to contend, to emphasize, to insist, to maintain, to proclaim, to pronounce, to report, to reveal, to state, to testify.

decline 1 *Logan declined the invitation to Tony's party.* to refuse, to reject, to turn down. 2 *Their enthusiasm declined after a while.* to decrease, to degenerate, to deteriorate, to die, to diminish, to fail, to flag, to lessen, to sink, to weaken, to wilt, to worsen.

decode *We tried to decode their signal.* to decipher, to explain, to interpret, to understand.

decompose *The dead bird had begun to decompose.* to decay, to disintegrate, to go bad, to perish, to rot.

decorate 1 *We decorated the church with flowers.* to adorn, to make beautiful. 2 *Mr Brunswick decorated Tony's room.* to paint, to paper. 3 *The soldier was decorated for bravery.* to honour, to reward.

decoration 1 *Christmas decorations.* adornment, ornament. 2 *a decoration for bravery.* award, badge, medal.

decorator painter. SEE ALSO **job.**

decoy *We had to decoy Logan away from the sweet stall.* to bait, to entice, to lure, to tempt.

decrease 1 *They ought to decrease the bus fares for a change.* to cut, to lessen, to lower, to reduce. 2 *The number of children in our school decreased this term.* to contract, to decline, to diminish, to dwindle, to fall, to lessen, to shrink, to wane.

decree 1 *an official decree.* command, declaration, order, proclamation. 2 *The government decreed that income tax* *would go up.* to command, to declare, to direct, to order, to proclaim.

decrepit *a decrepit old building.* broken down, derelict, dilapidated, old, ramshackle, worn out.

dedicated 1 *Mrs Brunswick was a dedicated fan of the Beatles.* devoted, faithful, loyal. 2 *This part of the church is dedicated to private prayer.* devoted to, set aside for.

deduct *Mr Brunswick threatened to deduct £1 from Lucy's pocket-money.* to subtract, to take away.

deed 1 *a heroic deed.* act, action, adventure, exploit, feat. 2 *the deeds of a house.* documents, papers, records.

deep 1 *deep feelings.* earnest, intense, profound, serious, sincere. 2 *a deep conversation.* intellectual, learned, thoughtful. 3 *a deep colour.* dark, strong. 4 *a deep note.* base, low. 5 *deep snow.* thick.

deer SEE **animal**.

deface *Vandals defaced the statue.* to disfigure, to mar, to spoil.

defeat *to defeat an enemy.* to beat, to conquer, to crush, to destroy, (informal) to flatten, (informal) to lick, to master, to outdo, to overcome, to overpower, to overthrow, to overwhelm, to rout, to subdue, to suppress, to thrash, to triumph over, to vanquish.

defect 1 *a defect in a piece of work, a defect in a person's character.* blemish, failing, fault, flaw, imperfection, mark, spot, stain, weakness. 2 *The traitor defected to the enemy's side.* to desert, to go over.

defective *Our TV set was defective.* faulty, imperfect, out of order.

defence 1 *When you accused him, what was his defence?* excuse, explanation, justification. 2 *We built a defence against the cold wind.* guard, protection, shelter, shield.

defend 1 *They did what they could to defend their homes from the hurricane.* to fortify, to guard, to keep safe, to protect, to safeguard, to shelter, to shield. 2 *He defended himself before the judge.* to speak up for, to stand up for, to support.

defer *We deferred the match until the weather got better.* to adjourn, to delay, to postpone, to put off.

defiant *Logan was defiant when Mrs Angel told him to clear up.* disobedient, mutinous, obstinate, rebellious, unyielding.

deficient *Their diet is deficient in vitamins.* lacking, scarce, short.

defile 1 *We thought the sewage works might defile our water supply.* to contaminate, to corrupt, to infect, to poison, to pollute, to soil. 2 *The horsemen rode down the steep path into the defile.* canyon, gorge, pass, ravine, valley.

define *A thesaurus simply lists words, whereas a dictionary defines them.* to clarify, to explain.

definite 1 *Mrs Brunswick has definite views about where to go on holiday.* assured, certain, confident, fixed, positive, settled, sure. 2 *We saw a definite improvement in granny's health.* clear, distinct, noticeable, obvious, plain, pronounced.

deformed *a deformed tree.* disfigured, distorted, grotesque, mis-shapen, twisted, ugly, warped.

defraud *He's in court because he tried to defraud the bank.* to cheat, to dupe, to swindle, to trick.

defrost to de-ice, to unfreeze.

deft *deft movements.* agile, clever, nimble, quick, skilful.

defy 1 *It isn't wise to defy the head.* to confront, to disobey, to face up to, to resist, to stand up to. 2 *I defy you to come any further.* to challenge, to dare.

degenerate *The sick man's condition degenerated.* to decline, to deteriorate, to sink, to weaken, to worsen.

degree 1 SEE **measure**. 2 *Lucy's cousin got a degree at Trent Polytechnic.* SEE **qualification**.

dehydrated *dehydrated food.* dried, dry.

de-ice *to de-ice the fridge.* to defrost, to unfreeze.

deity *Ancient tribes worshipped many deities.* divinity, god, goddess.

dejected *Tony was dejected when he didn't get into the swimming team.* crestfallen, depressed, discouraged, downcast, down-hearted, gloomy, melancholy, unhappy. SEE ALSO **sad**.

delay 1 *The snow delayed the traffic.* to detain, to hinder, to hold up, to keep, to obstruct, to slow down. **2** *We delayed the start of our journey.* to defer, to postpone, to put off. **3** *Don't delay if you want to catch that bus.* to hang back, to hesitate, to pause, to stall, to wait.

delete *Lucy was away ill, so we deleted her name from the list.* to cancel, to cross out, to erase, to remove, to wipe out.

deliberate 1 *a deliberate insult.* calculated, conscious, intentional, planned, premeditated, wilful. **2** *deliberate planning.* careful, cautious, methodical, painstaking, slow.

deliberately *He hit me deliberately.* intentionally, purposely.

delicacy SEE **food**.

delicate 1 *delicate material.* dainty, exquisite, fine, flimsy, fragile, frail, soft, tender. **2** *delicate health.* feeble, sickly, unhealthy, weak. **3** *delicate machinery.* intricate, sensitive. **4** *a delicate flavour.* faint, gentle, mild, subtle.

delicatessen SEE **shop**.

delicious appetizing, luscious, tasty. SEE ALSO **taste**.

delight 1 *The play delighted the children.* to amuse, to captivate, to charm, to enchant, to entertain, to entrance, to fascinate, to please, to thrill. **2** *Mum's greatest delight is a nice hot bath.* bliss, ecstasy, enjoyment, joy, pleasure, rapture.

delinquent *a juvenile delinquent.* criminal, culprit, hooligan, offender, wrongdoer.

delirious *Lucy was delirious with joy when she got in the county team.* crazy,

demented, excited, frantic, frenzied, hysterical, mad, wild.

deliver *to deliver letters.* to convey, to distribute, to give out, to hand over, to present, to take round.

delivery *The greengrocer has a fresh delivery of vegetables each day.* batch, consignment.

delta SEE **geography**.

delude *Logan deliberately tried to delude us.* to deceive, to fool, to hoax, to mislead.

deluge *We got soaked in the deluge.* downpour, flood, rainstorm.

delusion *The boy who said he met a Martian must have suffered a delusion.* hallucination, illusion.

demand *He demanded to have his money back.* to ask, to beg, to claim, to command, to order, to request, to require.

demented *The dog was demented when the wasp stung him.* berserk, crazy, delirious, deranged, frantic, frenzied, insane, lunatic, mad, wild.

demerara SEE **sugar**.

democracy SEE **country, government**.

Democrat SEE **politics**.

demolish *They demolished a block of old flats.* to destroy, to dismantle, to knock down, to raze.

demon devil, imp, spirit.

demonstrate 1 *The local garage demonstrated a new car.* to display, to exhibit, to show. **2** *She demonstrated how to make a cake.* to describe, to explain, to illustrate, to show. **3** *They demonstrated that smoking does affect your health.* to establish, to prove. **4** *We demonstrated against experiments on live animals.* to march, to protest.

demonstration 1 *a cookery demonstration.* display, exhibition, presentation, show. **2** *a political demonstration.* demo, march, protest, rally.

demure *a demure expression.* bashful, coy, modest, quiet, retiring, shy.

den *We made a den in the garden.* hide-out, hiding-place, lair.

denim SEE **cloth.**

denounce *At the end of the play, the detective denounced the murderer.* to accuse, to blame, to complain about, to condemn, to inform against, to report, to reveal, to tell of.

dense 1 *dense fog.* heavy, impenetrable, thick. **2** *a dense crowd.* packed, solid. **3** *a dense pupil.* dim, dull, foolish, obtuse, slow, stupid, (informal) thick, unintelligent.

dent *Dad dented the wing of the car.* to bend, to buckle, to crumple, to knock in.

dentist SEE **job, medicine.**

denture SEE **tooth.**

deny 1 *Do you deny the accusation?* to contradict, to disclaim, to dispute, to reject. **2** *Within reason, grandad doesn't deny us anything.* to deprive of, to refuse.

deodorant SEE **cosmetics.**

depart *Are you ready to depart?* to embark, to emigrate, to go away, to leave, to quit, to set off, to set out.

department branch, part, section.

depend *Lucy depends on dad to drive her to the gym.* to bank on, to count on, to need, to rely on, to trust.

dependable *a dependable bus service, a dependable friend.* consistent, faithful, regular, reliable, safe, sound, steady, true, trustworthy.

depict *We depicted a snowy scene.* to describe, to draw, to illustrate, to paint, to picture, to portray, to represent, to show.

deplorable *deplorable behaviour.* regrettable, reprehensible, unfortunate. SEE ALSO **bad.**

deport *They used to deport people for stealing.* to banish, to exile, to expel, to send away.

depose *to depose a monarch.* to get rid of, to remove.

deposit 1 *Deposit your dirty plates by the hatch.* to leave, to place, to put down, to set down. **2** *I deposited some money in the building society.* to pay in, to save. **3** *There's a dirty deposit in the bottom of the cup.* dregs, sediment.

depot *The climbers established a depot at the foot of the mountain.* base, cache, dump, headquarters, hoard, store.

depraved *Only a depraved person would torture a fellow human being.* base, corrupt, evil, immoral, vicious, wicked. SEE ALSO **bad.**

depress 1 *His dog's death depressed him.* to dishearten, to grieve, to sadden. **2** *depressed*: dejected, desolate, despondent, disconsolate, gloomy, heart-broken, low, melancholy, miserable, mournful, unhappy, wretched. SEE ALSO **sad. 3** *depressing*: black, discouraging, disheartening, dismal, gloomy, sombre, tragic. **4** SEE **sad.**

depression 1 *a mood of depression.* despair, gloom, hopelessness, melancholy, sadness. **2** SEE **weather. 3** *a depression in the ground.* dent, dip, hollow.

deprive *Would a vegetarian deprive a dog of his bone?* to deny, to refuse, to rob, to take away.

deputy *The mayor was ill, so he sent a deputy.* assistant, replacement, reserve, representative, stand-in, substitute.

derailment accident, crash.

deranged *He was so odd that we thought he was deranged.* crazy, demented, insane, (informal) loony, lunatic, mad.

derelict *a derelict farmhouse.* abandoned, broken down, decrepit, deserted, dilapidated, forsaken, ruined, tumbledown.

derive *Grandpa derives a lot of pleasure from his garden.* to acquire, to get, to obtain, to procure, to receive.

dermatitis SEE **illness.**

derrick crane.

descant SEE **sing.**

descend to come doxvn, to climb down, to drop, to fall, to move down, to sink.

descendants heirs, offspring, posterity.

describe *An eyewitness described what happened.* to depict, to explain, to express, to narrate, to portray, to recount, to relate, to represent, to tell.

description account, commentary, depiction, narration, portrait, representation, sketch, story.

desert 1 *The camels crossed the desert.* wasteland, wilderness. **2** *a desert island.* barren, uninhabited, wild. **3** *Don't desert your friends.* to abandon, to forsake, to leave. **4** *They deserted him on an island.* to maroon, to strand. **5** *The soldiers deserted.* to defect, to run away.

deserter fugitive, outlaw, renegade, traitor.

deserve *Does he deserve a prize?* to earn, to merit.

design 1 *a design for a dress.* drawing, pattern, plan, sketch. **2** *Our car is an old design.* model, type, version. **3** *An architect designs buildings.* to draw, to plan, to plot, to scheme, to sketch.

designer SEE **job**.

desire 1 *What do you desire most?* to fancy, to hanker after, to long for, to want, to wish for, to yearn for. **2** *He stole because of his desire for money.* ambition, appetite, craving, hunger, itch, longing, love, lust, passion, thirst, urge, wish.

desk SEE **furniture**.

desolate 1 *The desolate house was haunted.* bleak, barren, deserted, dreary, empty, isolated, lonely, remote, windswept. **2** *He was desolate after his dog died.* depressed, forlorn, forsaken, neglected, unhappy, wretched. SEE ALSO **sad**.

despair *a state of despair.* depression, desperation, hopelessness.

desperado brigand, criminal, crook, gangster, gunman, ruffian.

desperate 1 *The shipwrecked sailors were desperate.* despairing, hopeless. **2** *a desperate situation.* bad, serious. **3** *a desperate criminal.* dangerous, reckless, violent.

despicable *a despicable crime.* base, contemptible, detestable, hateful.

despise *We sometimes despise people who can't do what we can.* to be contemptuous of, to detest, to disdain, to dislike, to hate, to look down on, to scorn, to sneer at.

despondent *Tony was despondent when he didn't get into the swimming team.* depressed, desolate, gloomy, melancholy, unhappy. SEE ALSO **sad**.

dessert SEE **meal**.

dessert-spoon SEE **cutlery**.

destination *This train's destination is London.* terminus.

destined *Logan's resolutions were destined to fail.* doomed, fated, intended.

destiny chance, doom, fate, fortune, luck, providence.

destitute 1 *destitute beggars.* deprived, homeless, impoverished, needy, penniless, poor, poverty-stricken. **2** *the destitute*: beggars, paupers, tramps, vagrants.

destroy WAYS TO DESTROY THINGS ARE to abolish, to annihilate, to crush, to demolish, to devastate, to dismantle, to eliminate, to end, to eradicate, to exterminate, to finish off, to flatten, to get rid of, to knock down, to raze, to ruin, to stamp out, to uproot, to wipe out, to wreck. SEE ALSO **defeat**, **kill**.

destroyer SEE **vessel**.

destruction *a scene of destruction.* damage, devastation, havoc.

destructive *destructive animals.* dangerous, harmful, violent.

detach *We helped dad detach the caravan from the car.* to disconnect, to divide, to part, to remove, to separate, to undo, to unfasten.

detached 1 *a detached house.* separate. **2** *a detached attitude.* disinterested, impartial, neutral, unbiased, unemotional, uninvolved, unprejudiced.

detail *The policeman noticed every detail.* circumstance, fact, feature, particular.

detain 1 *What detained you?* to delay, to hold up, to keep. **2** *The police detained* *the suspect.* to arrest, to capture, to confine, to gaol, to hold, to imprison.

detect *Did the garage detect anything wrong with the car?* to diagnose, to discern, to discover, to find, to identify, to notice, to observe, to sense.

detective SEE **job, police**.

detention SEE **punishment**.

deter *We put up a scarecrow to deter the birds.* to daunt, to discourage, to dismay, to hinder, to impede, to obstruct, to prevent.

detergent soap. SEE ALSO **wash**.

deteriorate *His health deteriorated in the winter.* to decay, to decline, to degenerate, to disintegrate, to get worse, to weaken, to worsen.

determination *Marathon runners show great determination.* courage, (informal) grit, (informal) guts, spirit, will.

determined *He was determined that he would succeed.* adamant, firm, resolute, resolved, strenuous.

detest *Our dog detests snow.* to despise, to dislike, to hate, to loathe.

detestable *a detestable crime.* contemptible, despicable, hateful, horrible, loathsome, odious. SEE ALSO **unpleasant**.

detonate *to detonate a bomb.* to blow up, to discharge, to explode, to fire, to let off, to set off.

detour diversion.

devastate *The hurricane devastated the town.* to demolish, to destroy, to flatten, to ravage, to wreck.

develop 1 *Lucy's technique in gymnastics is developing well.* to advance, to evolve, to improve, to move on, to progress. 2 *The local shop plans to develop next year.* to build up, to expand, to grow, to increase. 3 *Leave the apples on the tree to develop.* to age, to mature, to ripen. 4 *Your story starts well: you ought to develop it.* to amplify, to enlarge, to strengthen.

device *That tin-opener is a clever device.* appliance, contraption, contrivance, gadget, implement, instrument, invention, machine, tool, utensil.

devil demon, fiend, imp, spirit.

devious 1 *We came home by a devious route.* indirect, roundabout. 2 *You can't always trust Logan: he can be very devious.* deceitful, dishonest, sly, sneaky, wily.

devise *Logan says he's devising a scheme to make lots of money!* to concoct, to design, to invent, to make up, to plan, to think up.

devoted *That dog is Tony's devoted companion.* constant, dedicated, devout, enthusiastic, faithful, loving, loyal, reliable.

devour *The lions devoured the meat greedily.* to consume, to gobble, to gulp. SEE ALSO **eat**.

devout *a devout worshipper.* committed, dedicated, devoted, genuine, religious, sincere.

dew SEE **weather**.

dhow SEE **vessel**.

diabetes SEE **illness**.

diabolical *diabolical behaviour.* devilish, fiendish, hellish.

diadem coronet, crown. SEE ALSO **hat**.

diagnose *The doctor diagnosed mumps.* to detect, to find, to identify.

diagram chart, graph, figure, plan, outline, sketch.

dial *Did you dial the right number?* to call, to phone, to ring, to telephone.

dialect *a London dialect, a northern dialect.* accent, brogue, language.

dialogue *The play contained a funny dialogue between a giant and an elf.* conversation, discussion, talk.

diamond 1 *a diamond ring.* SEE **jewellery**. 2 SEE **shape**. 3 *the ace of diamonds.* SEE **cards**.

diarrhoea SEE **illness**.

diary *Lucy writes a diary every day.* journal, log, record. SEE ALSO **book**.

dice SEE **game**.

dictator SEE **ruler**.

dictatorial *He's very dictatorial and*

won't let us say anything. bossy, domineering, tyrannical.

dictatorship SEE **country, government.**

dictionary SEE **book.**

die 1 *All mortal creatures must die.* to expire, to pass away, to perish. 2 *Our enthusiasm began to die after a while.* to decline, to decrease, to fail, to lessen, to stop, to weaken.

diesel SEE **engine.**

diet *You need a good diet to keep healthy.* food, nourishment.

differ 1 *I wonder how our school differs from the one granny went to?* to contrast with. 2 *We often differ about what to watch on TV.* to argue, to disagree, to quarrel.

difference 1 *What's the difference between the cheap jeans and the expensive ones?* comparison, contrast, distinction. 2 *We told Logan to stop messing about, but it didn't make any difference.* alteration, change, modification. 3 *There was a difference between Tony and Lucy about what to watch on TV.* argument, disagreement, quarrel.

different 1 *Have the chocolates got different centres?* assorted, contrasting, dissimilar, miscellaneous, mixed, unlike, varied, various. 2 *Everyone's handwriting is different.* distinct, particular, personal, separate, special, specific, unique. 3 *Tony and Lucy have different views about music.* conflicting, contradictory, incompatible, opposite.

difficult 1 *a difficult problem.* advanced, complicated, hard, thorny, ticklish, tricky. 2 *a difficult climb.* arduous, laborious, strenuous, tough.

difficulty *Have you got a difficulty?* adversity, complication, dilemma, fix, hardship, hindrance, jam, obstacle, plight, predicament, problem, snag, trouble.

dig *to dig a hole.* to burrow, to excavate, to gouge out, to hollow out, to mine, to scoop, to tunnel.

digest SEE **eat.**

digit figure, integer, number, numeral.

dignified *a dignified ceremony.* calm, elegant, formal, grave, noble, proper, sedate, serious, sober, solemn, stately, tasteful.

dike 1 *They dug a dike across the marsh.* channel, ditch. 2 *They built a dike as a defence against flooding.* dam, embankment.

dilapidated *a dilapidated old building.* broken down, decrepit, derelict, ramshackle, rickety, ruined, tumbledown.

dilemma *Tony was in a dilemma because he was invited to two parties on the same day.* difficulty, fix, jam, plight, predicament, problem.

diligent *a diligent worker.* careful, conscientious, earnest, hardworking, persevering, scrupulous, thorough.

dilute *You dilute orange squash with water.* to thin, to water down, to weaken.

dim 1 *We saw a dim outline in the mist.* blurred, cloudy, dark, faint, gloomy, hazy, indistinct, misty, murky, obscure, shadowy, unclear. 2 (informal) *You are dim if you can't understand that!* dense, dull, foolish, obtuse, slow, stupid, (informal) thick.

dimensions *If you're having a new carpet, we need to know the dimensions of your bedroom.* magnitude, measurements, proportions, size, volume.

diminish *Our supply of sweets diminished rather quickly.* to contract, to decline, to reduce, to shrink, to subside.

diminutive *We saw a diminutive figure in the distance.* little, miniature, minute, short, small, (informal) teeny, tiny, undersized, wee.

din *We were deafened by the din.* bedlam, clamour, commotion, hubbub, hullabaloo, noise, pandemonium, racket, row, rumpus, shouting, tumult, uproar.

dine SEE **eat.**

dinghy SEE **vessel.**

dingy *This room is dingy: it needs*

decorating. depressing, dirty, dismal, drab, dull, gloomy, grimy.

dining-room SEE **house**.

dinner banquet, feast. SEE ALSO **meal**.

dinosaur SEE **animal**.

dip 1 *to dip in water*. to dive, to drop, to immerse, to lower, to plunge, to submerge. 2 *a dip in the sea*. plunge, swim. 3 *a dip in the ground*. dent, depression, hollow.

diphtheria SEE **illness**.

diploma *Tony got a diploma in the swimming gala*. award, certificate. SEE ALSO **qualification**.

diplomat ambassador, consul, representative.

diplomatic *Lucy was diplomatic about not wanting to go to granny's*. discreet, polite, tactful.

dire *a dire calamity*. appalling, awful, calamitous, dreadful, serious, terrible. SEE ALSO **bad**.

direct 1 *a direct line*. straight, unswerving. 2 *a direct answer*. blunt, candid, frank, honest, outspoken, plain, straight, straightforward, uncomplicated. 3 *Can you direct me to the station?* to guide, to indicate, to show. 4 *Their guns were directed at us*. to aim, to point, to turn. 5 *The head directed us to come in*. to command, to instruct, to order, to tell. 6 *The fireman directed the rescue*. to administer, to command, to control, to govern, to manage, to regulate, to supervise.

director *the director of a business*. administrator, boss, captain, controller, executive, governor, head, manager, overseer, ruler, supervisor.

directory *a telephone directory*. catalogue, index, list, register.

dirge SEE **music**.

dirt dust, filth, grime, (informal) muck, mud, pollution.

dirty 1 *a dirty room, dirty shoes, etc.* dingy, dusty, filthy, foul, grimy, grubby, messy, (informal) mucky, muddy, soiled, sooty, sordid, squalid, unclean. 2 *dirty language*. coarse, crude, improper, indecent, obscene, offensive, rude, smutty, vulgar.

disable 1 to damage, to weaken. 2 *disabled*: crippled, handicapped, lame, maimed.

disadvantage *It's a disadvantage to be short if you play basketball*. drawback, handicap, hindrance, inconvenience.

disagree *Logan disagrees with nearly everything we say*. to argue, to differ, to quarrel.

disagreeable *a disagreeable remark, a disagreeable smell, etc.* distasteful, nasty, offensive, rude, unfriendly. SEE ALSO **unpleasant**.

disagreement *Was there any disagreement about Tony playing in goal?* argument, controversy, debate, dispute, opposition, quarrel.

disappear *The fog disappeared quickly*. to clear, to dwindle, to evaporate, to fade, to melt away, to pass, to vanish.

disappointed *We were disappointed when our team lost*. crestfallen, dejected, discontented, dissatisfied, downcast, down-hearted, let down, unhappy. SEE ALSO **sad**.

disapproval *Mrs Angel showed her disapproval of our behaviour*. censure, condemnation, criticism, dissatisfaction, reprimand, reproach.

disaster 1 *We had a disaster when our water pipes burst last winter*. accident, calamity, catastrophe, fiasco, mishap. 2 VARIOUS DISASTERS ARE air crash, avalanche, derailment, earthquake, flood, landslide, road accident, shipwreck, tidal wave, volcanic eruption.

disbelieving *Dad was disbelieving when I said I didn't want any pocket-money*. incredulous, sceptical.

disc 1 circle, counter, token. 2 *Do you buy discs or cassettes?* album, LP, single. SEE ALSO **record**. 3 *a disc drive*. SEE **computer**.

discard *It's time we discarded these old comics*. to dispose of, to dump, to

eliminate, to get rid of, to reject, to scrap, to shed, to throw away.

discern *We discerned a change in the weather.* to detect, to distinguish, to mark, to notice, to observe, to perceive, to recognize, to see, to spy, to understand.

discharge 1 *The judge discharged him.* to acquit, to excuse, to free, to let off, to liberate. 2 *His boss discharged him because he was lazy.* to dismiss, to fire, to sack. 3 *to discharge a gun.* to detonate, to fire, to shoot. 4 *The chimney discharged black smoke.* to belch, to eject, to emit, to expel, to give out, to release, to send out.

disciple admirer, apostle, follower.

discipline *Usually the discipline in our class is good.* control, management, obedience, order, system.

disclaim *Everyone disclaimed responsibility for the broken window.* to deny, to disown, to renounce.

disclose *Whatever you do, don't disclose our secret to anyone!* to bare, to betray, to divulge, to expose, to make known, to reveal, to uncover.

disco SEE **entertainment**.

discolour *The spilt acid discoloured the table.* to bleach, to stain, to tarnish, to tinge.

discomfort *Tony hates the discomfort of wearing new shoes.* ache, distress, pain, soreness, uncomfortableness, uneasiness.

disconsolate *Tony was disconsolate when his dog disappeared.* desolate, despondent, gloomy, melancholy, unhappy. SEE ALSO **sad**.

discontented *How can we cheer up this discontented crowd?* disappointed, disgruntled, displeased, dissatisfied, miserable, unhappy. SEE ALSO **sad**.

discontinue *They discontinued the Sunday bus service.* to cease, to end, to finish, to stop, to terminate.

discord 1 *Was there any discord, or did you all agree?* argument, conflict, disagreement, dispute, quarrelling. 2 SEE **music**.

discount *Did you pay the full price, or did they give you a discount?* concession, reduction.

discourage *The climbers were discouraged by the bad weather.* to daunt, to deter, to dishearten, to dismay, to dissuade, to frighten, to intimidate, to put off, to scare.

discourteous *It was discourteous to go into Mrs Wilson's garden without asking.* bad-mannered, cheeky, disrespectful, impertinent, impolite, impudent, insolent, rude, uncouth.

discover *We were in the library seeing what we could discover about dinosaurs.* to come across, to detect, to explore, to find out, to identify, to learn, to locate, to notice, to observe, to perceive, to reveal, to search out, to track down, to uncover, to unearth.

discoverer creator, explorer, inventor.

discreet *Could you ask a few discreet questions about what mum wants for her birthday?* careful, diplomatic, polite, prudent, tactful.

discretion *You showed great discretion in choosing those nice colours.* good sense, judgement.

discriminate 1 *Can you discriminate between instant coffee and ground coffee?* to distinguish, to tell apart. 2 *It is wrong to discriminate against people because of their religion or colour or sex.* to be biased, to be intolerant, to be prejudiced, to show favouritism.

discrimination *racial discrimination.* bias, favouritism, intolerance, prejudice, racialism, racism.

discus SEE **athletics**.

discuss *Let's discuss the problem.* to argue about, to consider, to debate, to examine, to talk about.

discussion argument, conversation, debate, dialogue, talk.

disdain *That cat's too fussy: he disdains everything we give him.* to despise, to dislike, to look down on, to scorn, to snub.

disdainful *a disdainful smile.* arrogant, contemptuous, haughty, proud, scornful, snobbish, stuck-up.

disease *to suffer from a disease.*
affliction, ailment, blight, (informal)
bug, complaint, disorder, infection,
infirmity, malady, sickness. SEE
ALSO **illness**.

disembark *to disembark from a ship.* to
go ashore, to land.

disentangle *to disentangle a piece of
string.* to untie, to untwist.

disfigured *He was disfigured in the fire.*
defaced, deformed, scarred.

disgrace 1 *If you do something wrong,
you suffer the disgrace of being punished.*
dishonour, embarrassment,
humiliation, shame. 2 *The way that
man treats his dog is a disgrace!* outrage,
scandal.

disgraceful *disgraceful behaviour.*
dishonourable, embarrassing,
humiliating, shameful.

disgruntled *A disgruntled old gentleman
complained about the food.* bad-
tempered, cross, discontented,
dissatisfied, grumpy.

disguise 1 *The bird-watchers disguised
their hide-out.* to camouflage, to
conceal, to cover up, to hide, to
mask. 2 *to disguise yourself as*: to
counterfeit, to dress up as, to pretend
to be.

disgust 1 *He couldn't hide his disgust for
the rotten food.* aversion, contempt,
dislike, hatred, loathing, revulsion.
2 *The rotten food disgusted him.* to
appal, to horrify, to nauseate, to
offend, to repel, to revolt, to shock, to
sicken. 3 *disgusting*: SEE **unpleasant**.

dish basin, bowl, plate. SEE ALSO
container.

dishearten *They were disheartened by
losing four games in a row.* to depress,
to deter, to discourage, to dismay, to
put off, to sadden.

dishevelled *dishevelled hair.*
bedraggled, messy, scruffy, tangled,
uncombed, unkempt, untidy.

dishonest cheating, corrupt, criminal, crooked, deceitful, deceptive,
false, fraudulent, insincere, lying,
misleading, underhand,
unscrupulous, untrustworthy.

dishonour disgrace, shame.

dishwasher SEE **kitchen**.

disinclined *As we couldn't see any shops,
we were disinclined to walk any further.*
hesitant, reluctant, unwilling.

disinfect *When Lucy had measles, Mrs
Brunswick disinfected all her things.* to
purify, to sterilize.

disintegrate *The wrecked ship soon
disintegrated.* to break up, to crumble,
to decay, to degenerate, to
deteriorate, to fall apart, to shatter,
to smash up.

disinterested *A referee is supposed to be
disinterested.* detached, impartial,
neutral, unbiased, uninvolved,
unprejudiced.

disjointed *I didn't like that programme:
the story seemed disjointed.* broken up,
confused, incoherent, jumbled,
mixed up, muddled.

dislike 1 *I dislike shopping.* to despise,
to detest, to hate, to loathe, to scorn.
2 *He couldn't hide his dislike.* aversion,
contempt, disgust, distaste, hatred,
loathing, revulsion.

disloyal *a disloyal friend.* treacherous,
unfaithful.

disloyalty *We found it hard to forgive his
disloyalty.* betrayal, infidelity,
treachery, treason, unfaithfulness.

dismal *Our garden looks dismal in the
winter.* bleak, cheerless, depressing,
dingy, dreary, gloomy, sombre. SEE
ALSO **sad**.

dismantle *They dismantled the old
factory chimney.* to demolish, to take
down.

dismay 1 *He realized with dismay that
the brakes were not working.* alarm,
anxiety, consternation, dread, fear,
horror. 2 *They were dismayed to see a
rhinoceros charging towards them.* to
alarm, to appal, to daunt, to
discourage, to disgust, to dishearten,
to distress, to frighten, to horrify, to
scare, to shock, to terrify.

dismiss 1 *The head dismissed us at the
end of the lesson.* to let go, to release, to
send away. 2 *The boss dismissed him
because he was lazy.* to discharge, to

fire, to sack. 3 *We dismissed the idea of going abroad because it was too expensive.* to discard, to disregard, to get rid of, to reject, to set aside.

disobedient *disobedient children, a disobedient crew.* contrary, defiant, insubordinate, mutinous, obstinate, perverse, rebellious, stubborn, troublesome, unmanageable, unruly.

disobey 1 *to disobey an order.* to defy, to disregard, to ignore. 2 *to disobey a rule.* to break, to infringe, to violate. 3 *to disobey your leader.* to mutiny, to rebel, to revolt.

disorder 1 *The police wanted to prevent disorder in the streets.* anarchy, chaos, confusion, lawlessness, rioting, unrest. 2 *The burglars left the house in great disorder.* mess, muddle, shambles. 3 *There was a bit of disorder in the playground when Logan started a fight.* commotion, disturbance, fuss, rumpus, turmoil.

disorderly 1 *That disorderly class next door is making a lot of noise!* badly-behaved, boisterous, lawless, noisy, obstreperous, riotous, rough, rowdy, turbulent, undisciplined, unruly, wild. 2 *Your work is very disorderly.* SEE **disorganized**.

disorganized *Your work is very disorganized.* careless, chaotic, confused, disorderly, haphazard, jumbled, messy, muddled, scatter-brained, slapdash, sloppy, slovenly, unsystematic, untidy.

disown *Tony disowned his dog when it misbehaved.* to renounce.

disparaging *disparaging remarks.* insulting, mocking, rude, uncomplimentary.

dispatch 1 *Have you dispatched that parcel yet?* to convey, to post, to send, to transmit. 2 *They decided they would have to dispatch the wounded animal.* (informal) to finish off, to put an end to. SEE ALSO **kill**. 3 *A messenger arrived with important dispatches.* bulletin, communiqué, letter, message, report.

dispensary SEE **medicine**.

dispense 1 *The chemist is qualified to dispense medicine.* to distribute, to give out, to provide. 2 *It's time we dispensed with that old bike in the garage.* to do without, to get rid of, to remove.

disperse *The crowd dispersed when it rained.* to scatter, to spread out.

display 1 *a gymnastics display.* demonstration, exhibition, presentation, show. 2 *to display your knowledge.* to air, to demonstrate, to exhibit, to present, to produce, to reveal, to show.

displease *Our noise displeased Mrs Angel.* to annoy, to exasperate, to irritate, to offend, to trouble, to upset, to vex, to worry.

dispose 1 *Can we dispose of that old bike?* to discard, to dump, to get rid of, to give away, to sell, to throw away. 2 *Do you think dad's disposed to give me a new bike?* to be inclined to, to be liable to, to be likely to, to be ready to, to be willing to.

disposition *Our dog has a friendly disposition.* attitude, character, manner, mood, nature, personality, temperament.

dispute 1 *There was a dispute between Tony and Logan.* argument, debate, quarrel. 2 *No one disputed the referee's decision.* to argue against, to contradict, to deny, to oppose, to question.

disregard 1 *Tony usually disregards Lucy's advice.* to dismiss, to disobey, to forget, to ignore, to neglect, to overlook, to reject. 2 *Logan disregarded the hard sums.* to leave out, to miss out, to omit, to skip.

disreputable *a disreputable-looking character.* dubious, shady, suspicious, untrustworthy.

disrespectful *Logan is sometimes disrespectful to the teachers.* cheeky, discourteous, impertinent, impolite, impudent, insolent, rude.

disrupt *The arrival of the visitors disrupted our work.* to break up, to interrupt, to upset.

dissatisfied *a dissatisfied customer.*

disappointed, discontented, displeased.

dissimilar *The teams need to wear dissimilar colours.* contrasting, different, distinct, unalike.

dissolve *Sugar dissolves in tea.* to disappear, to melt.

dissuade *Lucy dissuaded Tony from buying the record she hated.* to advise against, to discourage.

distance *What's the distance between us and the moon?* gap, interval, length, space, stretch. SEE ALSO **measure**.

distant 1 *distant places.* far, far-away, outlying, remote. **2** *a distant manner.* cool, reserved, unenthusiastic, unfriendly.

distasteful *The job of clearing up when the cat was sick was distasteful.* disagreeable, horrid, nasty, objectionable, repellent, revolting. SEE ALSO **unpleasant**.

distended bloated, bulging, swollen.

distinct 1 *We saw distinct footprints in the mud.* clear, definite, obvious, plain. **2** *Tony's handwriting is distinct from Lucy's.* contrasting, different, dissimilar, separate. **3** *Tony has a distinct kind of handwriting.* individual, special.

distinction 1 *Is there any distinction between different brands of soap powder?* contrast, difference. **2** *Lucy has the distinction of being in the county team.* excellence, fame, honour, importance, renown.

distinctive *Mrs Angel has distinctive handwriting.* characteristic, different, distinct, individual, personal, special, typical, unique.

distinguish 1 *Can you distinguish butter from margarine?* to discriminate, to tell apart. **2** *In the dark we couldn't distinguish who the visitor was.* to discern, to make out, to perceive, to recognize, to see. **3** *distinguished: a distinguished actor.* celebrated, eminent, famous, foremost, great, important, leading, notable, noted, outstanding, prominent, renowned, well-known.

distort *to distort the truth.* to bend, to deform, to twist, to warp.

distract *The flashing lights distracted us.* to bewilder, to confuse, to divert, to trouble, to worry.

distress 1 *The trapped animal was in distress.* agony, anguish, discomfort, pain, suffering, torment, torture. **2** *The phones by the motorway are for the use of motorists in distress.* adversity, danger, difficulty, trouble. **3** *The news of the disaster distressed us.* to afflict, to alarm, to dismay, to frighten, to grieve, to hurt, to perturb, to scare, to shake, to shock, to terrify, to torment, to torture, to trouble, to upset, to worry.

distribute *Mrs Angel asked Tony to distribute the papers.* to allot, to circulate, to deal out, to deliver, to dispense, to divide, to give out, to hand round, to issue, to share out.

district *There are plenty of shops in our district.* area, locality, neighbourhood, region, vicinity, zone.

distrust *I distrust dogs that bark.* to doubt, to mistrust, to suspect.

disturb 1 *Don't disturb granny.* to annoy, to bother, to interrupt, to worry. **2** *A fox disturbed the chickens.* to agitate, to alarm, to excite, to frighten, to perturb, to scare, to stir up, to upset.

disused *a disused railway line.* abandoned, obsolete.

ditch channel, dike, drain, gutter, trench.

divan SEE **bed**.

dive *to dive into the water.* to dip, to go under, to nosedive, to plunge, to sink, to submerge, to subside, to swoop.

diver frogman. SEE ALSO **job**.

diverge *The motorways diverge.* to branch, to divide, to fork, to separate, to split.

diverse *a diverse collection of things.* assorted, different, miscellaneous, mixed, varied, various.

diversion 1 *a traffic diversion.* detour. **2** *Can you organize some diversions for the* *guests?* amusement, entertainment, game, hobby, pastime, recreation.

divert 1 *Because of the fog they diverted the plane to another airport.* to change direction. **2** *Dad diverted us with funny stories.* to amuse, to cheer up, to distract, to entertain.

divide 1 *The road divides: which way do we go?* to branch, to diverge, to fork, to separate. **2** *How shall we divide these sweets?* to allot, to deal out, to distribute, to give out, to halve, to share out. **3** *We'll divide the class into two.* to part, to separate, to split.

dividers SEE **mathematics**.

divine celestial, god-like, heavenly, holy, religious, sacred.

division 1 *The box has divisions for different tools.* compartment, part, section, segment. **2** *a division of a business.* branch, department.

divorce to separate, to split up.

divulge *Don't divulge our secret, will you?* to betray, to disclose, to expose, to make known, to publish, to reveal, to tell.

DIY SEE **shop**.

dizzy *I feel dizzy when I look down from a height.* confused, faint, giddy, reeling, unsteady.

DJ SEE **entertainment**.

do 1 *Have you done your work?* to accomplish, to achieve, to carry out, to commit, to complete, to execute, to finish, to perform. **2** *Will you do the potatoes?* to attend to, to cope with, to deal with, to handle, to look after, to manage. **3** *Will four big potatoes do?* to be enough, to be satisfactory, to be sufficient, to be suitable. ! *Do* can mean many things. The words given here are only some of the other words you can use.

docile *a docile animal.* gentle, meek, obedient, patient, tame.

dock 1 *The ship came in to the dock.* berth, dockyard, harbour, haven, jetty, landing-stage, pier, port, quay, wharf. **2** *The prisoner stood in the dock.* SEE **law**.

docker SEE **job**.

doctor SEE **job, medicine**.

document VARIOUS DOCUMENTS ARE certificate, deed, form, licence, paper, passport, records, visa, warrant, will.

documentary SEE **film**.

dodder SEE **walk**.

dodge 1 *I dodged out of the way of the snowball.* to avoid, to duck, to elude, to evade, to swerve, to turn, to veer. **2** *I know a dodge for opening lemonade bottles.* knack, trick.

dodgems SEE **fun-fair**.

doe SEE **female**.

dog 1 bitch, cur, hound, mongrel, pedigree, puppy. **2** VARIOUS BREEDS ARE Alsatian, beagle, bloodhound, bulldog, collie, dachshund, Dalmatian, foxhound, greyhound, husky, Labrador, mastiff, Pekingese, poodle, pug, retriever, sheepdog, spaniel, terrier, whippet. **3** SEE **animal, pet**.

dogged *dogged persistence.* determined, firm, obstinate, persistent, resolute, stubborn, unwavering, wilful.

dole 1 social security, unemployment benefit. **2** *to be on the dole*: to be out of work, to be unemployed.

doleful *a doleful expression.* dismal, gloomy, sorrowful, unhappy. SEE ALSO **sad**.

doll SEE **toy**.

dollop *a dollop of ice-cream.* chunk, hunk, lump, mass.

dolphin SEE **animal**.

dome SEE **building**.

domestic *domestic animals.* domesticated, house-trained, tame.

dominant 1 *The teacher is usually the dominant influence in a class.* chief, main, outstanding, prevailing, principal, ruling. **2** *The church is the dominant feature in the landscape.* biggest, highest, largest, tallest.

dominate *Their captain dominated the game.* to control, to govern, to influence, to manage, to rule.

domineering *a domineering personality.* bossy, dictatorial, tyrannical.

dominoes SEE **game**.

donate *A local business donated £100 to keep the team going*. to contribute, to give, to grant, to provide, to supply.

donation *a donation to OXFAM*. contribution, gift, offering, present.

donkey SEE **animal**.

donor *The donors were very generous when we raised money for cancer research*. benefactor, contributor, giver, provider, sponsor.

doodle *I wasn't drawing properly, just doodling*. to jot, to scribble. SEE ALSO **picture**.

doom 1 *We shall never know the doom of the missing ship*. destiny, fate. 2 *The dying woman faced her doom bravely*. death, end.

door doorway, entrance, entry, exit, French windows, gate. SEE ALSO **house**.

dope 1 *to take dope*. SEE **drug**. 2 *You're a dope!* SEE **fool**.

dormant *Many plants are dormant in winter*. asleep, hibernating, inactive, resting, sleeping.

dormitory SEE **school**.

dormouse SEE **animal**.

dot mark, point, speck, spot.

dote *Tony dotes on his dog*. to adore, to idolize, to love, to worship.

dotty (informal) *That was a dotty thing to do*. SEE **mad**.

double 1 dual, twice. 2 *I saw Tony's double in town*. copy, duplicate, twin.

double-bass SEE **strings**.

double-cross to betray, to cheat.

double-decker bus. SEE ALSO **vehicle**.

doubt 1 *Have you any doubt about whether we can trust him?* anxiety, hesitation, misgiving, qualm, suspicion, uncertainty, worry. 2 *Do you doubt my word?* to distrust, to mistrust, to question, to suspect.

doubtful *The weather made us doubtful about our picnic*. dubious, hesitant, uncertain, undecided, unsure.

doughnut SEE **cake**.

dove SEE **bird**.

dowdy *dowdy clothes*. colourless, drab, dull, shabby, sloppy, unattractive.

down *a pillow filled with down*. feathers.

downcast *We were downcast after losing 12-0*. dejected, depressed, down-hearted, unhappy. SEE ALSO **sad**.

downpour *Tony got soaked in the downpour*. deluge, rainstorm, shower.

downs fells, hills, moors. SEE ALSO **geography**.

downtrodden *downtrodden slaves*. exploited, oppressed.

downy *The jacket was made of downy material*. feathery, fleecy, furry, fuzzy, soft, woolly.

doze *Dad often dozes in the evening*. to nod off, to sleep, to snooze, to take a nap.

dozen SEE **number**.

drab *drab colours*. cheerless, colourless, dingy, dismal, dowdy, dreary, dull, grimy, shabby, sombre, unattractive.

drag 1 *The tractor dragged a load of logs*. to draw, to haul, to lug, to pull, to tow, to tug. 2 *Time drags when you are bored*. to crawl, to creep, to pass slowly.

dragon SEE **legend**.

dragon-fly SEE **insect**.

drain 1 *They are repairing the drains*. ditch, drainage, gutter, pipe, sanitation, sewer. 2 *Mr Brunswick drained the oil out of his engine*. to clear, to draw off, to empty, to take off. 3 *The long game drained our energy*. to consume, to exhaust, to sap, to spend, to use up. SEE ALSO **exhaust**.

drake SEE **male**.

drama 1 *Drama is one of our favourite lessons*. acting, improvisation, plays, the stage, theatre. SEE ALSO **entertainment, theatre**. 2 *We had a drama today when Logan fell off the roof*. action, excitement, suspense.

dramatist SEE **author, writer**.

draper SEE **shop**.

drastic *It would be drastic to have all your teeth out*. extreme, severe.

draught breeze, wind.

draughts *a game of draughts.* SEE **game**.

draw 1 *to draw with crayons.* to depict, to portray, to represent, to sketch. SEE ALSO **picture**. **2** *The locomotive was drawing eleven coaches.* to drag, to haul, to lug, to pull, to tow, to tug. **3** *The dentist drew two of my teeth.* to extract, to remove, to take out. **4** *The show drew a big crowd.* to attract, to bring in, to entice, to lure. **5** *Even after extra time they still drew.* to be equal, to tie. **6** *Lucy draws out her chewing-gum like a bit of string.* to elongate, to extend, to lengthen, to prolong, to stretch. **7** *The bus drew up.* to halt, to pull up, to stop. **8** *a prize draw.* competition, lottery, raffle.

drawback *Being tall can be a drawback when you are exploring caves.* disadvantage, handicap, hindrance, inconvenience.

drawbridge SEE **castle**.

drawer SEE **furniture**.

drawers SEE **underclothes**.

drawing design, pattern, sketch. SEE ALSO **picture**.

drawing-room living-room, lounge, sitting-room. SEE ALSO **house**.

dread 1 *These days, there's no need to dread going to the dentist.* to be afraid of, to fear. **2** *Tony has a dread of spiders.* anxiety, fear, horror, terror.

dreadful 1 *a dreadful accident.* alarming, appalling, awful, fearful, frightening, frightful, ghastly, grisly, horrifying, monstrous, shocking, terrible, tragic. **2** *Logan's work is dreadful!* SEE **bad**.

dream 1 *Extraordinary things happen in dreams.* day-dream, fantasy, hallucination, illusion, nightmare, reverie, vision. **2** *She dreamed that she was flying.* to fancy, to imagine.

dreary *dreary weather.* boring, cheerless, depressing, dismal, drab, dull, gloomy, joyless, melancholy, sombre, unhappy. SEE ALSO **sad**.

dredger SEE **vessel**.

dregs *the dregs at the bottom of a bottle.* deposit, remains, sediment.

drench *The rainstorm drenched us.* to saturate, to soak, to wet.

dress 1 frock, gown. SEE ALSO **clothes**. **2** *Can a man's dress tell you the sort of person he is?* attire, clothes, clothing, costume, garments. **3** *You must dress when you come in from the beach.* to clothe yourself, to cover yourself, to wear clothes. **4** *A nurse dressed my wound.* to attend to, to bandage, to care for, to treat.

dresser SEE **furniture**.

dressing 1 *a dressing on a wound.* SEE **medicine**. **2** *salad dressing.* SEE **food, sauce**.

dressing-gown SEE **clothes**.

dribble *Blood dribbled down his face.* to drip, to flow, to leak, to ooze, to run, to seep, to trickle.

drift 1 *The boat drifted down the river.* to float. **2** *We had nowhere special to go, so we drifted about.* to ramble, to wander.

drill 1 *an electric drill.* SEE **tool**. **2** *to drill through something.* to bore, to penetrate, to pierce.

drink 1 WAYS TO DRINK ARE to gulp, to guzzle, to lap, to sip, to swallow, (informal) to swig. **2** VARIOUS DRINKS ARE alcohol, ale, beer, brandy, champagne, cider, cocktail, cocoa, coffee, cordial, gin, juice, lager, lemonade, lime-juice, milk, mineral water, nectar, orangeade, pop, port, punch, rum, shandy, sherbet, sherry, soda-water, squash, tea, vodka, water, whisky, wine. **3** CONTAINERS YOU DRINK FROM ARE beaker, cup, glass, goblet, mug, tankard, tumbler, wineglass.

drip 1 *The water dripped onto the floor.* to dribble, to leak, to sprinkle, to trickle. **2** *I felt a few drips of rain.* bead, drop.

dripping SEE **fat**.

drive 1 *The starving people were driven to stealing.* to compel, to force, to oblige, to press. **2** *The dog drove the sheep into a pen.* to propel, to push, to urge. **3** *Is it easy to drive a car?* to control, to operate, to pilot, to steer. **4** *He drove the ball over the boundary.* to hit, to strike. **5** *We went for a drive in the car.* excursion, journey, outing, trip. **6** *Park the car in the drive.* SEE **road**. **7** *Lucy does well because she's got lots of drive.* ambition, determination, energy, enthusiasm, keenness, zeal.

drivel *Don't talk drivel!* (informal) balderdash, (informal) bilge, gibberish, nonsense, rubbish, (informal) tripe, (informal) twaddle.

driver chauffeur. SEE ALSO **job**.

drizzle mist, rain. SEE ALSO **weather**.

dromedary camel. SEE ALSO **animal**.

drone 1 *a drone bee.* SEE **male**. **2** *a droning noise.* SEE **sound**.

droop *The flag drooped in the windless air.* to be limp, to dangle, to flop, to hang, to sag, to wilt.

drop 1 *a drop of liquid.* bead, drip, tear. **2** *to drop to the ground.* to collapse, to descend, to dip, to dive, to fall, to lower, to plunge. **3** *They dropped Logan from the team.* to eliminate, to exclude, to leave out, to omit. **4** *It isn't nice when a friend drops you.* to abandon, to desert, to dump, to forsake, to leave. **5** *We dropped our plan when we knew what it would cost.* to give up, to scrap. **6** *Some trees drop their leaves in autumn.* to discard, to shed.

drought SEE **weather**.

drown 1 SEE **kill**. **2** *The floods drowned everything for miles around.* to engulf, to flood, to immerse, to inundate, to overwhelm, to sink, to submerge, to swamp. **3** *The music drowned our voices.* to overpower, to overwhelm.

drowsy *Go to bed: you look drowsy.* sleepy, tired, weary.

drudgery *Rich people used to have servants to do all their drudgery.* chores, labour, toil, work.

drug 1 ADDICTIVE DRUGS ARE (informal) dope, heroin, marijuana, narcotic, nicotine, opium. **2** *Doctors use drugs to cure illnesses.* cure, remedy, treatment. SEE ALSO **medicine**.

drum 1 SEE **percussion**. **2** *an oil drum.* barrel. SEE ALSO **container**.

drunk *He sounded drunk.* fuddled, intoxicated, (informal) tight.

drunkard alcoholic.

dry 1 *In the desert everything is dry.* arid, dehydrated, parched, thirsty. **2** *a dry book.* boring, dull, tedious, uninteresting. **3** *The flowers dried up.* to shrivel, to wither.

dual *a dual carriageway.* double.

dubious 1 *Mrs Brunswick looked dubious when Lucy offered to wash up.* disbelieving, doubtful, incredulous, sceptical, uncertain, unconvinced. **2** *Tony saw a dubious character loitering about.* shady, suspicious, unreliable, untrustworthy.

duchess SEE **title**.

duck 1 drake, duckling. SEE ALSO **bird, poultry**. **2** *We ducked under the low branches.* to bend, to crouch, to dodge, to stoop, to swerve.

duckling SEE **young**.

dud (informal) *a dud battery.* unusable, useless, worthless.

due 1 *Your club subscription is due.* outstanding, owed, owing, unpaid. **2** *I gave the matter due consideration.* appropriate, decent, fitting, proper, right, suitable. **3** *Is the bus due?* expected, scheduled.

duel *to fight a duel.* bout, combat, contest, fight.

duet SEE **music**.

duffle coat SEE **clothes**.

duke SEE **title**.

dull 1 *a dull pupil.* dense, dim, obtuse, slow, stupid, (informal) thick, unintelligent. **2** *a dull film.* boring, dry, stodgy, tame, tedious, uninteresting. **3** *a dull sky.* cloudy, grey, overcast, sunless. **4** *dull colours.* dingy, dowdy, drab, gloomy, shabby, sombre. **5** *a dull sound.* deadened, indistinct, muffled.

dumb mute, silent, speechless, tongue-tied. SEE ALSO **handicap**.

dumbfounded *When we heard we had won £1000 we were dumbfounded.* amazed, astonished, astounded, nonplussed, speechless, stunned, thunderstruck.

dummy 1 *a dummy revolver.* imitation, model. 2 *a ventriloquist's dummy.* doll, puppet.

dump 1 *a rubbish dump.* rubbish-heap, tip. 2 *an ammunition dump.* cache, depot, hoard, store. 3 *We dumped that old bike.* to discard, to dispose of, to get rid of, to reject, to scrap, to throw away. 4 *Just dump your things on the table.* to drop, to place, to throw down, to unload.

dumpling SEE **food**.

dumpy *a dumpy figure.* chubby, fat, plump, podgy, portly, short, squat, stocky.

dunce ass, blockhead, dope, fool, half-wit, idiot, ignoramus, imbecile, moron. ! These words are usually insulting.

dune SEE **seaside**.

dung manure, muck.

dungarees SEE **clothes**.

dungeon gaol, prison. SEE ALSO **castle**.

dupe *Logan duped me into buying a dud radio.* to cheat, to deceive, to defraud, to fool, to hoax, to hoodwink, to swindle, to take in, to trick.

duplicate 1 *a duplicate of the original painting.* copy, double, imitation, likeness, replica, reproduction, twin. 2 *Mrs Angel duplicated our poems so that we could take them home.* to copy, to photocopy, to print, to reproduce.

durable *durable shoes.* hard-wearing, indestructible, lasting, strong, sturdy, tough, unbreakable, well-made.

dusk evening, gloom, sunset, twilight. SEE ALSO **time**.

dust 1 *Wipe the dust off the shelf.* dirt, grit, powder, sawdust. 2 *I dusted the shelf.* to clean, to wipe.

dustbin SEE **container**.

dustcart SEE **vehicle**.

dustman SEE **job**.

dusty *The spare room is dusty.* dirty, filthy, grimy, gritty, grubby, (informal) mucky, sooty.

dutiful *a dutiful worker.* conscientious, diligent, faithful, hard-working, loyal, reliable, responsible, scrupulous, thorough, trustworthy.

duty 1 *a sense of duty towards your country.* allegiance, faithfulness, loyalty, obligation, responsibility. 2 *When we go camping, we each have a special duty.* assignment, function, job, task. 3 *customs duty:* customs, tax.

dwarf midget, pigmy. ! These words may be insulting.

dwell to inhabit, to live in, to occupy, to reside in.

dwelling abode, home, house, residence.

dwindle *Our stock of sweets seems to have dwindled.* to contract, to decrease, to diminish, to disappear, to fade, to lessen, to shrink, to shrivel, to subside, to wane.

dye to colour, to paint, to stain, to tint. SEE ALSO **colour**.

dynamic *The team's new manager is a dynamic person.* active, energetic, forceful, powerful, vigorous.

dynamite SEE **explosive**.

dynamo SEE **electricity**.

dysentery SEE **illness**.

E e

eager *an eager pupil.* anxious, avid, earnest, enthusiastic, excited, fervent, impatient, intent, interested, keen, passionate, zealous.

eagle SEE **bird**.

ear SEE **body, head**.

earache SEE **illness**.

earl SEE **title**.

early 1 *an early motor car.* ancient, antiquated, old, primitive. 2 *The baby was born early.* prematurely. 3 *earlier:* before, previously. 4 *earliest: the earliest motor car.* first, initial, original.

earn 1 *Lucy earned her success with hard training.* to deserve, to merit. 2 *How much do you earn doing a paper round?* to clear, to gain, to get, to make, to receive, to take home.

earnest *an earnest worker.*
conscientious, determined, diligent,
grave, hard-working, industrious,
serious, sincere, solemn, zealous.

earnings income, pay, salary, wages.

earphone SEE **audio equipment**.

ear-ring SEE **jewellery**.

earth 1 *We live on the earth.* globe,
world. **2** *Plants grow in the earth.*
ground, land, loam, soil.

earthenware china, crockery,
porcelain, pottery.

earthquake *The earthquake rocked the
town.* shock, tremor. SEE ALSO
disaster.

earwig SEE **insect**.

ease 1 *Grandad hopes for a life of ease
when he retires!* comfort, leisure,
luxury, relaxation, repose, rest.
2 *Take an aspirin to ease the pain.* to
calm, to comfort, to lessen, to
quieten, to relieve, to soothe. **3** *Ease
the tension in the guy ropes.* to relax, to
slacken.

easel SEE **furniture**.

east SEE **geography**.

Easter SEE **church, time**.

easy 1 *easy work.* effortless, elementary, light, painless. **2** *easy to use.*
foolproof, simple, straightforward,
uncomplicated. **3** *an easy life.*
carefree, comfortable, contented,
cosy, leisurely,peaceful, relaxed,
relaxing, restful, soft, tranquil,
untroubled.

easygoing *Our teacher last year was
easygoing, but Mrs Angel is strict.*
carefree, casual, genial, indulgent,
informal, lenient, liberal, patient,
relaxed, tolerant, unexcitable.

eat 1 WAYS TO EAT THINGS ARE to
bite, to bolt, to chew, to consume, to
devour, to digest, to dine, to feast, to
feed on, to gnaw, to gobble, to graze,
to gulp, to gorge, to guzzle, to live
on, to munch, to nibble, to peck, to
swallow, to taste, (informal) to tuck
in. **2** SEE ALSO **food, meal**. **3** *Acid
can eat into metal.* to corrode, to rot, to
rust. **4** *The river ate the bank away.* to
erode, to wear away.

eatable *Is the food eatable?* edible.

eaves SEE **building**.

eavesdrop *It isn't polite to eavesdrop on
other people's conversations.* to listen, to
overhear.

ebb *When the tide ebbed we walked out onto
the beach.* to flow back, to go down, to
recede, to retreat.

ebony SEE **wood**.

eccentric *eccentric behaviour.* cranky,
odd, peculiar, strange,
unconventional, weird, zany.

echo 1 *The sound echoed back across the
valley.* to resound, to reverberate.
2 *The parrot echoed everything I said.* to
imitate, to mimic.

éclair SEE **cake**.

eclipse SEE **astronomy**.

ecology SEE **subject**.

economical 1 *It's more economical to
walk than to go by bus.* careful with
money, sparing, thrifty. **2** *Mum buys
economical kinds of meat.* cheap,
inexpensive, reasonable.

ecstasy *Lucy's idea of ecstasy is to lie in a
hot bath.* bliss, delight, happiness, joy,
pleasure, rapture.

ecstatic *They gave their heroes an ecstatic
welcome.* delighted, elated, exultant,
gleeful, joyful, overjoyed, rapturous.
SEE ALSO **happy**.

eddy *an eddy in the water.* swirl, whirl,
whirlpool.

edge 1 *the edge of a field.* border,
boundary. **2** *the edge of the road.* side,
verge. **3** *the edge of a crowd.* fringe.
4 *the edge of a picture.* frame, margin.
5 *the edge of a cup.* brim, brink, lip,
rim. **6** *We edged cautiously away.* to
creep, to slink.

edgy *The dog seems edgy: will he bite?*
highly-strung, jittery, jumpy,
irritable, nervous, tense, touchy,
(informal) uptight.

edible *I don't think conkers are edible.*
digestible, eatable.

edifice building, structure.

edit *We edited our articles for the
magazine.* to adapt, to alter, to
compile, to revise, to rewrite.

edition *When will the next edition of the magazine be ready?* issue, number, publication.

editor SEE **job, writer**.

editorial SEE **writing**.

educate 1 to bring up, to coach, to indoctrinate, to inform, to instruct, to lecture, to teach, to train. **2** *educated: an educated person.* cultivated, cultured, knowledgeable, learned, literate, well-bred. **3** PLACES WHERE YOU CAN BE EDUCATED ARE academy, college, kindergarten, play-group, polytechnic, SEE **school**, university. **4** PEOPLE WHO EDUCATE US ARE coach, guru, instructor, lecturer, professor, SEE **teacher**, trainer, tutor.

eel SEE **fish**.

eerie *The castle looked eerie in the moonlight.* creepy, frightening, ghostly, scary, spooky, uncanny, unearthly, weird.

effect 1 *Did the head's warning have any effect?* consequence, impact, influence, outcome, result, sequel. **2** *The new wallpaper in the bathroom gives a nice effect.* impression.

effective *an effective goalkeeper, an effective cure for colds, etc.* capable, competent, efficient, powerful, productive, proficient, strong, successful.

effervescent *effervescent drinks.* bubbling, bubbly, fermenting, fizzy, foaming, sparkling.

efficient *an efficient worker.* capable, competent, effective, productive, proficient, useful.

effort 1 *You deserve a rest after all that effort.* exertion, labour, struggle, toil, trouble, work. **2** *We made a real effort to win.* attempt, endeavour, try.

effortless *Lucy makes gymnastics look effortless.* easy, painless, simple.

egg 1 *a hen's egg.* SEE **food**. **2** (informal) *to egg someone on.* to encourage, to inspire, to prompt, to urge.

eiderdown SEE **bedclothes**.

eject *Logan was ejected from the youth club because of his behaviour.* to banish, to discharge, to dismiss, to evict, to expel, (informal) to kick out, to send out, to throw out.

elaborate 1 *an elaborate plan.* complex, complicated, detailed, intricate, involved. **2** *elaborate embroidery.* decorated, fancy, intricate, showy.

elapse *A lot of time has elapsed since we met.* to go by, to pass.

elastic *an elastic band.* springy, stretching.

elated *We were elated by our win.* delighted, ecstatic, joyful, overjoyed. SEE ALSO **happy**.

elbow SEE **body, joint**.

elder SEE **tree**.

elderly aged, old.

elect *The gymnastics team elected Lucy as captain.* to appoint, to choose, to name, to nominate, to pick, to select, to vote for.

election *We had an election to choose a captain.* ballot, poll, vote.

electrician SEE **job**.

electricity 1 WORDS TO DO WITH ELECTRICITY ARE adaptor, battery, bell, bulb, cable, charger, circuit, dynamo, element, flex, fuse, generator, insulation, lead, meter, negative, plug, positive, power-point, power-station, pylon, socket, switch, terminal, torch, transformer, volt, watt, wire, wiring. **2** SEE **fuel**.

electrifying *an electrifying performance.* exciting, stimulating, thrilling.

electrocute SEE **kill**.

electronics SEE **science**.

elegant *an elegant palace, an elegant dance, etc.* dignified, graceful, handsome, noble, (informal) posh, refined, stately, tasteful. SEE ALSO **beautiful, splendid**.

element 1 *the main elements of a subject.* component, ingredient, part. **2** *The explorers battled against the elements.* weather.

elementary *an elementary problem.*

basic, easy, fundamental, simple, uncomplicated.

elephant SEE **animal**.

elevate 1 *The gunners elevated the angle of the big guns.* to lift, to raise. 2 *elevated: an elevated position.* high, raised.

elf SEE **legend**.

eligible *Tony won't be eligible to swim in the junior race after his next birthday.* acceptable, allowed, authorized, qualified, suitable.

eliminate 1 *How can Mrs Brunswick eliminate the ants from her garden?* to abolish, to annihilate, to destroy, to end, to eradicate, to exterminate, to finish off, to get rid of, to remove, to stamp out. 2 *Our team was eliminated in the first round.* to knock out. 3 *I was eliminated because I wasn't fit.* to drop, to leave out, to omit, to reject.

elk SEE **animal**.

ellipse SEE **shape**.

elm SEE **tree**.

elongated *Lucy described an ellipse as an elongated circle.* drawn out, extended, lengthened, stretched.

eloquent *an eloquent speaker.* fluent, persuasive.

elude *The thieves couldn't elude the police.* to avoid, to dodge, to escape, to evade.

emaciated *The refugees were terribly emaciated.* bony, gaunt, scraggy, skinny, thin, wasted away.

emancipate *to emancipate slaves.* to free, to liberate.

embankment bank, dam.

embark 1 *The sailors embarked at high tide.* to board, to depart, to go, to leave, to set out. 2 *Mr Brunswick embarked on the building of his extension.* to begin, to commence, to start, to undertake.

embarrass 1 *Tony was embarrassed when mum bought him pink underwear.* to disgrace, to distress, to humiliate. 2 *embarrassing:* humiliating, shameful. 3 *embarrassed:* ashamed, distressed, flustered, humiliated, self-conscious, shy, upset.

embedded *My wellingtons were embedded in the mud.* fixed, set.

embers ashes, cinders.

embittered *Tony was not embittered by being beaten in the last race.* bitter, envious, resentful, sour.

emblem badge, crest, seal, sign, symbol.

embrace *They embraced each other lovingly.* to clasp, to cling to, to cuddle, to fondle, to grasp, to hold, to hug, to kiss.

embroidery needlework, sewing. SEE ALSO **art**.

embryo foetus.

emerald SEE **jewellery**.

emerge *It's nice to see the flowers emerge in the spring.* to appear, to come out, to evolve, to issue, to materialize, to show, to surface.

emergency *We knew there was an emergency when we heard the fire-engine.* crisis, danger, predicament.

emigrate *Many people emigrated from Europe to America.* to depart, to leave, to quit.

eminent *an eminent TV personality.* celebrated, distinguished, famous, great, important, notable, outstanding, prominent, renowned, well-known.

emit *The exhaust of your car emits a lot of smoke. That fire emits a lot of heat.* to belch, to discharge, to expel, to give out, to radiate, to send out, to transmit.

emotion feeling, passion, sentiment.

emotional *Saying goodbye was an emotional moment.* moving, passionate, romantic, sentimental, touching.

emperor SEE **ruler**.

emphasize *Mrs Angel emphasized that we must not wander off.* to assert, to insist, to stress, to underline.

employ 1 *The school employs a special teacher to teach music.* to give work to, to pay. 2 *Our doctor employs the most modern methods.* to apply, to use, to utilize. 3 *to be employed in something:* to be active, to be busy, to be engaged, to be involved, to be occupied.

employer boss, chief, head, manager, owner.

employment *Tony's uncle is looking for employment.* business, job, occupation, profession, trade, work.

empty 1 *an empty space.* hollow, unfilled, void. **2** *an empty room.* bare, unfurnished. **3** *an empty house.* deserted, desolate, forsaken, uninhabited, unoccupied, vacant. **4** *an empty page.* blank, clean, unused. **5** *Empty the cup. Empty the room.* to clear, to drain, to evacuate.

emu SEE **bird**.

emulsion SEE **paint**.

enable 1 *A little more money will enable us to have a really good time.* to aid, to assist, to help. **2** *A passport enables you to travel to certain countries.* to allow, to authorize, to entitle, to permit.

enamel SEE **paint**.

enchant 1 *The ballet enchanted us.* to allure, to bewitch, to captivate, to charm, to delight, to entrance, to fascinate. **2** *enchanted*: spellbound.

enchantment *The witch's enchantment held them in its power.* charm, magic, spell, witchcraft, wizardry.

encircle *We encircled the area where the tortoise was last seen.* to besiege, to circle, to enclose, to ring, to surround.

enclose *The lions were enclosed behind a high fence.* to confine, to encircle, to envelop, to fence in, to hedge in, to hem in, to imprison, to pen, to restrict, to ring, to shut in, to surround, to wall in.

enclosure *an enclosure for animals.* cage, compound, corral, courtyard, farmyard, fold, pen, run.

encounter 1 *a violent encounter.* battle, clash, confrontation, fight, meeting, struggle. **2** *The plan to close the school encountered fierce opposition.* to clash with, to confront, to face, to meet, to run into.

encourage 1 *The supporters encouraged their team.* to cheer up, (informal) to egg on, to inspire, to reassure, to support. **2** *Advertising encourages sales.* to boost, to help, to promote. **3** *Encourage people to pay their subscriptions.* to invite, to prompt, to urge. **4** *encouraging*: favourable, hopeful, promising, reassuring. SEE ALSO **kind**.

encouragement *The team needs encouragement.* boost, incentive, reassurance, support.

encyclopaedia SEE **book**.

end 1 *the end of a film.* close, conclusion, ending, finale, finish. **2** *the end of an ambition.* collapse, death, destruction, downfall, fall, passing, ruin. **3** *the end of a train.* back, rear, tail. **4** *the end of a pin.* point, tip. **5** *What was the end of all your efforts?* consequence, effect, outcome, result. **6** *What end did you have in mind when you started?* aim, intention, objective, purpose. **7** *When does your club membership end?* to cease, to close, to expire, to finish, to stop. **8** *Do you want to end your club membership?* to discontinue, to terminate. **9** *Please end your work now.* to break off, to cut off, to halt, to round off. **10** *We have the power to end all life on earth.* to abolish, to destroy, to eliminate, to get rid of, to kill.

endanger *If you don't keep your bike in good condition, you could endanger your life.* to threaten.

endearing *an endearing puppy.* appealing, attractive, charming, lovable.

endeavour *Logan endeavoured to behave.* to attempt, to exert yourself, to make an effort, to strain, to strive, to try.

endless 1 *an endless journey into space.* boundless, eternal, immeasurable, infinite, limitless, unlimited. **2** *We are sick of Logan's endless chattering.* ceaseless, constant, continual, everlasting, incessant, interminable, persistent, unending.

endure 1 *Some people have to endure a lot of pain.* to abide, to bear, to cope with, to experience, to put up with, to stand, (informal) to stick, to suffer, to tolerate, to undergo, to withstand. **2** *We hope that life on earth will endure for a long time yet.* to carry on, to continue, to exist, to last, to live on, to remain, to stay, to survive.

enemy adversary, antagonist, attacker, foe, opponent, opposition, rival.

energetic *an energetic player.* active, animated, brisk, dynamic, enthusiastic, forceful, hard-working, lively, powerful, spirited, sprightly, vigorous.

energy *The winning team played with tremendous energy.* force, liveliness, might, power, strength, vigour, vitality, zeal, zest.

enforce *The referee enforces the rules.* to carry out, to impose, to inflict, to insist on.

engaged 1 *an engaged couple.* betrothed. **2** *What are you engaged in?* busy, employed, involved, occupied.

engagement 1 *I can't come because I have another engagement.* appointment, date, fixture, meeting. **2** *a fierce engagement between two armies.* battle, clash, encounter, fight, struggle.

engine 1 KINDS OF ENGINE ARE diesel engine, electric motor, internal combustion engine, jet engine, outboard motor, steam engine, turbine. **2** *a railway engine.* locomotive.

engineer SEE **job**.

engraving SEE **picture**.

engulf *A tidal wave engulfed the town.* to flood, to inundate, to overwhelm, to submerge, to swallow up, to swamp.

enjoy *Do you enjoy snooker?* to admire, to appreciate, to be pleased by, to delight in, to like, to love, to relish, to revel in.

enjoyable agreeable, amusing, delightful, diverting, entertaining, likeable, pleasant, satisfying.

enjoyment *They ate the food with great enjoyment.* appreciation, delight, pleasure, satisfaction, zest.

enlarge *Tony is enlarging his collection of records.* to amplify, to build up, to develop, to expand, to extend, to fill out, to increase, to inflate, to lengthen, to magnify, to swell, to widen.

enlargement SEE **photograph**.

enlist *to enlist in the army.* to enrol, to join up, to register, to sign on, to volunteer.

enormous *an enormous elephant.* gigantic, gross, huge, immense, mammoth, massive, mighty, monstrous, towering, tremendous, vast. SEE ALSO **big**.

enough *Was there enough food?* adequate, sufficient.

enquire WAYS TO ENQUIRE ARE to ask, to beg, to demand, to entreat, to implore, to inquire, to query, to question, to request.

enrage *Logan's silly questions enrage us.* to anger, to exasperate, to incense, to inflame, to infuriate, to madden, to provoke, to vex. SEE ALSO **angry**.

enrol 1 *to enrol in the army.* to enlist, to join up, to register, to sign on, to volunteer. **2** *How many people have we enrolled for the youth club outing?* to accept, to recruit, to sign up, to take on.

ensemble *a recorder ensemble.* band, group, orchestra. SEE ALSO **music**.

ensign *a ship's ensign.* banner, colours, flag, standard.

ensnare *to ensnare animals.* to ambush, to capture, to catch, to entangle, to trap.

ensure *Will you ensure that the goldfish gets fed?* to guarantee, to make certain, to secure. ! This is not the same word as *insure*.

enter *to enter a cave.* to come in, to go in, to penetrate.

enterprising *Several enterprising children organized a sponsored walk.* adventurous, ambitious, bold, courageous, daring, energetic, enthusiastic, hard-working, industrious, intrepid, keen, resourceful.

entertain 1 *The comedian entertained the audience.* to amuse, to delight, to divert, to please. **2** *We usually entertain some friends at Christmas.* to cater for, to give hospitality to, to greet, to receive, to welcome.

entertainment 1 amusement, diversion, enjoyment, fun, recreation. **2** KINDS OF ENTERTAINMENT ARE aerobatics, ballet, cabaret, casino, cinema, circus, comedy, concert, dance, disco, drama, fair, gymkhana, musical, night-club, night-life, opera, pageant, pantomime, play, recital, recitation, radio, rodeo, show, tap-dancing, tattoo, television, variety show, waxworks, zoo. **3** VARIOUS ENTERTAINERS ARE acrobat, actor, actress, ballerina, broadcaster, clown, comedian, comic, compère, conjurer, contortionist, dancer, DJ, jester, juggler, lion-tamer, magician, matador, minstrel, musician, question-master, singer, star, stunt man, superstar, toreador, trapeze artist, ventriloquist. SEE ALSO **music, theatre**.

enthusiasm 1 *You need plenty of enthusiasm to succeed in sport*. ambition, drive, eagerness, excitement, fervour, keenness, zeal. **2** *Mr Brunswick's enthusiasms include water-skiing*. craze, diversion, pastime.

enthusiast *Logan is a pop music enthusiast*. addict, fan, fanatic, supporter.

enthusiastic *The team needs an enthusiastic new manager*. avid, eager, energetic, fervent, keen, lively, passionate, spirited.

entice *I enticed the rabbit into the hutch with a carrot*. to attract, to bribe, to coax, to lure, to tempt.

entire *Did you read the entire book?* complete, full, intact, total, unbroken, whole.

entitle 1 *Grandad's bus pass entitles him to travel free of charge*. to allow, to authorize, to enable, to permit. **2** *What did you entitle your story?* to call, to name.

entrance 1 *You pay at the entrance*. access, door, entry, gate, opening, turnstile, way in. **2** *The ballet entranced everyone*. to bewitch, to captivate, to charm, to delight, to enchant, to fascinate, to spellbind.

entrant *How many entrants are there for the swimming gala?* applicant, candidate, competitor, contestant, participant, rival.

entreat *The captain entreated the passengers to remain calm*. to appeal to, to ask, to beg, to implore, to plead, to request.

entry access, door, entrance, gate, opening, turnstile, way in.

entwine *The wires became entwined*. to coil, to entangle, to tangle, to twist, to wind.

envelop *Fog enveloped the town*. to conceal, to cover, to encircle, to enclose, to surround, to wrap up.

envelope cover, wrapper. SEE ALSO **container**.

envious bitter, grudging, jealous, resentful.

environment *What kind of environment do you live in?* surroundings.

envy *Tony doesn't envy Lucy's success*. to begrudge, to resent.

epic SEE **poem, writing**.

epidemic *an epidemic of measles*. outbreak, plague.

epilepsy SEE **illness**.

epilogue SEE **book**.

episode *What happened in the last episode?* instalment, passage, scene, section.

epistle letter.

epitaph *an epitaph on a tombstone*. inscription.

equal *equal amounts*. equivalent, even, identical, level, matching, the same.

equalize *to equalize the scores*. to balance, to even up.

equator SEE **geography**.

equilateral SEE **mathematics**.

equilibrium *to keep your equilibrium*. balance, poise, stability, steadiness.

equip *They equipped the hall with new lighting*. to furnish, to provide, to supply.

equipment *Mr Brunswick has a lot of decorating equipment*. apparatus, furnishings, gear, hardware, instruments, kit, machinery, outfit, paraphernalia, supplies, tackle.

equivalent *They'll refund the money or give you something of equivalent value.* equal, matching, the same.

era *The Roman era.* age, period, time.

eradicate *Mrs Brunswick wants to eradicate those ants!* to abolish, to annihilate, to destroy, to eliminate, to end, to exterminate, to get rid of, to remove, to uproot.

erase *It's easy to erase mistakes when you're using a word-processor.* to blot out, to cancel, to delete, to remove, to rub out, to wipe out.

erect 1 *to erect a tent.* to build, to construct, to pitch, to put up, to raise, to set up. 2 *Human beings stand erect.* upright, vertical.

erode *The river is eroding the bank.* to corrode, to eat away, to grind down, to wear away.

err *It is better to err by arriving early than by arriving late.* to do wrong, to go wrong, to misbehave, to miscalculate.

errand *She sent Tony on an errand to the shops.* job, mission, task.

erratic *The team's performance has been erratic lately.* changeable, fickle, inconsistent, irregular, unpredictable, variable.

error *Mrs Angel corrected the errors in Logan's work.* blunder, fallacy, fault, (informal) howler, inaccuracy, miscalculation, misconception, mistake, misunderstanding, oversight, (informal) slip-up.

erupt *A flow of lava erupted from the volcano.* to be discharged, to be emitted, to belch, to burst out, to gush, to issue, to pour out.

eruption *an eruption of laughter, a volcanic eruption.* explosion, outburst.

escalate *The trouble escalated as more people joined in.* to become worse, to increase, to multiply, to step up.

escalator lift, staircase, stairs.

escapade *Don't get involved in any escapades!* adventure, mischief, prank, scrape.

escape 1 *The prisoner escaped.* to abscond, to bolt, to elope, to flee, to run away, to slip away. 2 *Lucy always escapes the washing-up.* to avoid, to dodge, to elude, to evade, to get away from, to shirk. 3 *His escape wasn't noticed until the morning.* getaway, flight, retreat, running away.

escort 1 *The security man has an escort if he's carrying a lot of money.* companion, guard, guide, protector. 2 *Dad escorted the little ones home after the party.* to accompany, to conduct, to see.

espionage intelligence, spying.

esplanade SEE **seaside**.

essay SEE **writing**.

essential 1 *the essential facts.* basic, chief, fundamental, important, indispensable, main, primary, principal. 2 *It's essential that you come.* imperative, necessary, vital.

establish 1 *Mr Brunswick established a new business.* to base, to begin, to construct, to create, to found, to initiate, to install, to introduce, to originate, to set up. 2 *We must establish what to do first.* to agree, to decide, to fix, to settle. 3 *Can you establish where you were last night?* to confirm, to demonstrate, to prove, to show, to verify.

establishment *What sort of establishment does uncle run?* business, company, concern, factory, firm, institution, office, organization, shop.

estate 1 *a housing estate.* area, development. 2 *a family estate.* fortune, inheritance, possessions, property, wealth.

estate agent SEE **job**.

estate car SEE **vehicle**.

estimate *We estimated how many sandwiches we needed for the party.* to assess, to calculate, to guess, to reckon, to work out.

estuary SEE **geography**.

eternal 1 *eternal life.* endless,

everlasting, immortal, infinite, limitless, timeless, unending. 2 *I'm tired of your eternal quarrelling.* ceaseless, constant, continual, frequent, incessant, interminable, non-stop, perennial, permanent, perpetual, persistent, recurrent, relentless, repeated.

ethnic *ethnic music.* national, racial.

eucalyptus SEE **tree**.

evacuate 1 *The police evacuated everyone from the area.* to clear, to move out, to remove. 2 *The family had to evacuate the blazing house.* to abandon, to desert, to forsake, to leave, to quit.

evade *Lucy tries to evade the washing-up.* to avoid, to dodge, to elude, to escape from, to shirk.

evangelist SEE **church, preacher**.

evaporate *The dew evaporates during the morning.* to disappear, to dry up, to vaporize.

even 1 *even ground.* flat, level, smooth. 2 *an even temper.* calm, placid, serene, steady. 3 *the even ticking of the clock.* consistent, regular. 4 *even scores.* balanced, equal, identical, level, the same. 5 *Logan played for the opposition to even up the teams.* to balance, to equalize. 6 *We evened out the wrinkled carpet.* to flatten, to level.

evening dusk, sunset, twilight. SEE ALSO **time**.

event 1 *a special event.* affair, ceremony, entertainment, experience, function, happening, incident, occasion, occurrence, proceedings. 2 *a sporting event.* championship, competition, contest, match, meeting, tournament.

eventually finally, ultimately.

evergreen SEE **tree**.

everlasting 1 *everlasting life.* endless, eternal, immortal, infinite, limitless, timeless, unending. 2 *We get tired of their everlasting quarrelling.* ceaseless, constant, continual, frequent, incessant, interminable, non-stop, perennial, permanent, perpetual, persistent, recurrent, relentless, repeated.

evermore always, eternally, for ever, unceasingly.

everyday *an everyday happening.* accustomed, common, commonplace, conventional, customary, familiar, habitual, normal, ordinary, orthodox, regular, routine, standard, typical, usual.

evict *The landlord evicted them for not paying the rent.* to eject, to expel, (informal) to kick out, to remove, to throw out, to turn out.

evidence *The judge examined the evidence.* data, facts, grounds, information, proof, sign, statistics, testimony.

evident *It is evident that Logan doesn't like work.* apparent, clear, obvious, plain, self-explanatory, unmistakable.

evil *an evil deed, an evil person.* atrocious, base, foul, hateful, immoral, infamous, malevolent, sinful, sinister, vicious, villainous, wicked, wrong. SEE ALSO **bad**.

evolve *Animals have evolved over millions of years.* to emerge, to develop, to grow, to improve, to progress.

ewe lamb, sheep. SEE ALSO **female**.

exact *the exact time.* accurate, correct, precise, right, specific, true.

exaggerate to overdo it.

examination 1 *a school examination.* exam, test. 2 *a medical examination.* check-up, inspection, investigation, scrutiny.

examine 1 *We examined the evidence.* to analyse, to check, to inquire into, to inspect, to investigate, to probe, to study, to test. 2 *The police examined the witness.* to cross-examine, to interrogate, to question.

example 1 *Give an example of what you mean.* case, illustration, instance, sample, specimen. 2 *Can we have an example to copy?* model, pattern, prototype.

exasperate *Logan exasperated the head by dropping sweets all over the floor.* (informal) to aggravate, to anger, to annoy, to bother, to enrage, to incense, to infuriate, to irritate, to provoke, to vex. SEE ALSO **anger**.

excavate *to excavate a hole.* to burrow, to dig, to mine, to scoop, to tunnel, to uncover, to unearth.

exceed *to exceed a target.* to beat, to excel, to go over, to outdo, to outnumber, to surpass, to top.

exceedingly *This is exceedingly good cake: can I have some more?* exceptionally, extremely, outstandingly, specially, unusually, very.

excel *Our team excelled theirs in nearly every event.* to beat, to exceed, to outdo, to surpass, to top.

excellent *excellent advice, excellent food, etc.* admirable, brilliant, esteemed, exceptional, (informal) fabulous, fantastic, fine, first-class, gorgeous, great, impressive, magnificent, marvellous, outstanding, (informal) super, superb, (informal) terrific, tremendous, wonderful.

except *Everyone behaved well, except Logan.* besides, excluding.

exceptional 1 *exceptional weather.* abnormal, extraordinary, peculiar, rare, remarkable, special, uncommon, unusual. **2** *an exceptional performance.* SEE **excellent**.

excerpt *an excerpt from 'Treasure Island'.* clip, extract, quotation.

excessive 1 *excessive prices.* exorbitant, extreme, high, uncalled-for, unreasonable. **2** *an excessive amount of food.* extravagant, superfluous, unnecessary.

exchange *Tony exchanged his old bike for some roller-skates.* to change, to replace, to substitute, to swop, to trade, to trade in.

exchequer SEE **government**.

excite 1 *The smell of blood excited the tiger.* to agitate, to arouse, to disturb, to electrify, to move, to provoke, to rouse, to stimulate, to stir, to thrill. **2** *excited*: animated, boisterous, delirious, exuberant, frenzied, hysterical, lively, spirited, vivacious, wild.

excitement action, activity,

adventure, drama, (informal) kicks, stimulation, suspense, thrill.

exclaim to call, to cry out, to shout, to yell. SEE ALSO **talk**.

exclamation mark SEE **punctuation**.

exclude *Mrs Angel excluded Logan because he was rude.* to ban, to bar, to keep out, to omit, to prohibit, to shut out.

excruciating *excruciating pain.* agonizing, painful, unbearable.

excursion *an excursion to the seaside.* expedition, jaunt, outing, tour, trip.

excuse 1 *Have you any excuse for what you did?* explanation, defence, justification, pretext, reason. **2** *After hearing the facts, the judge excused him.* to forgive, to free, to let off, to overlook, to pardon.

execute 1 *The pilot executed a difficult manoeuvre.* to accomplish, to carry out, to complete, to do, to perform. **2** *to execute a criminal.* to put to death. **3** WAYS TO EXECUTE PEOPLE ARE to behead, to crucify, to decapitate, to electrocute, to gas, to guillotine, to hang, to lynch, to shoot, to stone. SEE ALSO **punishment**.

executive *an executive in big business.* administrator, director, manager. SEE ALSO **chief, job**.

exercise 1 *Exercise helps to keep you fit.* activity, aerobics, games, gymnastics, PE, sport. **2** *army exercises.* drill, manoeuvres, training. **3** *Mr Brunswick likes to exercise several times a week.* to jog, to keep fit, to practise, to train. **4** *Please exercise a little more self-control.* to display, to employ, to show, to use, to wield.

exercise book jotter, notebook, pad.

exert *to exert yourself*: to attempt, to endeavour, to strain, to strive, to try.

exertion *The exertion made us sweat.* effort, energy, labour, toil, work.

exhaust 1 *The car gives out a lot of exhaust.* fumes, gases, smoke. **2** *We exhausted our money.* to consume, to spend, to use up. **3** *Don't exhaust yourselves.* to drain, to sap, to strain, to tire, to weaken, to wear out, to weary. 4 *exhausted*: breathless, (informal) done in, drained, gasping, panting, tired out, weary, worn out. 5 *exhausting*: arduous, gruelling, hard, laborious, strenuous, tiring.

exhaustive *an exhaustive search*. careful, complete, meticulous, thorough.

exhibit *We exhibited our art work*. to demonstrate, to display, to present, to produce, to show.

exhibition *an exhibition of paintings*. demonstration, display, presentation, show.

exile 1 *to exile someone from his country*. to banish, to deport, to eject, to expel, to send away. 2 *An exile longs to be back in her own country*. outcast, refugee, wanderer.

exist 1 *Do dragons exist?* to be, to occur. 2 *We can't exist without water*. to endure, to keep going, to live, to remain, to survive.

exit door, outlet, way out.

exorbitant *exorbitant prices*. excessive, high, unreasonable.

expand *Mr Brunswick hopes his business will expand. Can you expand your story?* to amplify, to build up, to enlarge, to fill out, to grow, to increase, to lengthen, to swell, to widen.

expanse *an expanse of water*. area, sheet, surface.

expect 1 *We are expecting snow*. to anticipate, to forecast, to foresee, to hope for, to wait for. 2 *expecting a baby*: expectant, pregnant.

expedition *a hunting expedition*. excursion, exploration, journey, mission, outing, safari, tour, trek, trip, voyage. SEE ALSO **travel**.

expel *to expel someone from the country*. to banish, to deport, to discharge, to dismiss, to eject, to evict, to exile, (informal) to kick out, to send away, to throw out.

expense cost, expenditure, payment, price.

expensive *expensive jewellery*. costly, dear, exorbitant, extravagant, lavish, luxurious, precious, priceless, (informal) pricey, valuable.

experience 1 *He has a lot of experience*. knowledge, wisdom. 2 *Flying in a helicopter is an exciting experience*. event, happening, incident, occurrence. 3 *to experience pain*. to endure, to feel, to go through, to know, to live through, to see, to suffer, to undergo.

experienced *an experienced craftsman*. accomplished, competent, expert, knowledgeable, proficient, qualified, skilled, trained.

experiment *a scientific experiment*. test, trial.

expert 1 *an expert mechanic*. clever, experienced, knowledgeable, professional, proficient, qualified, skilful, skilled, talented, trained. 2 *Ask an expert*. authority, professional, specialist.

expire 1 *My club membership expires this month*. to cease, to end, to finish, to run out, to stop, to terminate. 2 *The wounded animal expired*. to die, to pass away, to perish.

explain *Can you explain how a computer works?* to account for, to analyse, to clarify, to define, to demonstrate, to describe, to illustrate, to interpret, to justify, to make clear, to show.

explanation *Do you believe his explanation?* account, answer, definition, description, excuse, justification, reason, theory.

explode to blow up, to burst, to detonate, to go off, to set off.

exploit 1 *the exploits of King Arthur*. act, adventure, deed, feat. 2 *The owners exploited the slaves*. to take advantage of, to use, to utilize. 3 *exploited*: downtrodden, oppressed.

explore 1 *We explored the woods*. to discover, to look around, to travel about. 2 *We explored the problem*. to examine, to inquire into, to investigate, to probe.

explorer discoverer, pioneer, prospector.

explosion bang, blast, eruption, outburst, report.

explosive KINDS OF EXPLOSIVE ARE dynamite, gelignite, gunpowder, TNT.

expose *to expose a secret.* to bare, to disclose, to display, to divulge, to make known, to reveal, to show, to uncover.

express *We expressed our thanks.* to communicate, to describe, to make known, to put into words, to say, to speak, to talk, to utter.

expression 1 *Her expression shows she's had bad news.* countenance, face, look. **2** EXPRESSIONS ON PEOPLE'S FACES ARE beam, frown, glare, glower, grimace, grin, laugh, leer, pout, scowl, smile, smirk, sneer, wince, yawn. **3** *We learned a few French expressions before we went abroad.* phrase, remark, saying, statement, word.

expressionless *an expressionless face.* blank, vacant.

exquisite *an exquisite piece of jewellery.* beautiful, dainty, delicate, elegant, fine, lovely, perfect.

extend 1 *The pier extends into the sea.* to project, to reach out, to stick out, to stretch out. **2** *You can extend this ladder to twice its length.* to draw out, to elongate, to enlarge, to lengthen, to prolong, to stretch. **3** *We extend a warm welcome to all.* to give, to offer.

extension *an extension to a house.* addition, annexe, enlargement, wing.

extensive 1 *an extensive forest.* broad, large, vast, wide. **2** *extensive damage.* general, wholesale, widespread.

extent *the extent of a person's wealth, the extent of a piece of land.* amount, area, breadth, degree, dimensions, distance, length, limit, magnitude, measure, measurement, range, reach, scope, size.

exterior *the exterior of a house.* outside, shell, skin, surface.

exterminate *Dad exterminated an ant's nest.* to annihilate, to destroy, to eliminate, to eradicate, (informal) to finish off, to kill, to slaughter, to wipe out.

external *The external appearance of the house was attractive.* exterior, outer, outside, outward.

extinct *Dinosaurs are extinct.* dead, died out.

extinguish *to extinguish a candle.* to put out, to quench, to snuff.

extra 1 *We need extra milk for the weekend.* additional, further, more, spare, supplementary. **2** *When Mrs Brunswick grows more beans than she can use, she puts the extra in the freezer.* excess, remainder, surplus.

extract 1 *The dentist extracted the bad tooth.* to draw out, to pull out, to remove, to take out. **2** *Mrs Angel read an extract from 'Oliver Twist'.* clip, excerpt, passage, quotation.

extraordinary *We hardly believed his extraordinary story.* abnormal, amazing, curious, exceptional, fantastic, funny, incredible, miraculous, notable, odd, peculiar, phenomenal, queer, rare, remarkable, singular, special, strange, stupendous, unbelievable, uncommon, unusual.

extravagant *It was extravagant to buy the biggest ice-creams.* excessive, expensive, lavish, prodigal, wasteful.

extreme 1 *the extreme end of the runway.* farthest, furthest, furthermost, ultimate. **2** *extreme difficulties.* acute, drastic, excessive, great, intense, severe. **3** *This unsettled weather goes from one extreme to the other.* end, limit, maximum, opposite.

exuberant *The winning team was in an exuberant mood.* animated, boisterous, cheerful, energetic, excited, lively, spirited, sprightly.

exultant *Lucy was exultant when she won the cup.* delighted, ecstatic, elated, gleeful, joyful, overjoyed, rapturous. SEE ALSO **happy**.

eye SEE **body, head**.

eye-shadow SEE **cosmetics**.

eyesore *The quarry is an eyesore.* blemish, blot.

eyewitness *The police asked the eyewitnesses to describe the accident.* bystander, observer, onlooker, spectator, witness.

eyrie *an eagle's eyrie.* nest.

F f

fable SEE **writing**.

fabric cloth, material, textile. SEE ALSO **cloth**.

fabulous 1 *fabulous monsters.* fictional, imaginary, legendary, mythical, non-existent. 2 FOR FABULOUS CREATURES SEE **legend**. 3 (informal) *a fabulous record.* SEE **excellent**.

face 1 *He made a funny face.* countenance, features, look. SEE ALSO **expression**. 2 *A cube has six faces.* front, side, surface. 3 *Our house faces the pie factory.* to look at, to overlook. 4 *The explorers faced many dangers.* to confront, to encounter, to meet.

facetious *Mrs Angel hates Logan's facetious remarks.* amusing, comic, funny, humorous, joking, witty.

fact *I want the full facts.* circumstances, data, details, evidence, information, reality, statistics, truth.

factory 1 VARIOUS PLACES WHERE THINGS ARE MADE ARE forge, foundry, manufacturing plant, mill, refinery, workshop. 2 SEE **building**.

fade 1 *The sun faded the curtains.* to bleach, to discolour, to whiten. 2 *The light faded.* to decline, to diminish, to disappear, to dwindle, to fail, to melt away, to vanish, to wane, to weaken.

fail 1 *His attempt to beat the record failed.* to be unsuccessful, to fall through. 2 *The old man's health was failing.* to decline, to diminish, to disappear, to dwindle, to fade, to melt away, to vanish, to wane, to weaken. 3 *Don't fail to phone us!* to neglect, to omit.

failing *Lucy's main failing is that she is untidy.* defect, fault, imperfection, shortcoming, vice, weakness.

failure *Our attempt to cook a cake was a failure.* disaster, fiasco.

faint 1 *a faint picture.* blurred, dim, faded, hazy, indistinct, misty, pale, shadowy, unclear, weak. 2 *a faint smell.* delicate, slight. 3 *a faint sound.* low, soft. 4 *to feel faint.* dizzy, exhausted, giddy, unsteady, weak. 5 *to faint:* to become unconscious, to collapse.

faint-hearted *He made a faint-hearted attempt to stop the thieves.* cowardly, fearful, shy, spineless, timid, timorous, unheroic.

fair 1 carnival, fun-fair. SEE ALSO **entertainment**. 2 *a Christmas fair.* bazaar, exhibition, festival, fête, market, sale. 3 *fair hair.* blond, light. 4 *a fair referee, a fair decision.* honest, impartial, just, proper, right, unbiased, unprejudiced. 5 *a fair performance.* indifferent, mediocre, middling, moderate, ordinary, reasonable, satisfactory. 6 *fair weather.* bright, cloudless, fine, pleasant, sunny. SEE ALSO **weather**. 7 (old-fashioned) *a fair maiden.* attractive, beautiful, pretty.

fairly moderately, (informal) pretty, rather.

fairy SEE **legend**.

fairy-tale SEE **writing**.

faith 1 *Your dog has faith in you.* belief, confidence, trust. 2 *a religious faith.* conviction, creed, religion.

faithful *The dog is his faithful companion.* consistent, constant, dependable, devoted, dutiful, loyal, reliable, true, trustworthy.

fake 1 *He faked her signature.* to copy, to counterfeit, to feign, to forge, to imitate, to pretend, to reproduce. 2 *faked:* artificial, bogus, false, (informal) phoney, synthetic, unreal. 3 *The £5 note was a fake.* copy, counterfeit, duplicate, forgery, fraud, hoax, imitation, replica, reproduction.

falcon SEE **bird**.

fall 1 *He fell into the river.* to collapse, to drop, to overbalance, to plunge, to tumble. **2** *The temperature falls at night.* to decrease, to decline, to diminish, to lessen. **3** *Millions fell in the First World War.* to be killed, to die, to perish.

fallacy *There's a fallacy in your reasoning.* error, inaccuracy, misconception, mistake, misunderstanding.

false 1 *a false idea.* deceptive, inaccurate, incorrect, misleading, mistaken, untrue, wrong. **2** *a false friend.* deceitful, dishonest, disloyal, lying, treacherous, unfaithful. **3** *a false £5 note.* artificial, bogus, counterfeit, fake, imitation, (informal) phoney, synthetic. **4** *a false name, a false story.* assumed, fictitious, made up, unreal.

falsehood (informal) fib, lie, untruth.

falter *He faltered when he saw the lion coming towards him.* to flinch, to hesitate, to quail, to stagger, to stumble, to totter.

fame *A superstar's fame spreads everywhere.* distinction, glory, importance, prestige, renown, reputation.

familiar 1 *a familiar sight.* common, everyday, normal, regular, usual, well-known. SEE ALSO **ordinary**. **2** *a familiar companion.* close, friendly, intimate. **3** *to be familiar with*: to be acquainted with, to know about.

family 1 brood, clan, generation, kin, kinsmen, litter, relations, relatives, tribe. **2** MEMBERS OF A FAMILY ARE adopted child, ancestor, aunt, brother, cousin, daughter, descendant, divorcee, father, fiancé, fiancée, forefather, foster-child, foster-parent, godchild, godparent, grandchild, grandparent, guardian, husband, mother, nephew, niece, orphan, parent, quadruplet, quintuplet, sextuplet, sister, son, stepchild, stepparent, triplet, twin, uncle, ward, widow, widower, wife.

famine *Why is there famine in the world*

when we have plenty to eat? hunger, malnutrition, starvation.

famished *We were famished after our long walk.* hungry, (informal) peckish, ravenous, starving.

famous *a famous person.* celebrated, distinguished, eminent, great, historic, important, legendary, notable, noted, outstanding, prominent, renowned, well-known.

fan *Mrs Brunswick was a Beatles fan.* addict, enthusiast, fanatic, follower, supporter.

fanatic *She was a Beatles fanatic.* addict, enthusiast, fan.

fanciful *We had a fanciful plan to sail to America.* fantastic, imaginary, make-believe, pretended, unreal.

fancy 1 *Mr Brunswick put fancy patterns on Lucy's birthday cake.* decorated, elaborate, ornamental. **2** *I fancied I saw a pink elephant.* to dream, to imagine. **3** *What do you fancy to eat?* to desire, to hanker after, to like, to long for, to prefer, to wish for.

fanfare SEE **music**.

fang *an animal's fang.* tooth.

fantastic 1 *a fantastic story about dragons and wizards.* amazing, extraordinary, fabulous, grotesque, incredible, odd, remarkable, strange, unbelievable, unreal, weird. **2** (informal) *We had a fantastic time.* fabulous, great, marvellous, sensational, wonderful. SEE ALSO **good**.

fantasy *Alice's adventures in Wonderland were a fantasy.* day-dream, dream, illusion, make-believe, reverie.

far far-away, distant, remote.

farce SEE **theatre**.

fare *How much is the fare to London?* charge, cost, payment, price.

farewell au revoir, goodbye.

far-fetched *The story about a singing dog is a bit far-fetched.* improbable, incredible, unbelievable, unconvincing, unlikely.

farm 1 croft, ranch. **2** CROPS GROWN ON FARMS ARE barley, cereals, corn, fodder, fruit, maize, oats, rye, sugar

beet, sweetcorn, vegetables, wheat.
SEE ALSO **fruit, vegetable**.
3 ANIMALS KEPT ON FARMS ARE
bantam, bull, bullock, calf, cattle,
chicken, cow, duck, goat, goose, hen,
horse, lamb, livestock, pig, poultry,
pullet, sheep, turkey. **4** FARM
BUILDINGS ARE barn, cow-shed,
farmhouse, farmyard, granary,
haystack, outhouse, pigsty, rick,
shed, silo, stable, sty. **5** KINDS OF
FARM EQUIPMENT ARE baler,
combine harvester, cultivator,
harrow, harvester, mower, pitchfork,
planter, plough, scythe, tractor,
trailer.

fascinate 1 *Snakes fascinate some people.*
to attract, to bewitch, to captivate, to
charm, to enchant, to entice, to
entrance, to interest, to spellbind.
2 *fascinating*: alluring, attractive,
glamorous.

fashion 1 *the latest fashion.* craze, style,
taste, trend, vogue. **2** *The headmaster
acts in a business-like fashion.* manner,
method, mode, style, way.

fashionable *fashionable clothes.*
contemporary, modern, smart,
sophisticated, stylish, tasteful,
(informal) trendy, up-to-date.

fast 1 *a fast pace.* brisk, (informal)
nippy, quick, rapid, smart, speedy,
swift. **2** *fast colours.* fixed, indelible,
permanent. **3** *The ship was fast on the
rocks.* firm, immobile, immovable,
secure. **4** *In some religions you fast on
certain days.* to go without food, to
starve.

fasten 1 WAYS OF FASTENING THINGS
ARE to adhere, to attach, to bind, to
cling, to close, to connect, to fix, to
hitch, to join, to knot, to lash, to link,
to lock, to moor, to seal, to secure, to
stick, to tether, to tie, to unite, to
weld. **2** THINGS USED TO FASTEN
ARE anchor, bolt, buckle, button,
cement, chain, clamp, clasp, clip,
glue, hook, knot, lock, nail, padlock,
paste, peg, pin, rivet, rope, safety-
pin, screw, sellotape, solder, staple,
strap, string, tack, tape, wedge, zip.

fastidious *Our cat is fastidious about his
food.* (informal) choosey, finicky,
funny, particular, squeamish.

fat 1 KINDS OF FAT ARE butter,
dripping, grease, lard, margarine,
oil, suet. SEE ALSO **food**. **2** *a fat
person.* chubby, dumpy, flabby, gross,
heavy, overweight, plump, podgy,
portly, squat, stocky, stout, tubby.
3 *a fat book.* thick. **4** *fat meat.* fatty,
greasy, oily.

fatal *a fatal illness.* deadly, lethal,
mortal, terminal.

fatality *There were no fatalities in the
accident.* casualty, death.

fate *Fate was kind to him.* chance,
destiny, doom, fortune, luck,
providence.

fated *He believes he was fated to miss that
train.* destined, doomed, intended.

father dad, daddy. SEE ALSO **family**.

fathom SEE **measure**.

fatigue exhaustion, tiredness,
weakness, weariness.

fault 1 *It was Logan's fault that Lucy fell.*
blame, guilt, responsibility. **2** *Look
for any faults in your own work.* blemish,
defect, error, failing, fallacy, flaw,
imperfection, inaccuracy, mistake,
shortcoming, slip, vice, weakness.

faulty *Take the faulty goods back.*
defective, imperfect, out of order.

favour *Will you do me a favour?* good
deed, kindness, service.

favourable 1 *a favourable wind.*
beneficial, helpful. **2** *a favourable
comment.* approving, encouraging,
friendly, generous, kind,
sympathetic.

favourite 1 *a favourite toy.* best,
chosen, popular, preferred, well-
liked. **2** *She's her mother's favourite.*
darling, pet.

fawn 1 SEE **young**. **2** SEE **colour**.

fear alarm, anxiety, awe, dread,
fright, horror, panic, terror.

fearful 1 *He's fearful of spiders.* afraid,
anxious, apprehensive, cowardly,
cowed, frightened, scared, terrified.
2 *The volcano was a fearful sight.*
alarming, appalling, awful,
fearsome, frightening, frightful,

horrifying, shocking, terrible, terrific, tremendous.

fearless *The fearless rescuer leapt into the sea.* adventurous, bold, brave, courageous, daring, heroic, intrepid, valiant.

feasible *Is the plan to build a twenty-mile bridge feasible?* possible, practicable, realistic, viable, workable.

feast banquet, dinner. SEE ALSO **meal.**

feat *The rescue of the wrecked sailors was a daring feat.* achievement, act, action, deed, exploit, performance.

feathers down, plumage, plumes.

feathery downy, fluffy, light.

feature 1 *One feature of the crime puzzled us.* aspect, characteristic, circumstance, detail. 2 *a person's features.* countenance, expression, face. 3 *a feature film.* SEE **film.**

fee *a fee of £1.* charge, cost, fare, payment, price, subscription, toll.

feeble 1 *I felt feeble after my illness.* delicate, frail, helpless, ill, listless, (informal) poorly, sickly, (informal) weedy. 2 *He put up a feeble defence.* puny, spineless, weak. 3 *She made some feeble excuse.* flimsy, lame, poor, tame, weak.

feed to nourish, to strengthen. SEE ALSO **eat.**

feel 1 *Feel this lovely velvet.* to finger, to handle, to manipulate, to stroke, to touch. 2 *Can you feel your way in the dark?* to grope. 3 *It feels colder today.* to seem. 4 *Do you feel the cold?* to detect, to experience, to know, to notice, to perceive, to sense, to suffer. 5 *I feel it's time to go home.* to believe, to consider, to think.

feeling 1 *What were your feelings when you won?* emotion, passion, sensation, sentiment. 2 *Lucy's feeling was that we ought to invite granny for dinner.* attitude, belief, impression, opinion, thought. 3 *There was a happy feeling at the party.* atmosphere, mood, tone. 4 *I have a feeling I'm going to be lucky.* guess, hunch, instinct, intuition.

feign *Logan feigned a cold to avoid going*

out. to act, to concoct, to counterfeit, to fake, to forge, to invent, to pretend.

fell 1 down, hill. SEE ALSO **geography.** 2 *A lumberjack fells trees.* to cut down, to knock down.

fellow (informal) bloke, chap, (informal) guy, man.

fellowship *Most people enjoy the fellowship of others.* companionship, company, friendship, society.

felt *a felt hat.* SEE **cloth.**

female FEMALE CREATURES ARE bitch, cow, doe, ewe, hen, lioness, mare, nanny-goat, sow, tigress, vixen.

feminine *feminine clothes.* female, girlish, ladylike, womanly.

fen bog, marsh, swamp. SEE ALSO **geography.**

fence 1 *a garden fence.* barrier, hedge, hurdle, obstacle, paling, palisade, railing, stockade, wall. 2 *We fenced in the animals.* to enclose, to encircle, to hedge in, to pen, to surround, to wall in.

fend *The boxer fended off his opponent's blows.* to keep off, to parry, to push away, to repel, to repulse, to ward off.

ferment *Mr Brunswick's wine is fermenting.* to bubble, to effervesce, to fizz, to foam.

fern SEE **plant.**

ferocious *a ferocious attack.* barbaric, barbarous, bloodthirsty, bloody, brutal, cruel, fierce, inhuman, merciless, murderous, pitiless, ruthless, sadistic, savage, vicious, violent.

ferret SEE **animal, pet.**

ferry 1 *The ship ferried us to the island.* to carry, to convey, to take, to transfer, to transport. 2 SEE **vessel.**

fertile *a fertile garden.* flourishing, fruitful, lush, productive.

fertilizer compost, manure.

fervent *Tony is a fervent follower of the local team.* avid, eager, enthusiastic, keen, passionate, zealous.

festering *a festering wound.* infected, inflamed, poisoned, putrid.

festival carnival, celebration, fair, feast, festivity, fête, gala, jamboree, jubilee.

festive *Christmas is supposed to be a festive occasion.* cheerful, gay, gleeful, happy, joyful, joyous, light-hearted, merry.

fetch *Our dog fetches the newspaper.* to bring, to carry, to collect, to get, to obtain, to retrieve.

fetching *a fetching dress.* appealing, attractive, charming, lovely, pretty. SEE ALSO **beautiful**.

fête carnival, fair, festival, gala, jamboree.

fetters *The prisoner was in fetters.* bonds, chains, handcuffs, irons, shackles.

feud *There was a bitter feud between the two families.* dispute, quarrel, strife, vendetta.

fever SEE **illness**.

fiancé, fiancée SEE **family**. ! A *fiancé* is a man; a *fiancée* is a woman.

fiasco *Our play was a fiasco.* disaster, failure, (informal) flop, (informal) mess-up.

fib SEE **lie**.

fibre strand, thread.

fibreglass SEE **material**.

fickle *Our weather is so fickle that you never know what clothes to wear.* changeable, erratic, inconsistent, unpredictable, unreliable, variable.

fiction SEE **book**.

fictional, fictitious *His story was fictitious.* fabulous, false, fanciful, imaginary, invented, legendary, made-up, mythical, unreal.

fiddle 1 violin. SEE ALSO **music, strings**. **2** *Please don't fiddle with the knobs on the TV.* to fidget, to twiddle.

fidelity faithfulness, honesty, integrity.

fidget *It irritates other people when you fidget all the time!* to be restless, to fiddle, to jerk, to twiddle, to twitch.

fidgety *The horses became fidgety as the storm approached.* impatient, jittery, jumpy, nervous, restless.

field 1 *Cows grazed in the field.* enclosure, meadow, paddock, pasture. **2** *a games field.* arena, ground, pitch, stadium.

field-glasses binoculars. SEE ALSO **optical**.

fiend demon, devil, imp, spirit.

fierce *a fierce attack, a fierce animal, etc.* angry, barbaric, bloodthirsty, brutal, cruel, ferocious, merciless, murderous, savage, vicious, violent.

fiery 1 *a fiery furnace.* blazing, burning, flaming, hot, red, red-hot. **2** *a fiery temper.* angry, furious, livid, mad, raging.

fig SEE **fruit**.

fight KINDS OF FIGHT ARE action, attack, battle, bout, boxing-match, brawl, clash, combat, competition, confrontation, conflict, contest, counter-attack, duel, encounter, engagement, feud, hostilities, joust, quarrel, raid, rivalry, row, scramble, scrap, scuffle, squabble, strife, struggle, tussle, vendetta, war, wrestling.

fighter VARIOUS FIGHTERS ARE archer, boxer, gladiator, guerrilla, gunman, knight, marine, mercenary, paratrooper, partisan, SEE **soldier**, troops, warrior, wrestler.

figure 1 *Write down the figures 1 to 10.* digit, integer, number, numeral. **2** *Ask Tony to add it up: he's good at figures.* mathematics, sums, statistics. **3** *He has a plump figure.* form, outline, shape. **4** *In the temple was a bronze figure of the goddess.* carving, image, statue. **5** *Figure out how much we owe.* to add up, to calculate, to compute, to reckon, to total, to work out.

file 1 SEE **tool**. **2** *Stand in single file.* column, line, queue, rank, row. **3** *Keep your papers in a file.* folder.

fill 1 *Fill the box with sweets.* to cram, to crowd, to load up, to pack, to occupy. **2** *The drain was filled with muck.* to block up, to jam, to obstruct, to plug, to stop up. **3** *Mrs Brunswick tells us not to pick the peas until the pods fill out.* to enlarge, to expand, to swell.

filling station SEE **building**.

film 1 VARIOUS CINEMA OR TV FILMS ARE cartoon, documentary, feature, movie, western. **2** *a film of oil.* coating, covering, layer, sheet, skin.

filter *You filter the liquid to remove the solid bits.* to sieve, to strain.

filth dirt, grime, (informal) muck, mud, pollution.

filthy 1 *filthy shoes, a filthy room, etc.* caked, dirty, dusty, foul, grimy, grubby, messy, (informal) mucky, muddy, soiled, sooty, sordid, squalid. **2** *filthy language.* coarse, crude, improper, indecent, offensive, rude, smutty, vulgar.

fin SEE **aircraft, fish**.

final *the final moments of the game.* closing, concluding, last, ultimate.

finally eventually, ultimately.

finch SEE **bird**.

find 1 *Where do you find fossils?* to come across, to discover, to dig up, to locate, to uncover, to unearth. **2** *Did mum find her handbag?* to get back, to recover, to regain, to retrieve, to trace. **3** *Did you find your friends?* to encounter, to meet. **4** *Did the garage find the fault in the car?* to detect, to diagnose, to identify, to notice, to observe.

fine 1 *a parking fine.* charge, penalty. SEE ALSO **punishment**. **2** *fine weather.* bright, cloudless, fair, pleasant, sunny. **3** *a fine thread.* narrow, slender, slim, thin. **4** *fine sand.* minute, powdered, powdery. **5** *fine embroidery.* beautiful, dainty, delicate, exquisite. **6** *a fine performance.* admirable, excellent, first-class. SEE ALSO **good**.

finger 1 SEE **body, hand**. **2** *Please don't finger the food.* to feel, to handle, to stroke, to touch.

finicky *Our cat's finicky about food.* (informal) choosey, fastidious, fussy, particular.

finish 1 *Finish your work.* to accomplish, to complete, to conclude, to end, to round off, to stop, to terminate. **2** *Did we finish that box of sweets?* to consume, to exhaust, (informal) to polish off, to use up. **3** *When did they finish dinner?* to break off, to cease, to discontinue, to halt. **4** (informal) *to finish off*: to destroy, to dispatch, to exterminate. SEE ALSO **kill**.

fiord inlet. SEE ALSO **geography**.

fir SEE **tree**.

fire 1 blaze, bonfire, conflagration, inferno. **2** *Modern houses don't always have a fire in the lounge.* fireplace, grate, hearth. **3** OTHER KINDS OF HEATING APPARATUS ARE boiler, central heating, convector, electric fire, forge, furnace, gas fire, heater, immersion heater, incinerator, kiln, oven, stove. **4** *The vandals fired a barn.* to burn, to ignite, to kindle, to light, to set fire to. **5** *to fire a gun.* to detonate, to discharge, to explode, to let off. **6** *The gunners fired at the ship.* to bombard, to shell. **7** *His boss fired him* to dismiss, to sack.

firearms 1 guns. **2** VARIOUS FIREARMS ARE machine-gun, pistol, revolver, rifle, shotgun, sub-machine-gun. SEE ALSO **weapon**.

fire-engine SEE **vehicle**.

fireman SEE **job**.

fireplace fire, grate, hearth.

firework VARIOUS FIREWORKS ARE banger, Catherine wheel, cracker, rocket, sparkler, squib.

firm 1 *Is the ice firm?* hard, rigid, solid, stable, stiff, unyielding. **2** *Is the nail firm?* fast, fixed, immovable, secure, steady, tight. **3** *She was quite firm that she didn't want to play.* adamant, decided, determined, dogged, obstinate, persistent, resolute, unwavering. **4** *a firm arrangement.* agreed, settled, unchangeable. **5** *a firm friend.* constant, dependable, devoted, faithful, loyal, reliable. **6** *Mr Brunswick wants to be boss of his own firm.* business, company, concern, corporation, establishment, organization.

first 1 *Who was the first to arrive?* earliest, soonest. **2** *Who made the first aeroplane?* initial, original. **3** *Who is your first choice?* foremost, leading, prime.

first-class SEE **excellent**.

fish 1 VARIOUS FISH ARE carp, chub, cod, eel, goldfish, haddock, herring, mackerel, minnow, perch, pike, pilchard, plaice, salmon, sardine, shark, sole, stickleback, tiddler, trout. SEE ALSO **shellfish**. **2** PARTS OF A FISH ARE dorsal fin, fin, gills, roe, scales, tail. **3** *fishing:* angling, trawling.

fishmonger SEE **shop**.

fist hand, knuckles.

fit 1 *Is that old house fit to live in?* appropriate, fitting, proper, right, suitable. **2** *Will Lucy be fit for the gymnastics display?* able, capable, healthy, prepared, ready, strong, well. **3** *Do casual clothes fit the occasion?* to become, to suit. **4** *Can you fit the pieces together?* to assemble, to build, to construct, to put together. **5** *She had a fit of coughing.* attack, bout, convulsion, outbreak, seizure, spasm. SEE ALSO **illness**.

fitting *Lucy waited for a fitting moment to mention the broken window.* appropriate, apt, due, proper, right, suitable, timely.

fix 1 *to fix something into place, to fix things together.* to attach, to bind, to join, to link, to make firm, to secure. SEE ALSO **fasten**. **2** *to fix a price for something.* to agree, to arrange, to decide, to establish, to settle. **3** *to fix a broken window.* to mend, to put right, to repair. **4** *to get into a fix.* difficulty, dilemma, jam, plight, predicament, problem.

fixture *Our team has a fixture at home this week.* appointment, engagement, meeting.

fizz to bubble, to effervesce, to fizzle, to foam, to froth.

fizzy *fizzy drinks.* bubbly, effervescent, foaming, sparkling.

flabby *a flabby tummy.* fat, feeble, overweight, out of condition, weak.

flag 1 *decorated with flags.* banner, colours, ensign, streamer. **2** *After two hours our interest flagged.* to decline, to flop, to sink, to weaken, to wilt, to worsen.

flake *flakes of old paint, flakes of flint.* bit, chip, scale, slice, splinter.

flame to blaze, to flare. SEE ALSO **burn**.

flamingo SEE **bird**.

flan SEE **cake**.

flannel SEE **cloth**.

flap *The flag flapped in the wind.* to flutter, to swing, to wave.

flare to blaze, to flame. SEE ALSO **burn**.

flash SEE **light**.

flashy *flashy clothes.* bright, elaborate, fancy, gaudy, showy.

flask bottle. SEE ALSO **container**.

flat 1 *a flat surface.* even, horizontal, level, smooth. **2** *a flat sea.* calm. **3** *to lie in a flat position.* prone, spread out. **4** *a flat voice.* boring, dull, monotonous, unexciting, uninteresting. **5** *to live in a flat.* SEE **house**.

flatten 1 *We must flatten the lawn if we want to play cricket on it.* to even out, to iron out, to level, to press, to roll, to smooth. **2** *The hurricane flattened the town.* to crush, to demolish, to destroy, to devastate, to knock down. **3** *Tony flattened Mrs Brunswick's geraniums.* to run over, to trample. **4** *We flattened the opposition.* SEE **defeat**.

flatter 1 to humour. **2** *flattering: a flattering remark.* complimentary.

flavour 1 SEE **taste**. **2** *Mrs Angel read an extract to give us the flavour of the book.* character, characteristic, quality.

flaw *a flaw in a piece of work.* blemish, crack, defect, error, fault, imperfection, inaccuracy, mistake, shortcoming, weakness.

flea SEE **insect**.

fledgeling SEE **bird, young**.

flee *We fled when the lion roared.* to abscond, to escape, to run away.

fleet *a fleet of ships.* armada, convoy, navy, squadron. SEE ALSO **group**.

flesh meat, muscle.

flex *The flex for our iron needs replacing.* cable, lead, wire. SEE ALSO **electricity**.

flexible bendable, (informal) bendy, floppy, pliable, soft, springy, supple.

flick to flip. SEE ALSO **hit**.

flicker *The candles flickered.* to blink, to flutter, to glimmer, to quiver, to tremble, to twinkle, to waver. SEE ALSO **light**.

flight 1 SEE **travel**. **2** escape, getaway, retreat, running away.

flimsy *A butterfly's wings seem so flimsy.* brittle, delicate, feeble, frail, fragile, rickety, shaky, slight, thin, weak.

flinch *Tony flinched when the dog rushed at him.* to cringe, to falter, to jerk away, to quail, to recoil, to shrink back, to wince.

fling *I flung a coin into the well.* to cast, (informal) to chuck, to hurl, to lob, to sling, to throw, to toss.

flint SEE **rock**.

flip to flick. SEE ALSO **hit**.

flipper SEE **limb**.

flit *Bats flitted about.* to dart, to fly, to skim. SEE ALSO **move**.

float 1 *to float on water.* to drift, to sail, to swim. **2** *to float in the air.* to drift, to hang, to hover. **3** *We're ready to float our raft.* to launch. **4** *a milk-float.* SEE **vehicle**.

flock *a flock of birds.* SEE **group**.

floe ice, iceberg.

flog 1 to beat, to cane, to lash, to scourge, to thrash, to wallop, to whip. SEE ALSO **hit**. **2** *flogging:* SEE **punishment**.

flood 1 *When the dam burst a flood of water swept through the valley.* deluge, inundation, spate, torrent. SEE ALSO **disaster**. **2** *The water flooded the whole town.* to drown, to engulf, to inundate, to overflow, to submerge, to swamp.

floodlights SEE **light**.

floor 1 SEE **building**. **2** VARIOUS FLOOR COVERINGS ARE carpet, lino, mat, matting, rug, tiles. **3** *The bedrooms are on the top floor.* deck, level, storey.

flop *The seedlings we forgot to water began to flop.* to collapse, to dangle, to droop, to drop, to fall, to flag, to sag, to wilt.

floppy *The cabbage seedlings have gone floppy.* bendable, (informal) bendy, flexible, limp, pliable.

floppy disc SEE **computer**.

florist SEE **shop**.

flounder *We floundered about in the mud.* to struggle, to wallow.

flour SEE **food**.

flourish 1 *Mrs Brunswick's plants are flourishing now that we've had some rain.* to be fruitful, to be successful, to bloom, to blossom, to flower, to grow, to prosper, to strengthen, to succeed, to thrive. **2** *He flourished his umbrella to attract our attention.* to brandish, to shake, to twirl, to wave

flow WAYS IN WHICH LIQUIDS FLOW ARE to dribble, to drip, to ebb, to gush, to leak, to move in a current, t ooze, to pour, to run, to seep, to stream, to trickle.

flower 1 *There are flowers in the garden.* bloom, blossom, petal. **2** *a bunch of flowers*: arrangement, bouquet, garland, posy, spray, wreath. **3** VARIOUS FLOWERS ARE bluebell, buttercup, carnation, catkin, chrysanthemum, cornflower, cowslip, crocus, daffodil, daisy, dandelion, forget-me-not, foxglove, geranium, hollyhock, hyacinth, iris, lilac, lily, lupin, marigold, orchid, pansy, peony, pink, poppy, primrose, rhododendron, rose, snowdrop, sunflower, tulip, violet, wallflower, water-lily.

flu SEE **illness**.

fluent *a fluent speaker of French.* eloquent, flowing, unhesitating.

fluffy *fluffy toys.* downy, feathery, fleecy, furry, fuzzy, woolly.

fluid *a fluid substance.* flowing, liquid, runny, sloppy, watery.

fluke *It was only a fluke that you scored.* accident, chance, luck.

flush 1 *to flush the lavatory.* to rinse out, to wash out. 2 *Mrs Angel flushed with embarrassment.* to blush, to colour, to glow, to redden.

flustered *Keep calm: don't get flustered.* confused, distressed, embarrassed, nervous.

flute SEE **woodwind**.

flutter *The leaves fluttered in the wind.* to flap, to flicker, to quiver, to tremble.

fly 1 *Most birds fly.* to flit, to glide, to hover, to rise, to soar, to swoop. 2 *A flag was flying.* to flap, to flutter, to wave. 3 SEE **move**. 4 *A lot of flies were buzzing about.* SEE **insect**.

fly-over SEE **road**.

foal SEE **horse, young**.

foam 1 froth, lather, scum, suds. 2 *What makes the water foam?* to bubble, to effervesce, to fizz, to froth, to lather.

fo'c'sle SEE **vessel**.

focus 1 SEE **photography**. 2 *Let's focus on the main problem.* to concentrate on, to look at, to think about. 3 *The market square is the main focus of the town.* centre, core, heart, hub.

fodder hay, silage.

foe adversary, antagonist, attacker, enemy, opponent, opposition, rival.

foetus embryo.

fog cloud, haze, mist. SEE ALSO **weather**.

foil 1 *The security officer foiled the thieves.* to block, to frustrate, to halt, to hamper, to hinder, to obstruct, to prevent, to stop. 2 *to fight with foils.* sword. SEE ALSO **weapon**.

fold 1 *Fold the paper.* to bend, to crease, to double over. 2 *My umbrella folds up.* to collapse. 3 *The curtains hung in folds.* crease, pleat, wrinkle. 4 *The dog drove the sheep into the fold.* compound, enclosure, pen.

folder *a folder to keep papers in.* cover, file.

foliage *We want some foliage to put with the flowers.* greenery, leaves.

folk human beings, humanity, people. SEE ALSO **person**.

folk-song SEE **sing**.

folk-tale SEE **writing**.

follow 1 *Follow the car in front!* to chase, to hound, to hunt, to pursue, to shadow, to stalk, to tag on to, to tail, to track, to trail. 2 *Another bus follows this one in a few minutes.* to come after, to replace, to succeed. 3 *Follow the instructions.* to heed, to keep to, to obey, to observe, to take notice of. 4 *Did you follow what he said?* to comprehend, to grasp, to understand. 5 *Do you follow football?* to be interested in, to know about, to support.

follower admirer, apostle, disciple, fan, supporter.

fond *a fond kiss.* affectionate, attached, loving, partial, tender.

fondle *He fondled the dog's ears.* to caress, to kiss, to pat, to pet, to stroke, to touch.

font SEE **church**.

food 1 delicacy, diet, fodder, (informal) grub, nourishment, protein, provisions, recipe, refreshments, swill, vitamins. SEE ALSO **drink, meal**. 2 KINDS OF FOOD ARE batter, beans, SEE **biscuit**, blancmange, bran, bread, broth, SEE **cake**, caviare, SEE **cereal**, cheese, chips, chop suey, cornflakes, cornflour, cream, crisps, curry, custard, dumplings, egg, SEE **fat**, SEE **fish**, flour, fritter, SEE **fruit**, glucose, goulash, greens, haggis, hash, health foods, honey, hot-pot, ice-cream, icing, jam, jelly, junket, kipper, kosher food, lasagne, macaroni, malt, marmalade, SEE **meat**, milk, mincemeat, mince pie, mousse, noodles, SEE **nut**, oatmeal, omelette, pancake, pasta, pastry, pasty, pâté, pie, pizza, porridge, pudding, quiche, rice, risotto, rissole, rusk, SEE **salad**, sandwich, sausage, sausage-roll, scampi, seafood, semolina, soufflé, soup, soya beans, spaghetti, stew, stock, stuffing, syrup, tart, toast, treacle, trifle, SEE **vegetable**, vegetarian food, wholemeal flour, yeast, yogurt.

3 THINGS YOU ADD TO FOOD ARE chutney, colouring, dressing, garlic, gravy, herbs, ketchup, mayonnaise, mustard, pepper, pickle, preservative, salt, sauce, seasoning, spice, sugar, vanilla, vinegar.

fool 1 ass, blockhead, booby, dope, dunce, half-wit, idiot, ignoramus, imbecile, moron, nit, nitwit, twerp.
! These words are mostly used informally and are often insulting.
2 *the king's fool.* clown, entertainer, jester. **3** *Logan fooled us by saying he'd won a prize.* to bluff, to cheat, to deceive, to dupe, to hoax, to hoodwink, to kid, to mislead, to swindle, to take in, to trick.

foolish *It was foolish of Logan to try to trick the headmaster.* absurd, crazy, frivolous, idiotic, irrational, ludicrous, misguided, ridiculous, silly, stupid, unwise.

foot 1 hoof, paw. SEE ALSO **body, leg**.
2 PARTS OF A FOOT ARE ankle, heel, instep, sole, toe. **3** *There are 12 inches in one foot.* SEE **measure**.

football 1 soccer. SEE ALSO **sport**.
2 WORDS USED IN FOOTBALL ARE ball, corner, cup tie, defender, draw, forward, foul, goal, goalkeeper, linesman, match, offside, penalty, pitch, referee, striker, touch-line.

footlights SEE **theatre**.

footman SEE **servant**.

footpath SEE **road**.

footplate SEE **railway**.

forbid *Mrs Brunswick forbids smoking in the house.* to ban, to bar, to deter, to outlaw, to prohibit, to veto.

forbidding *forbidding storm-clouds.* gloomy, grim, menacing, ominous, stern, threatening, unfriendly.

force 1 *We used all our force to open the door.* energy, might, power, pressure, strength, vigour. **2** *You can't force me to play with you.* to compel, to drive, to make, to oblige, to order. **3** *We had to force the door because it was locked.* to

break open, to burst open, to wrench.

forceful *a forceful leader.* dynamic, energetic, enthusiastic, masterful, powerful, strong, vigorous.

forceps SEE **medicine**.

ford SEE **road**.

foreboding *I had a foreboding that something nasty would happen.* omen, premonition, warning.

forecast 1 *They forecast rain.* to foresee, to foretell, to predict, to prophesy. **2** *the weather forecast.* outlook, prediction, prophecy.

forecastle SEE **vessel**.

forefather ancestor, predecessor. SEE ALSO **family**.

forehead SEE **body, head**.

foreign 1 *a foreign country.* alien, strange, unfamiliar. **2** *foreign goods.* imported.

foreigner *Many foreigners pass through the airport.* alien, immigrant, outsider, visitor.

foreman boss, controller, head, superintendent, supervisor. SEE ALSO **chief**.

foresee *Do they foresee any improvement in the weather?* to anticipate, to expect, to forecast, to foretell, to predict, to prophesy.

forethought planning.

forfeit *to pay a forfeit.* fine, penalty.

forge 1 *a blacksmith's forge.* furnace.
2 *to forge £5 notes.* to copy, to counterfeit, to fake, to imitate.

forgery copy, fake, fraud, imitation, replica, reproduction.

forget 1 *We almost forgot Mother's Day last year.* to disregard, to ignore, to leave out, to miss out, to neglect, to overlook, to skip. **2** *Logan forgot his money as usual.* to leave behind.

forgetful absent-minded, careless, inattentive, negligent, scatter-brained, thoughtless.

forget-me-not SEE **flower**.

forgive *Mrs Brunswick never forgave Tony for trampling on her geraniums.* to excuse, to pardon, to spare.

fork SEE **cutlery, garden.**

forked *a forked stick.* branched, divided, V-shaped.

forlorn *Lucy looked forlorn when the doctor said she couldn't play.* dejected, depressed, desolate, miserable, neglected, unhappy, wistful, wretched. SEE ALSO **sad.**

form 1 *a human form.* figure, outline, shape. **2** *What form of exercise do you like best?* kind, sort, type, variety. **3** *Tony is in Mrs Angel's form.* class, group, set. **4** *We sat on a form.* bench, seat. **5** *If you want a bus pass, you fill in a form.* document, paper. **6** *Tony formed the clay into a ball.* to cast, to mould, to shape. **7** *These players form an excellent team.* to compose, to constitute, to create, to make up, to produce. **8** *In cold weather, icicles form under the bridge.* to appear, to develop, to grow, to take shape.

formal *prize-giving was a formal occasion.* ceremonial, dignified, official, (informal) posh, proper, solemn, stately.

forsake *The dog never forsook his master.* to abandon, to desert, to evacuate, to give up, to leave, to quit, to renounce.

fort castle, citadel, fortress, garrison, stronghold.

forthwith directly, immediately, instantly, promptly.

fortify *We fortified our den against Logan's gang.* to defend, to protect, to reinforce, to strengthen.

fortitude *Lucy endured the pain with fortitude.* bravery, courage, heroism, patience, (informal) pluck, valour.

fortnight SEE **time.**

fortress castle, citadel, fort, garrison, stronghold.

fortunate *a fortunate accident.* favourable, happy, lucky.

fortune 1 *good fortune, bad fortune.* chance, destiny, fate, luck, providence. **2** *The duke lost his fortune by gambling.* estate, inheritance, possessions, property, wealth.

fortune-teller prophet.

forward *It was forward of you to yell 'Happy Christmas' at the headmaster.* bold, brazen, cheeky, impudent, insolent, shameless.

forwards ahead, onwards.

foster SEE **family.**

foul 1 *a foul mess.* dirty, disgusting, filthy, nasty, nauseating, obnoxious, repulsive, revolting. SEE ALSO **unpleasant.** **2** *foul weather.* rainy, rough, stormy, violent, windy. SEE ALSO **weather.** **3** *foul language.* blasphemous, coarse, common, crude, improper, indecent, offensive, rude, uncouth, vulgar. **4** *a foul crime.* atrocious, cruel, evil, monstrous, vicious, vile, villainous, wicked. **5** *foul air.* contaminated, impure, infected, polluted, smelly, unclean. **6** *a foul stroke.* illegal, prohibited.

found 1 *Mr Brunswick's dad founded a business in the High Street.* to begin, to create, to establish, to set up. **2** *They founded the castle on solid rock.* to base, to build, to construct, to erect.

foundation *the foundations of a building.* base, basis, bottom, foot.

foundry SEE **factory.**

fountain *a fountain of water.* jet, spray.

fountain pen SEE **write.**

four-poster SEE **bed.**

fowl bird, chicken, hen.

fox SEE **animal.**

foxglove SEE **flower.**

foxhound SEE **dog.**

foyer entrance, hall, lobby. SEE ALSO **theatre.**

fraction 1 *Only a fraction of the crowd could hear what was going on.* part, portion, section. **2** *to divide something into fractions.* shares.

fracture *to fracture a leg.* to break, to crack. SEE ALSO **wound.**

fragile *Eggshell is fragile.* breakable, brittle, delicate, frail, thin.

fragments 1 *Tony smashed granny's teapot into fragments.* atoms, bits, particles, smithereens. **2** *Please sweep up the fragments.* chips, crumbs, debris, pieces, remnants, scraps, snippets, specks.

frail 1 *As you get old, you get more frail.* delicate, feeble, infirm, unsteady, weak, (insulting) weedy. **2** *The first aircraft were frail machines.* brittle, flimsy, fragile, rickety.

frame 1 *a frame for a tent.* framework, skeleton. **2** *a frame for a picture.* border, edge, edging. **3** *Tony framed his picture in a coloured border.* to enclose, to mount, to surround.

framework frame, outline, plan, skeleton, structure.

frank *a frank reply.* candid, direct, honest, open, outspoken, plain, sincere, straightforward.

frantic *Dad went frantic when he lost his wallet.* berserk, crazy, demented, deranged, frenzied, hectic, hysterical, mad, wild.

fraud 1 *He was put in prison for fraud.* deceit, deception, dishonesty. **2** *The so-called magic was a fraud.* cheat, counterfeit, fake, hoax, ruse, sham, trick.

fraudulent cheating, crooked, deceitful, dishonest, false, lying, underhand, unscrupulous.

frayed *a frayed collar.* ragged, tattered, (informal) tatty, worn.

freak *freak weather conditions.* abnormal, exceptional, peculiar, queer, unusual.

freckle SEE **complexion**.

free 1 *Are you free to come?* able, allowed, permitted. **2** *The slaves wanted to be free.* emancipated, liberated, released. **3** *Uncle George is free with his money.* bounteous, generous, lavish, liberal. **4** *Is the lavatory free?* available, open, unoccupied. **5** *The judge freed him.* to acquit, to discharge, to let off, to let go, to pardon, to spare. **6** *Robin Hood freed his friends from the castle.* to liberate, to release, to rescue, to save, to set free.

freedom *The slaves wanted their freedom.* independence, liberty.

free-wheel *Tony free-wheeled downhill.* to coast, to drift, to glide.

freeze 1 *to freeze food.* to chill, to ice, to refrigerate. **2** *Will it freeze tonight?* SEE **weather**.

freezer SEE **kitchen**.

freight *Some aircraft carry passengers and some carry freight.* cargo, goods, load, merchandise.

frenzied *The frenzied fans screamed.* berserk, crazy, delirious, demented, frantic, hysterical, mad, wild.

frenzy *a frenzy of excitement.* hysteria, insanity, madness, mania.

frequent 1 *frequent bouts of illness, frequent trains.* constant, continual, countless, many, numerous, persistent, recurrent. **2** *The cuckoo is a frequent visitor to Britain.* common, habitual, regular.

fresh 1 *The detectives looked for fresh clues.* different, new, recent, up-to-date. **2** *We put fresh sheets on the bed.* airy, clean, unused, untouched. **3** *You feel fresh after a shower.* energetic, healthy, invigorated, lively, perky, rested. **4** *fresh water.* pure, unpolluted.

fret *The dog fretted while his master was away.* to grieve, to worry.

fretsaw SEE **tool**.

friar SEE **church**.

fridge SEE **kitchen**.

friend acquaintance, ally, chum, companion, comrade, (informal) mate, (informal) pal, partner, pen-friend.

friendly *a friendly girl, a friendly welcome, etc.* affectionate, agreeable, amiable, attached, close, familiar, good-natured, favourable, gracious, helpful, hospitable, intimate, kind, kind-hearted, loving, sociable, sympathetic, tender, warm, welcoming.

frieze *a decorative frieze.* border, edging.

frigate SEE **vessel**.

fright alarm, dread, fear, horror, panic, terror.

frighten 1 *Logan frightened the cat.* to alarm, to appal, to bully, to daunt, to dismay, to horrify, to intimidate, to make afraid, to menace, to persecute, to petrify, to scare, to shake, to shock, to startle, to terrify, to terrorize, to threaten. **2** *frightened*: afraid, apprehensive, fearful. **3** *frightening*: creepy, eerie, ghostly, hair-raising, scary, sinister, spooky, uncanny, weird.

frightful *a frightful accident*. appalling, awful, dreadful, fearful, fearsome, ghastly, grisly, hideous, horrible, horrid, horrifying, shocking, terrible. SEE ALSO **unpleasant**.

frill *a curtain with a frill round the bottom*. border, edging, fringe.

fringe 1 *a fringe round the bottom of a curtain*. border, edging, frill. **2** *the fringe of a town*. edge, outskirts.

frisk *Lambs were frisking in the field*. to caper, to dance, to jump about, to leap, to prance, to romp, to skip.

frisky jaunty, lively, perky, playful, spirited, sprightly.

fritter 1 SEE **food**. **2** *to fritter away your money*. to misuse, to squander, to waste.

frivolous *Mrs Angel hates Logan's frivolous questions*. foolish, ridiculous, silly, stupid, trivial, unimportant, worthless.

frock dress, gown. SEE ALSO **clothes**.

frog SEE **amphibious**.

frogman diver.

front *the front of an aircraft, the front of a house*. face, head, nose.

frontier *the frontier between two countries*. border, boundary.

frost, frosty SEE **cold, weather**.

frostbite SEE **illness**.

froth bubbles, foam, lather, scum, suds.

frown to glower, to scowl. SEE ALSO **expression**.

fruit VARIOUS FRUITS ARE apple, apricot, banana, berry, blackberry, cherry, citrus fruit, coconut, crab-apple, currant, damson, date, fig, gooseberry, grape, grapefruit, greengage, hip, lemon, lime, melon, olive, orange, peach, pear, pineapple, plum, prune, raisin, raspberry, rhubarb, strawberry, sultana, tangerine, tomato.

fruitful 1 *a fruitful search*. profitable, successful. **2** *a fruitful garden*. fertile, flourishing, lush, productive.

fruitless *a fruitless search*. futile, pointless, unsuccessful, useless.

frustrate *The police frustrated an attempted robbery*. to foil, to halt, to hinder, to prevent, to stop.

fry SEE **cook**.

frying-pan SEE **cook, kitchen**.

fuddled 1 *I'm always fuddled when I wake up*. confused, flustered, mixed up, muddled. **2** *fuddled with alcohol*. drunk, intoxicated.

fudge SEE **sweet**.

fuel KINDS OF FUEL ARE anthracite, butane, charcoal, coal, coke, electricity, gas, gasoline, logs, methylated spirit, nuclear fuel, oil, paraffin, peat, petrol, propane.

fugitive deserter, refugee, renegade.

fulfil 1 *I wonder if Lucy will fulfil her ambition to compete in the Olympics?* to accomplish, to achieve, to carry out, to complete, to perform. **2** *Did the shop fulfil your requirements?* to meet, to satisfy.

full 1 *The shops are full at Christmas*. bursting, congested, crammed, crowded, filled, jammed, packed, stuffed. **2** *My cup is full*. brimming, overflowing. **3** *Tell us the full story*. complete, entire, total, whole. **4** *She ran at full speed*. greatest, highest, maximum.

full stop SEE **punctuation**.

fumble *He fumbled the ball*. to grope at, to mishandle.

fume 1 *fuming chimneys*. to smoke. **2** *He was fuming because his money had been stolen*. SEE **angry**.

fumes exhaust, gases, smoke, vapour.

fun amusement, jokes, laughter, merriment, pastimes, play, pleasure, recreation. SEE ALSO **entertainment, game**.

function 1 *The function of the police is to keep order*. aim, duty, job, purpose, task, use. **2** *Uncle Rick's wedding was a* *happy function*. ceremony, event, gathering, occasion, party, reception. **3** *This computer isn't functioning properly*. to act, to behave, to operate, to perform, to work.

fundamental *Lucy learned the fundamental skills of windsurfing*. basic, elementary, essential, important, main, primary, principal.

funds *Mr Brunswick needs more funds to start his business*. capital, money, resources, savings, wealth.

funeral 1 burial, cremation. **2** WORDS TO DO WITH FUNERALS ARE cemetery, coffin, crematorium, grave, graveyard, hearse, memorial, mortuary, mourner, tomb, undertaker, wreath.

fun-fair SOME ENTERTAINMENTS AT A FUN-FAIR ARE dodgems, merry-go-round, roundabout, side-show.

fungus mushroom, toadstool. SEE ALSO **plant**.

funny 1 *a funny joke*. absurd, amusing, comic, crazy, facetious, farcical, hilarious, humorous, hysterical, laughable, ludicrous, (informal) priceless, ridiculous, uproarious, witty, zany. **2** *Tony had a funny pain in his stomach*. abnormal, curious, odd, peculiar, queer, strange, unusual.

funny-bone SEE **body**.

fur 1 *Many animals are covered in fur*. bristles, down, fleece, hair. **2** *Primitive people used to dress in furs*. hide, skin.

furious *a furious bull*. angry, cross, enraged, fuming, incensed, indignant, infuriated, irate, livid, mad, raging.

furlong SEE **measure**.

furnace SEE **fire**.

furnish *Mr Brunswick has a workshop furnished with the latest gadgets*. to equip, to fit up, to provide, to supply.

furniture KINDS OF FURNITURE ARE antique, armchair, bed, bench, bookcase, bunk, bureau, cabinet, chair, chest of drawers, cot, couch, cradle, cupboard, cushion, deck-chair, desk, divan, drawer, dresser, easel, fender, fireplace, mantelpiece, pew, pouffe, rocking-chair, settee, sideboard, sofa, stool, suite, table, trestle table, wardrobe, workbench.

furrow crease, groove, rut, wrinkle.

furry *furry animals*. bristly, downy, feathery, fleecy, fuzzy, hairy, woolly.

further *We'd like further information*. additional, extra, more, supplementary.

furthermore additionally, also, besides, moreover, too.

furtive *The shopkeeper didn't like the furtive way Logan was looking round the shop*. crafty, deceitful, mysterious, secretive, shifty, sly, sneaky, stealthy, tricky, untrustworthy, wily.

fury *We were frightened by the fury of the storm*. anger, rage, violence, wrath.

fuse SEE **electricity**.

fuselage SEE **aircraft**.

fuss *Logan made a fuss when he didn't win*. ado, bother, commotion, excitement, to-do, trouble, turmoil, uproar.

fussy *fussy about food*. (informal) choosey, fastidious, finicky, particular.

futile *It's futile to complain if you've lost the receipt*. fruitless, ineffective, pointless, unsuccessful, useless, vain, worthless.

future *future events*. approaching, coming.

fuzzy 1 *a fuzzy beard*. downy, feathery, fleecy, woolly. **2** *We get a fuzzy picture on our TV*. blurred, cloudy, dim, faint, hazy, indistinct, misty, unclear.

G g

gabble *I can't understand what you say if you gabble*. to babble, to jabber, to mutter. SEE ALSO **talk**.

gable SEE **building**.

gadget *a gadget for opening lemonade bottles*. contraption, contrivance, device, implement, instrument, invention, machine, tool, utensil.

gag 1 *The comedian told some old gags.* jest, joke. **2** *The gang tied him up and gagged him.* to silence.

gain 1 *What did they gain by fighting a terrible war?* to acquire, to earn, to get, to obtain, to procure, to receive, to win. **2** *The explorers gained their objective.* to achieve, to get to, to reach. **3** *At the end of the day we added up our gains.* advantage, asset, benefit, profit.

gala carnival, fair, festival, fête.

galaxy SEE **astronomy, group.**

gale *The gale blew our TV aerial down.* blast, wind. SEE ALSO **weather.**

gallant *a gallant knight.* brave, chivalrous, courageous, fearless, gentlemanly, heroic, noble, polite, valiant.

galleon SEE **vessel.**

gallery SEE **theatre.**

galley SEE **vessel.**

gallon SEE **measure.**

gallop to race, to run, to rush. SEE ALSO **horse, move.**

gallows *to be hanged on a gallows.* scaffold.

galvanized iron SEE **metal.**

gamble 1 WAYS OF GAMBLING ARE betting, bingo, cards, dice, drawing lots, lottery, pools, raffle, wager. **2** *She gambled her life to save the drowning man.* to risk, to venture.

game 1 *What's your favourite game?* amusement, entertainment, fun, joke, pastime, playing, sport. **2** *Let's have another game of chess.* competition, contest, match, tournament. **3** VARIOUS GAMES ARE billiards, bingo, SEE **cards,** charades, chess, crossword puzzle, darts, dice, dominoes, draughts, hide-and-seek, hopscotch, jigsaw puzzle, leap-frog, ludo, marbles, pool, skittles, snooker, table-tennis, tiddlywinks. **4** FOR MORE ACTIVE GAMES SEE **sport.**

gamekeeper SEE **job.**

gammon bacon, ham. SEE ALSO **meat.**

gander SEE **male.**

gang *a gang of workmen.* band, company, crew, horde. SEE ALSO **group.**

gangster brigand, criminal, crook, desperado, gunman, robber, ruffian.

gaol 1 dungeon, prison. SEE ALSO **punishment.** **2** *He was gaoled for fraud.* to confine, to detain, to imprison, to intern, to shut up.

gap 1 *a gap in the fence.* break, hole. SEE ALSO **opening.** **2** *a gap between lessons.* interval, lapse, lull, pause, respite, rest. **3** *Is the gap between the posts wide enough for the car?* distance, space.

gape to gaze, to stare. SEE ALSO **look.**

garage SEE **building.**

garbage *Put the garbage in the dustbin.* junk, litter, refuse, rubbish, trash, waste.

garbled *a garbled message.* confused, incoherent, jumbled, misleading, mixed up.

garden 1 *Mrs Brunswick loves her garden.* allotment, patch, plot. **2** THINGS FOUND IN A GARDEN ARE bed, border, butt, compost heap, flagstones, SEE **flower,** SEE **fruit,** hedge, lawn, orchard, path, patio, pond, rockery, rock garden, shrubbery, terrace, SEE **tree,** trellis, turf, SEE **vegetable,** window-box. **3** GARDEN TOOLS ARE broom, cultivator, fork, hoe, rake, riddle, secateurs, shears, shovel, sieve, spade, trowel, watering-can. **4** SUBSTANCES USED IN A GARDEN ARE compost, fertilizer, insecticide, manure, peat, pesticide, weed-killer.

gardener SEE **job.**

gargle SEE **medicine.**

gargoyle SEE **church.**

garland SEE **flower.**

garlic SEE **food.**

garment attire, clothing, costume, dress. FOR VARIOUS GARMENTS SEE **clothes.**

garrison citadel, fort, fortress.

garter SEE **clothes**.

gas 1 *A car engine gives off poisonous gas.* exhaust, fumes, vapour. **2** VARIOUS GASES ARE hydrogen, nitrogen, oxygen, tear gas. **3** SEE **fuel**.

gash *The broken bottle made a gash in Tony's foot.* cut, slash, slit, wound. SEE ALSO **cut, opening**.

gasoline petrol. SEE ALSO **fuel**.

gasp 1 *The smoke made them gasp.* to choke, to pant, to puff, to wheeze. **2** *gasping*: breathless, exhausted, puffed, tired out.

gastric flu SEE **illness**.

gate door, entrance, entry, exit, gateway, turnstile.

gather 1 *A crowd gathered. We gathered our belongings. Gather your team together.* to accumulate, to assemble, to bring together, to cluster, to collect, to come together, to concentrate, to congregate, to crowd, to get together, to group, to herd, to hoard, to mass, to meet, to mobilize, to muster, to pile up, to round up, to store up, to swarm, to throng. **2** *We gathered strawberries.* to harvest, to pick, to pluck. **3** *I gather you've been ill.* to conclude, to learn, to understand.

gathering 1 *a gathering of people.* bunch, company, congregation, crowd, mass, swarm, throng. SEE ALSO **group**. **2** *The grown-ups are having some sort of gathering at Christmas.* assembly, function, meeting, party, social.

gaudy *gaudy colours.* bright, colourful, flashy, lurid, showy, tawdry.

gauge *a narrow gauge railway.* measurement, size.

gaunt *The old man looked gaunt after his illness.* bony, emaciated, lean, skinny, starving, thin, wasted away.

gauntlet glove. SEE ALSO **clothes**.

gauze SEE **cloth**.

gawky *The ostrich looked a gawky bird.* awkward, blundering, clumsy, ungainly.

gay 1 *gay colours, gay laughter.* bright, cheerful, joyful, light-hearted, merry. SEE ALSO **happy**. **2** homosexual, (impolite) queer.

gaze *We gazed at the sunset.* to contemplate, to eye, to observe, to regard, to stare at, to view, to watch. SEE ALSO **look**.

gear 1 *to change gear.* SEE **vehicle**. **2** *camping gear.* apparatus, equipment, instruments, kit, paraphernalia, rig, tackle.

gelignite SEE **explosive**.

gem jewel, precious stone. SEE ALSO **jewellery**.

general 1 *The bad weather is general this year.* common, communal, global, shared, universal, widespread. **2** *Smoking used to be more general than it is now.* customary, everyday, familiar, habitual, regular, usual. **3** *He only gave us a general idea of where we were going.* broad, indefinite, unclear, vague.

generally chiefly, mainly, mostly, predominantly, usually.

generate *to generate electricity, to generate business, etc.* to breed, to bring about, to create, to make, to produce.

generation SEE **family**.

generator SEE **electricity**.

generous 1 *a generous sponsor.* bounteous, charitable, free, kind, lavish, liberal, public-spirited, unselfish. **2** *generous portions of food.* abundant, ample, copious, large, liberal, plentiful, sizeable.

genial *Our friends gave us a genial welcome.* cheerful, cordial, easy-going, friendly, pleasant, relaxed, warm-hearted. SEE ALSO **kind**.

genius 1 *He is a mathematical genius.* expert, know-all, master-mind. **2** *He has a genius for maths.* gift, intellect, talent.

gentle 1 *a gentle person.* good-tempered, kindly, merciful, mild, pleasant, soft-hearted, tender. **2** *gentle music.* peaceful, quiet, relaxing, soft, soothing. **3** *a gentle dog.* docile, manageable, meek, obedient, tame. **4** *a gentle wind.* balmy, delicate, faint, light. 5 *a gentle hint.* indirect, subtle. 6 *a gentle hill.* gradual, moderate, steady.

gentleman SEE **person**.

genuine 1 *a genuine £5 note.* actual, authentic, real. 2 *genuine feelings.* devout, honest, sincere, true.

geo-board SEE **mathematics**.

geography 1 SOME GEOGRAPHICAL WORDS ARE Antarctic, archipelago, Arctic, bay, borough, canyon, cape, capital, city, climate, continent, contour, conurbation, country, county, creek, dale, delta, downs, east, equator, estate, estuary, fells, fen, fiord, geyser, glacier, glen, gulf, hamlet, heath, hemisphere, highlands, hill, industry, inlet, island, isthmus, lagoon, lake, land, latitude, longitude, mainland, nation, north, oasis, parish, pass, peninsula, plain, plateau, pole, prairie, province, reef, relief map, river, sea, south, strait, suburb, tide, town, tributary, tropics, valley, village, volcano, west, world.
2 SEE **subject**.

geology SEE **science**.

geometry SEE **mathematics**.

geranium SEE **flower**.

gerbil SEE **animal, pet**.

germ bacteria, (informal) bug, microbe, virus. ! *Bacteria* is a plural word.

germinate *Our seeds have germinated.* to grow, to shoot, to spring up, to sprout, to start growing.

gesture 1 action, movement, sign.
2 WAYS TO MAKE GESTURES ARE to beckon, to nod, to point, to salute, to shake your head, to shrug, to wave, to wink.

get 1 *What did you get for Christmas? What can I get for £10?* to acquire, to be given, to buy, to gain, to get hold of, to obtain, to procure, to purchase, to receive. 2 *Tell the dog to get the ball.* to bring, to fetch, to pick up, to retrieve. 3 *Did you get a prize?* to earn, to take, to win. 4 *Lucy got a cold.* to catch, to contract, to develop, to

suffer from. 5 *Get Tony to do the washing-up.* to cause, to persuade.
6 *Let's get tea now.* to make ready, to prepare. 7 *I don't get what he means.* to comprehend, to follow, to grasp, to understand. 8 *What time do you get to school?* to arrive at, to reach. 9 *How do you get to school?* to go, to travel.
10 *It's getting cold.* to become, to grow, to turn. ! *Get* can mean many things. The words given here are only some of the other words you could use.

getaway *They made their getaway in a fast car.* escape, flight, retreat.

geyser SEE **geography**.

ghastly *a ghastly disaster.* appalling, awful, dreadful, fearful, frightful, grim, grisly, horrible, horrifying, shocking, terrible.

ghetto SEE **town**.

ghost apparition, hallucination, illusion, phantom, poltergeist, spectre, spirit, (informal) spook, vision.

ghostly *Tony heard a ghostly noise in the churchyard.* creepy, eerie, frightening, scary, spooky, uncanny, unearthly, weird.

giant 1 monster, ogre. 2 *a giant statue.* colossal, enormous, gigantic, huge, immense, massive, mighty, monstrous, vast.

gibberish (informal) balderdash, drivel, nonsense, rubbish, (informal) tripe, (informal) twaddle.

giddy *Heights make me feel giddy.* dizzy, faint, reeling, unsteady.

gift 1 *Mrs Brunswick sent some beans as a gift for the harvest festival.* contribution, donation, offering, present.
2 *Lucy has a gift for gymnastics.* ability, genius, knack, talent.

gifted *a gifted musician.* able, accomplished, brilliant, clever, masterly, skilful, skilled, talented, versatile.

gigantic *a gigantic monster.* colossal, enormous, giant, huge, immense, mammoth, massive, mighty, monstrous, vast. SEE ALSO **big**.

giggle to snigger, to titter. SEE ALSO **laugh**.

gill SEE **fish**.

gilt SEE **colour**.

gin SEE **drink**.

ginger SEE **spice**.

gingerbread SEE **cake**.

giraffe SEE **animal**.

girder *a framework of girders*. bar, beam, joist, rafter.

girdle belt. SEE ALSO **underclothes**.

girl lass. OLD-FASHIONED WORDS ARE damsel, maid, maiden, virgin. SEE ALSO **person**.

girth SEE **horse**.

give 1 *The headmaster gave Lucy her prize.* to award, to hand over, to offer, to pass, to present. 2 *How much did she give to you?* to allot, to allow, to contribute, to donate, to deal out, to distribute, to grant, to pay, to provide, to ration out, to supply. 3 *Give me the facts.* to display, to reveal, to show, to tell. 4 *Be careful: the roof might give.* to buckle, to collapse, to fall in, to fold up, to yield.

glacier SEE **geography**.

glad *We were glad to hear your good news.* delighted, joyful, pleased. SEE ALSO **happy**.

gladiator SEE **fighter**.

glamorous 1 *a glamorous TV star.* alluring, attractive, beautiful, good-looking, gorgeous, lovely. 2 *a glamorous place for a holiday.* colourful, exciting, fascinating.

glance SEE **look**.

gland SEE **body**.

glare 1 *glaring*: bright, dazzling, harsh. SEE ALSO **light**. 2 *an angry glare.* SEE **expression**.

glass 1 pane, plate-glass. 2 *a glass ball.* crystal. 3 *a glass of water.* tumbler, wine-glass. SEE ALSO **container**, **drink**.

glasses bifocals, goggles, spectacles, sun-glasses. SEE ALSO **optical**.

glasshouse greenhouse.

glass-paper sandpaper. SEE ALSO **tool**.

glazier SEE **job**.

gleam 1 *a gleam of light.* beam, flash, glimmer, glow, ray. SEE ALSO **light**. 2 *gleaming*: bright, brilliant, shining, shiny, sparkling.

gleeful *Lucy was gleeful when she beat her nearest rival.* delighted, ecstatic, exultant, joyful, merry, overjoyed, pleased. SEE ALSO **happy**.

glen dale, valley. SEE ALSO **geography**.

glide *to glide across the ice.* to coast, to drift, to fly, to skid, to slide, to slip. SEE ALSO **move**.

glider SEE **aircraft**.

glimmer *A distant light glimmered in the darkness.* to flicker, to gleam, to glow, to twinkle. SEE ALSO **light**.

glimpse *We glimpsed someone moving between the trees.* to discern, to distinguish, to make out, to notice, to observe, to see, to sight, to spot. SEE ALSO **look**.

glint *The light glinted on the bright metal.* to flash, to sparkle. SEE ALSO **light**.

glisten *The lights glistened on the wet road.* to gleam, to shine. SEE ALSO **light**.

glitter 1 *The diamond necklace glittered.* to flash, to sparkle, to twinkle. SEE ALSO **light**. 2 *glittering: The grand banquet was a glittering occasion.* brilliant, colourful, glamorous, resplendent, sparkling. SEE ALSO **splendid**.

gloat *Logan gloats when he wins.* to boast, to brag, to show off.

global *Do you think there's any danger of a global war?* general, universal, wholesale, widespread, worldwide.

globe 1 *the shape of a globe.* ball, sphere. 2 *the globe we live on.* earth, world.

glockenspiel SEE **percussion**.

gloom *We could hardly see in the gloom.* dimness, dusk, twilight.

gloomy 1 *a gloomy house, gloomy weather.* cheerless, cloudy, dark, depressing, dingy, dismal, dull, heavy, murky, overcast, shadowy, sombre. **2** *a gloomy person*. depressed, down-hearted, glum, grave, lugubrious, melancholy, miserable, morbid, unhappy. SEE ALSO **sad**.

glorious 1 *glorious scenery, glorious weather, etc*. beautiful, brilliant, excellent, gorgeous, grand, impressive, lovely, magnificent, majestic, marvellous, resplendent, spectacular, splendid, super, superb, wonderful. **2** *a glorious victory*. celebrated, distinguished, famous, heroic, noble.

gloss *We polished the table until we got a good gloss*. brightness, lustre, polish, sheen, shine.

glossy *glossy paint*. bright, gleaming, shiny, sleek.

glove gauntlet. SEE ALSO **clothes**.

glow 1 *A fire glowed in the hearth*. to gleam, to glimmer, to radiate, to shine. SEE ALSO **light**. **2** *We enjoyed the glow from the fire*. brightness, colour, redness, heat, warmth.

glower to frown, to scowl. SEE ALSO **expression**.

glow-worm SEE **insect**.

glucose SEE **food**.

glue 1 *We need some glue to stick the pictures onto card*. adhesive, gum, paste. **2** *Can we glue the broken bits together?* to paste, to stick. SEE ALSO **fasten**.

gluey adhesive, gummed, sticky, tacky.

glum *The defeated team looked glum*. depressed, down-hearted, gloomy, lugubrious, melancholy, miserable, unhappy. SEE ALSO **sad**.

gluttonous greedy.

gnarled *a gnarled old tree*. distorted, knobbly, lumpy, rough, twisted.

gnat SEE **insect**.

gnaw *The dog gnawed a bone*. to bite, to chew, to munch. SEE ALSO **eat**.

gnome dwarf, goblin. SEE ALSO **legend**.

go 1 *Let's go!* to advance, to begin, to be off, to commence, to depart, to disappear, to embark, to get away, to leave, to proceed, to retire, to retreat, to set out, to start, to withdraw. SEE ALSO **move**. **2** *I'd love to go to America*. to journey to, to travel to, to visit. SEE ALSO **travel**. **3** *This road goes to the rubbish dump*. to extend to, to lead to, to reach, to stretch to. **4** *The car won't go*. to act, to function, to operate, to perform, to run, to work. **5** *A holiday always goes quickly*. to elapse, to pass. **6** *Is he going mad?* to become, to grow, to turn. **7** *The bomb went off*. to blow up, to detonate, to explode. **8** *How long can you go on running?* to carry on, to continue, to keep on, to last, to persevere, to persist. **9** *She has gone through a serious illness*. to endure, to experience, to undergo. **10** *Who'll go with me to the shops?* to accompany, to escort. **!** *Go* can be used in many ways. The words given here are just some of the other words you can use.

goal 1 SEE **sport**. **2** *to have a goal in life*. aim, ambition, objective, purpose, target.

goalkeeper SEE **football**.

goat billy-goat, kid, nanny-goat. SEE ALSO **animal**.

gobble *She gobbled her food greedily*. to bolt, to devour, to gulp, to guzzle. SEE ALSO **eat**.

goblet beaker, cup. SEE ALSO **drink**.

goblin brownie. SEE ALSO **legend**.

god deity, divinity.

godparent SEE **family**.

goggles glasses, spectacles.

go-kart SEE **vehicle**.

gold SEE **colour, jewellery, metal**.

goldfinch SEE **bird**.

goldfish SEE **fish, pet**.

goldsmith SEE **art**.

golf, golf-course SEE **sport**.

gondola SEE **vessel**.

gong SEE **percussion**.

good 1 *a good deed, a good person*. admirable, appropriate, benevolent, caring, commendable, considerate, creditable, dutiful, esteemed, fair, great, helpful, holy, honest, honourable, humane, innocent, just,

kind, kind-hearted, law-abiding, marvellous, moral, noble, obedient, outstanding, praiseworthy, proper, reliable, religious, right, righteous, saintly, thoughtful, upright, virtuous, well-behaved, wonderful, worthy. 2 *a good musician, a good worker*. able, accomplished, capable, clever, conscientious, creditable, efficient, (informal) fabulous, gifted, proficient, skilful, skilled, talented, thorough. 3 *a good holiday, good weather*. agreeable, delightful, enjoyable, excellent, fine, heavenly, lovely, nice, pleasant, pleasing, satisfactory, (informal) terrific.
! *Good* can mean many different things. The words given here are only some of the other words you could use.

goodbye au revoir, farewell.

good-humoured amiable, cheerful, friendly, genial, kind, likeable, sympathetic, warm-hearted. SEE ALSO **happy**.

good-looking attractive, handsome, lovely, pretty. SEE ALSO **beautiful**.

good-natured friendly, helpful, kind-hearted, sympathetic. SEE ALSO **kind**.

goods *a train carrying goods*. cargo, freight, merchandise.

good-tempered gentle, mild, nice. SEE ALSO **kind**.

goose gander, gosling. SEE ALSO **bird, poultry**.

gooseberry SEE **fruit**.

gore *gored by a bull*. SEE **wound**.

gorge 1 *Logan was sick after gorging himself on ice-cream*. to feast, to gobble, to guzzle. SEE ALSO **eat**. 2 *A river runs along the gorge*. canyon, defile, pass, ravine, valley.

gorgeous *a gorgeous dress, a gorgeous view*. colourful, glorious, lovely, magnificent. SEE ALSO **beautiful, splendid**.

gorilla SEE **animal**.

gorse SEE **shrub**.

gory *a gory battle*. blood-stained, bloody, grisly, gruesome.

gosling goose. SEE ALSO **young**.

gospel SEE **church**.

gossip 1 *Don't gossip while I'm reading to you!* to chatter, to prattle. SEE ALSO **talk**. 2 *Don't listen to unkind gossip*. rumour, scandal.

gouge *to gouge out a hole*. to dig, to scoop.

goulash SEE **food**.

govern *to govern a country*. to administer, to be in charge of, to command, to control, to direct, to guide, to head, to look after, to manage, to master, to regulate, to rule, to run, to supervise.

government WORDS CONNECTED WITH GOVERNMENT ARE administration, ambassador, cabinet, chancellor, civil service, commonwealth, constituency, constitution, consul, councillor, democracy, dictatorship, diplomat, embassy, empire, exchequer, kingdom, mayor, member of parliament, minister, ministry, monarchy, parliament, politician, politics, premier, president, prime minister, republic, statesman. SEE ALSO **politics**.

governor *Who is the governor here?* boss, chief, controller, director, head, manager, ruler, supervisor.

gown dress, frock. SEE ALSO **clothes**.

grab *Grab the end of that rope!* to catch, to clutch, to grasp, to hold, to pluck, to seize, to snatch.

grace 1 *God's grace*. forgiveness, goodness, mercy. 2 *grace before dinner*. blessing, prayer.

graceful 1 *A gymnast's movements are very graceful*. agile, deft, flowing, nimble, supple. 2 *She has a graceful figure*. attractive, beautiful, dignified, elegant, slim, slender.

gracious *a gracious lady*. agreeable, courteous, friendly, good-natured, kind, polite.

grade *Our butcher sells top grade meat*. category, class, quality, standard.

gradient *a steep gradient*. ascent, hill, incline, slope.

gradual *They say there will be a gradual improvement in the weather.* gentle, moderate, slow, steady.

graffiti SEE **picture.**

grain 1 *Many farmers grow grain.* corn. SEE ALSO **cereal.** 2 *a grain of sand.* bit, granule, particle, speck.

gram SEE **measure.**

grammar SEE **language.**

gramophone SEE **audio equipment.**

granary SEE **building.**

grand *The opening of the new stadium was a grand occasion.* big, great, important, imposing, impressive, lordly, magnificent, majestic, noble, (informal) posh, regal, royal, stately. SEE ALSO **splendid.**

grandchild, grandparent SEE **family.**

grandstand SEE **sport.**

granite SEE **rock.**

grant 1 *a grant of money.* allowance, donation, expenses, loan, scholarship. 2 *The insurance company granted them the full value of the wrecked car.* to allow, to allot, to donate, to give, to pay, to provide. 3 *In the end he granted that I was right.* to acknowledge, to accept, to admit, to agree.

grape, grapefruit SEE **fruit.**

graph chart, diagram.

graphics SEE **art.**

grapple 1 *The police grappled with the intruder.* to struggle, to wrestle. 2 *Tony grappled with his maths.* to attend to, to cope with, to deal with, to handle, to manage.

grasp 1 *Grasp the bat firmly.* to catch, to clasp, to clutch, to grab, to grip, to hang on to, to hold, to seize. 2 *Lucy didn't grasp how to do her maths.* to comprehend, to follow, to learn, to master, to realize, to understand.

grasping *a grasping miser.* greedy, miserly, selfish, worldly.

grass 1 *Tony helped Mrs Brunswick cut the grass.* green, lawn. 2 PLANTS RELATED TO GRASS ARE bamboo, pampas grass, sugar-cane. 3 SEE **plant.**

grasshopper SEE **insect.**

grass-snake SEE **snake.**

grate 1 *There's a fire in the grate.* fireplace, hearth. SEE ALSO **fire.** 2 *to grate cheese.* to shred. SEE ALSO **cut.** 3 *a grating noise.* SEE **sound.**

grateful *He was grateful for the gift.* appreciative, thankful.

grave 1 *She looked grave when she heard the bad news.* dignified, earnest, gloomy, pensive, sedate, serious, sober, solemn, subdued, thoughtful. SEE ALSO **sad.** 2 *Stealing is a grave offence.* important, momentous, serious, weighty. 3 *There are some old graves in the churchyard.* burial-place, gravestone, memorial, tomb. SEE ALSO **funeral.**

gravel grit, pebbles, shingle, stones.

graveyard cemetery, churchyard. SEE ALSO **funeral.**

gravy SEE **food, sauce.**

graze *grazing cattle.* to feed.

grease oil. SEE ALSO **fat.**

greasy fatty, oily.

great 1 *a great mountain.* enormous, huge, immense, large, tremendous. SEE ALSO **big.** 2 *great pain.* acute, excessive, extreme, intense, severe. 3 *a great event.* grand, important, large-scale, momentous, serious, significant, spectacular. SEE ALSO **splendid.** 4 *a great piece of music.* brilliant, classic, excellent, (informal) fabulous, famous, (informal) fantastic, fine, outstanding, wonderful. 5 *a great composer.* celebrated, distinguished, eminent, gifted, notable, noted, prominent, renowned, talented, well-known. 6 *a great friend.* chief, close, main, valued.

greedy 1 *That greedy crowd ate everything before we arrived!* avid, eager, famished, gluttonous, hungry, ravenous, starving. 2 *Don't be greedy: share things with the others.* grasping, miserly, selfish, worldly.

green SEE **colour.**

greenery foliage, leaves.

greengage SEE **fruit.**

greengrocer SEE **shop**.

greenhouse glasshouse.

greens SEE **food, vegetable**.

greet *We greeted our visitors at the door.* to receive, to welcome.

grenade SEE **weapon**.

grey SEE **colour**.

greyhound SEE **dog**.

grief misery, regret, remorse, sadness, sorrow, unhappiness.

grievance *If you have a grievance, see the manager.* complaint.

grieve 1 *He grieved terribly when his dog died.* to fret, to lament, to mope, to mourn, to weep. 2 *It grieved us to see how cruelly the animal had been treated.* to depress, to distress, to hurt, to sadden.

grill SEE **cook, kitchen**.

grim *a grim expression, grim weather, etc.* bad-tempered, cruel, forbidding, frightful, ghastly, gloomy, grisly, gruesome, harsh, horrible, menacing, ominous, severe, stern, terrible, threatening, unfriendly.

grimace *to make a grimace.* face, look. SEE ALSO **expression**.

grimy *grimy windows.* dirty, dusty, filthy, grubby, sooty.

grin to beam, to smile. SEE ALSO **expression, laugh**.

grind 1 *to grind corn.* to crush, to pound, to powder. 2 *to grind a knife.* to polish, to sharpen. 3 *to grind something away.* to eat away, to erode, to wear away.

grip *He gripped her hand.* to clasp, to clutch, to grab, to grasp, to hold, to seize.

grisly *a grisly accident.* appalling, dreadful, frightful, ghastly, gory, grim, gruesome, hideous, horrible, terrible. SEE ALSO **bad**.

gristly *gristly meat.* leathery, rubbery, tough.

grit 1 *I had some grit in my eye.* dust, gravel, sand. 2 (informal) *You need grit to climb that mountain.* bravery, courage, determination, (informal)

guts, (informal) pluck, spirit. 3 *to grit your teeth.* to clench.

grizzle *The baby grizzled.* to cry, to weep, to whimper.

grizzly bear SEE **animal**.

groan to moan, to wail. SEE ALSO **sound**.

grocer SEE **shop**.

groom 1 *The groom looks after the horses.* SEE **job**. 2 bridegroom. SEE ALSO **wedding**.

groove cut, furrow, scratch, slot.

grope *We groped about in the dark.* to feel about, to fumble.

gross 1 SEE **number**. 2 *He was gross: he never stopped eating.* enormous, fat, flabby, huge, monstrous, overweight, ugly.

grotesque *grotesque carvings.* absurd, deformed, distorted, fantastic, mis-shapen, ugly, weird.

grotto cave, cavern.

ground 1 *We buried it in the ground.* earth, loam, soil. 2 *We showed our visitors round the grounds.* campus, estate, gardens, playing-fields, surroundings. 3 *Whose ground are we playing on next week?* arena, field, pitch, stadium. 4 *Have you any grounds for accusing her?* argument, cause, evidence, proof, reason.

groundsheet SEE **tent**.

groundsman SEE **job**.

group 1 *We formed a group for railway enthusiasts.* alliance, association, body, club, combination, company, league, organization, party, society, union. 2 OTHER GROUPS ARE accumulation, assortment, band, batch, brood, bunch, bundle, category, clan, class, clump, cluster, clutch, collection, colony, company, congregation, convoy, crew, crowd, fleet, flock, galaxy, gang, gathering, herd, hoard, horde, host, litter, mass, mob, multitude, pack, party, picket, posse, pride, rabble, school, set, shoal, swarm, team, throng, troop. 3 *Group the specimens according to size.* to arrange, to assemble, to bring together, to classify, to collect, to set out, to sort.

grouse 1 SEE **bird**. **2** *Logan grouses even when little things go wrong.* to complain, to grumble, to moan.

grove *a grove of small trees.* coppice, copse, forest, thicket, wood.

grovel *Stand up for yourself: don't grovel!* to cower, to cringe, to be too humble, to snivel.

grow 1 *The seeds have started to grow.* to emerge, to germinate, to spring up, to sprout. **2** *Many plants won't grow in cold weather.* to flourish, to live, to prosper, to survive, to thrive. **3** *Trees grow slowly.* to become longer, to become taller, to enlarge, to expand, to fill out, to increase in size, to lengthen, to swell. **4** *Her confidence grew when she started training seriously.* to build up, to develop, to improve, to increase. **5** *Mrs Brunswick grows lovely beans.* to cultivate, to produce, to raise.

growl SEE **sound**.

grown-up adult, mature, well-developed.

grub *There's a grub in this apple!* caterpillar, larva, maggot.

grubby *You need to wash that grubby shirt.* dirty, grimy, (informal) mucky, soiled.

grudging *Logan was grudging about Tony's success.* envious, jealous, resentful, ungracious, unkind.

gruelling *a gruelling climb.* arduous, exhausting, hard, laborious, stiff, strenuous, tiring, tough.

gruesome *a gruesome accident.* bloody, disgusting, grim, grisly, hideous, horrible, ghastly, gory, revolting, sickening.

gruff 1 *a gruff voice.* harsh, hoarse, husky, rough. **2** *a gruff answer.* bad-tempered, grumpy, surly, unfriendly.

grumble to complain, to grouse, to moan.

grumpy *He's grumpy because he's got toothache.* bad-tempered, cross, gruff, irascible, irritable, peevish, snappy, surly, testy.

grunt SEE **sound**.

guarantee 1 *He gave us his guarantee that it worked.* assurance, pledge, promise. **2** *He guarantees that it works.* to pledge, to promise, to swear, to vow. **3** *This ticket guarantees you a seat.* to ensure, to secure.

guard 1 *A mother always guards her young.* to care for, to defend, to keep safe, to look after, to preserve, to protect, to safeguard, to shelter, to shield, to tend. **2** *The sentry guarded the prisoners.* to prevent from escaping, to watch. **3** *A guard watched over the prisoner.* escort, look-out, patrol, sentinel, sentry, warder, watchman. **4** *a guard on a train.* SEE **railway**.

guardian 1 SEE **family**. **2** *The guardian of the treasure was a fierce dragon.* custodian, keeper, protector, warder.

guerrilla SEE **fighter**.

guess 1 *Make a guess.* assumption, estimate, guesswork, opinion, supposition, theory. **2** *I guess it will cost about £1.* to assume, to estimate, to suppose.

guest 1 *We had guests on Sunday.* caller, visitor. **2** *How many guests stay in this hotel?* boarder, customer, lodger, resident, tenant.

guest-house SEE **holiday**.

guide 1 *We need a guide to show us the way.* escort, pilot. **2** *Harris knows how to guide us out of the maze.* to conduct, to direct, to escort, to lead, to manoeuvre, to navigate, to pilot, to steer.

guillotine SEE **cut, execute**.

guilt *The evidence proved his guilt.* blame, fault, responsibility.

guilty 1 *The jury declared him guilty.* at fault, responsible. **2** *He looked guilty.* ashamed, regretful, remorseful, sheepish.

guinea-pig SEE **animal, pet**.

guitar SEE **music, strings**.

gulf bay. SEE ALSO **geography**.

gull SEE **bird**.

gullet throat. SEE ALSO **body**.

gulp *We gulped our food as fast as we could.* to bolt, to devour, to gobble. SEE ALSO **drink, eat**.

gum 1 *a pot of gum.* adhesive, glue, paste. 2 *We need healthy gums and healthy teeth.* SEE **body, head**.

gumboot SEE **shoe**.

gummed *gummed paper.* adhesive, gluey, sticky.

gumption (informal) *Haven't you any gumption?* judgement, sense, wisdom.

gum-tree SEE **tree**.

gun 1 VARIOUS GUNS ARE airgun, artillery, automatic, blunderbuss, cannon, machine-gun, mortar, musket, pistol, revolver, rifle, shotgun, small arms, sub-machine-gun. 2 PARTS OF A GUN ARE barrel, breech, butt, magazine, muzzle, sight, trigger.

gunboat SEE **vessel**.

gunman SEE **criminal, fighter**.

gunner SEE **soldier**.

gunpowder SEE **explosive**.

gurgle SEE **sound**.

guru leader, teacher.

gush 1 *Oil gushed out of the pipe.* to flow, to pour, to run, to spout, to spurt, to squirt, to stream. 2 *to come in a gush.* flood, jet, rush, stream.

gusty *gusty weather.* blustery, squally, windy. SEE ALSO **weather**.

guts 1 SEE **body**. 2 (informal) *They had guts to take the lifeboat out in that storm.* bravery, courage, determination, (informal) grit, nerve, (informal) pluck, spirit.

gutter *The water flows along the gutter.* channel, ditch, drain, sewer.

guy rope SEE **tent**.

guzzle *It's not polite to guzzle your food.* to bolt, to gobble, to gulp. SEE ALSO **drink, eat**.

gymkhana SEE **entertainment, horse**.

gymnasium SEE **building, sport**.

gymnastics SEE **sport**.

gypsy nomad, traveller.

H h

habit 1 *Don't let smoking become a habit!* addiction, compulsion. 2 *In our family, it's our habit to open presents on Christmas Eve.* custom, practice, routine.

habitual *We went home by our habitual route.* accustomed, conventional, common, customary, normal, ordinary, regular, routine, traditional, usual.

hack *We hacked down the undergrowth.* to chop, to hew, to slash. SEE ALSO **cut**.

hack-saw SEE **tool**.

haddock SEE **fish**.

haggis SEE **food**.

haggle *If you haggle with the man in the market, he'll knock a pound off the price.* to argue, to bargain, to discuss terms, to negotiate.

haiku SEE **poem**.

hail SEE **weather**.

hair 1 *Most animals have hairs on their skins.* bristles, fur. 2 *Does your mum do your hair?* curls, locks, tresses. 3 WAYS OF DOING HAIR ARE permanent wave, pigtail, plait, pony-tail. 4 WORDS TO DESCRIBE THE COLOUR OF HAIR ARE auburn, blond or blonde, brunette, dark, fair.

hairdresser barber. SEE ALSO **job, shop**.

hairless bald, bare.

hair-raising *The drive over the mountain road was hair-raising.* appalling, frightening, horrifying, scary, terrifying.

hairy *hairy skin.* bristly, downy, feathery, fleecy, fuzzy, shaggy, woolly.

half-hearted 1 *He made a half-hearted shot at goal.* feeble, ineffective, weak. 2 *She seems half-hearted about the party.* cool, indifferent, unenthusiastic.

half-wit blockhead, (informal) dope, dunce, fool, idiot, imbecile, moron. ! These words are usually insulting.

hall 1 *Wipe your feet before you come into the hall.* corridor, foyer, lobby, passage. **2** *We do the nativity play in the hall.* assembly hall, concert hall, theatre.

hallowed *hallowed ground.* blessed, consecrated, holy, sacred.

Hallowe'en SEE **time**.

hallucination apparition, delusion, dream, illusion, mirage, vision.

halt 1 *A red light halts the traffic.* to arrest, to block, to check, to stop. **2** *The traffic halts when the lights turn red.* to come to a standstill, to draw up, to pull up, to stop. **3** *All activity halted when the whistle went.* to break off, to cease, to end, to terminate.

halter SEE **horse**.

halve 1 *The two explorers halved their rations.* to divide, to share. **2** *Dad threatened to halve my pocket-money.* to cut, to decrease, to lessen, to reduce.

ham, hamburger SEE **meat**.

hamlet settlement, village. SEE ALSO **geography**.

hammer 1 *He hammered on the door.* to bash, to batter, to beat, to knock, to strike. SEE ALSO **hit**. **2** SEE **tool**.

hammock SEE **bed**.

hamper *Work on the Brunswicks' extension was hampered by bad weather.* to curb, to foil, to frustrate, to hinder, to hold back, to obstruct.

hamster SEE **animal, pet**.

hand 1 *She hit me with her hand.* fist. SEE ALSO **body**. **2** PARTS OF A HAND ARE finger, fingernail, index finger, knuckle, palm, thumb, wrist. **3** *to hand in, to hand over:* to deliver, to give, to present, to submit. **4** *to hand round:* to circulate, to deal out, to distribute, to give out, to pass round, to share.

handbag bag, purse. SEE ALSO **container**.

handicap 1 *It's a handicap to run a race in wellington boots!* disadvantage, drawback, hindrance, impediment, inconvenience, obstacle. **2** WAYS IN WHICH PEOPLE MAY BE PERMANENTLY HANDICAPPED ARE to be backward, blind, crippled, deaf, deformed, disabled, disfigured, dumb, lame, limbless, maimed, mute, paralysed, paraplegic, retarded, slow, spastic, to have a speech impediment. **!** These words may seem insulting if you use them carelessly.

handicraft art, craft, workmanship.

handkerchief tissue.

handle 1 *Hold it by the handle.* grip, hilt, knob. **2** *You must handle small animals carefully.* to feel, to finger, to stroke, to touch. **3** *Mrs Angel handled the rowdy class firmly.* to control, to cope with, to deal with, to look after, to manage, to manipulate.

handsome 1 *a handsome man.* attractive, good-looking. **2** *a handsome piece of furniture.* beautiful, elegant, tasteful. **3** *a handsome present.* big, generous, sizeable, valuable.

handy 1 *Dad always has his tools handy.* accessible, available, close at hand, convenient, easy to reach, ready. **2** *Mum is handy at mending the car.* capable, clever, competent, helpful, practical, proficient, skilful.

hang 1 *Hang the washing on the line.* to dangle, to suspend. **2** *The smoke hung in the still air.* to drift, to float, to hover. **3** *Don't hang about.* to dally, to dawdle, to linger, to loiter. **4** *Come on, there's no need to hang back.* to hesitate, to pause, to wait. **5** *Hang on to the rope!* to catch, to grasp, to hold, to keep, to retain, to seize. **6** *They used to hang murderers.* SEE **execute**.

hangar SEE **building**.

hang-glider SEE **aircraft**.

hangman executioner.

hanker *In winter we hanker after warm sunshine.* to desire, to fancy, to long for, to want, to wish for.

haphazard *The organization of the jumble sale was a bit haphazard.* accidental, chance, chaotic, confused, disorganized, random, unplanned, unsystematic.

happen *Did anything interesting happen to Emma?* to befall, to come about, to occur, to take place.

happening event, incident, occasion, occurrence, phenomenon.

happy 1 *a happy bride, a happy event, etc.* blissful, cheerful, contented, delighted, ecstatic, elated, exultant, festive, gay, glad, gleeful, good-humoured, joyful, joyous, laughing, light-hearted, lively, merry, overjoyed, pleased, proud, radiant, rapturous.**2** *a happy accident.* favourable, fortunate, lucky.

harass *The dogs harassed the sheep.* to annoy, to bother, to disturb, to molest, to pester, to plague, to trouble, to worry.

harbour 1 *The ships tied up in the harbour.* anchorage, dock, haven, jetty, landing-stage, marina, moorings, pier, port, quay, wharf. **2** *I'd be in trouble if I harboured a criminal.* to give asylum to, to give refuge to, to protect, to shelter.

hard 1 *hard concrete.* firm, inflexible, rigid, solid, unyielding.**2** *a hard climb.* arduous, difficult, exhausting, gruelling, harsh, heavy, laborious, stiff, strenuous, tough.**3** *a hard problem.* baffling, complicated, confusing, difficult, involved, puzzling.**4** *a hard heart.* cruel, harsh, heartless, merciless, pitiless, ruthless, severe, stern, strict, unfeeling.**5** *a hard knock.* forceful, heavy, powerful, strong, violent. **6** *hard up*: SEE **poor**.

hardly barely, only just, scarcely, with difficulty.

hardship *They suffered great hardship when their father died.* adversity, difficulty, misery, suffering, trouble, unhappiness.

hardware equipment, instruments, machinery, tools.

hard-wearing *You need hard-wearing shoes for walking in the hills.* durable, lasting, strong, sturdy, tough, well-made.

hare SEE **animal**.

harm to damage, to hurt, to injure, to misuse, to spoil, to wound.

harmful *Eating stale food can be harmful.* bad, damaging, dangerous, destructive, injurious, unhealthy.

harmless *Don't you know that grass-snakes are harmless?* innocent, innocuous, inoffensive, mild, safe.

harmonica, harmonium SEE **music**.

harmony 1 *Wouldn't it be nice if we could all live in harmony?* agreement, concord, friendliness, peace.**2** SEE **music**.

harness SEE **horse**.

harp SEE **music, talk**.

harpoon SEE **weapon**.

harpsichord SEE **keyboard**.

harrow SEE **farm**.

harsh 1 *a harsh noise.* grating, jarring, raucous, shrill.**2** *harsh light, harsh colours.* bright, brilliant, dazzling, gaudy, glaring, lurid.**3** *a harsh smell.* acrid, bitter, unpleasant.**4** *harsh conditions.* arduous, austere, difficult, hard, severe, tough.**5** *a harsh texture.* bristly, coarse, hairy, rough, scratchy.**6** *a harsh judge.* cruel, stern, strict, unkind.

harvest 1 *The farmers hope for a good harvest.* crop, produce, yield.**2** *They harvest the corn in the summer.* to gather, to reap.

hash goulash, stew. SEE ALSO **food**.

hasty 1 *a hasty decision.* abrupt, hurried, impetuous, impulsive, quick, rash, reckless, speedy, sudden.**2** *hasty work.* brief, careless, cursory, hurried, slapdash.

hat KINDS OF HEAD-DRESS ARE beret, bonnet, bowler, cap, coronet, crash-helmet, crown, diadem, helmet, hood, sou'wester, turban, wig. SEE ALSO **clothes**.

hatch 1 *to hatch eggs.* to brood, to incubate.**2** *to hatch a plot.* to concoct, to devise, to plan.

hatchet SEE **tool**.

hate *Logan hates cabbage.* to despise, to detest, to dislike, to loathe, to scorn.

hateful SEE **unpleasant**.

hatred *Logan made his hatred of vegetarian food quite obvious.* aversion, contempt, dislike, loathing, revulsion.

haughty *a haughty manner.* arrogant, boastful, bumptious, (informal) cocky, conceited, disdainful, proud, self-important, (informal) stuck-up.

haul *The explorers had dogs to haul the sledge.* to drag, to draw, to lug, to pull, to tow, to tug.

haunt *Tony and his friends haunt the area near the sweet shop most evenings.* to hang around, to loiter about, to visit.

have 1 *Lucy has her own radio.* to own, to possess. 2 *Our house has six rooms.* to consist of, to contain, to hold, to include, to incorporate, to involve. 3 *What did you have for Christmas?* to acquire, to be given, to gain, to get, to obtain, to receive. 4 *Who had the last biscuit?* to consume, to eat, to remove, to take. 5 *Did you have fun? Did you have any pain?* to endure, to enjoy, to experience, to feel, to go through, to know, to live through, to suffer, to undergo. ! *Have* has many meanings. These are only some of the other words you can use.

haven 1 *The ship reached the haven before the storm broke.* anchorage, harbour, port. 2 *The climbers found haven in a mountain hut.* asylum, refuge, retreat, safety, shelter.

haversack knapsack, rucksack. SEE ALSO **container**.

havoc *The storm created havoc along the coast.* damage, destruction, devastation.

hawk SEE **bird**.

hawser cable, cord, line, rope.

hawthorn SEE **tree**.

hay fodder.

hay fever SEE **illness**.

haystack rick. SEE ALSO **farm**.

hazard *Fog is one of the worst hazards for traffic.* danger, peril, risk, threat, trouble.

hazardous *Crossing the sea in a rowing boat is hazardous.* chancy, dangerous, perilous, risky, unsafe.

haze fog, mist. SEE ALSO **weather**.

hazel SEE **nut, tree**.

hazy *The view was hazy.* blurred, dim, faint, misty, unclear.

H-bomb SEE **weapon**.

head 1 PARTS OF YOUR HEAD ARE brain, cheek, chin, ear, eye, forehead, gums, hair, jaw, lip, mouth, nose, nostril, scalp, skull, teeth, tongue. SEE ALSO **body**. 2 *the head of a mountain.* apex, crown, top. 3 *the head of an organization.* boss, director, employer, leader, manager, ruler. SEE ALSO **chief**. 4 *the head of a school.* headmaster, headmistress, headteacher, principal. SEE ALSO **school**. 5 *Captain Scott headed an expedition to the South Pole.* to be in charge of, to command, to govern, to lead, to manage, to rule, to supervise. 6 *Tony headed the ball into the net.* SEE **hit**. 7 *the head waiter.* chief, leading, most important, senior.

headache SEE **illness**.

head-dress SEE **hat**.

heading *Mrs Angel told us to write the heading in big letters.* caption, headline, title.

headlight SEE **light, vehicle**.

headline *a newspaper headline.* caption, heading, title.

headlong *a headlong dash.* breakneck, hurried, impetuous, impulsive, reckless.

headphones SEE **audio equipment**.

headquarters 1 *the headquarters of an expedition.* base, depot. 2 *the headquarters of a business.* head office, main office.

heal 1 *They claim that this ointment heals cuts.* to cure, to make better, to remedy. 2 *Wounds heal in time.* to get better, to mend, to recover.

health 1 *We'd all like to have good health.* condition, fitness, strength, vigour. 2 SEE **medicine**.

healthy 1 *a healthy animal.* hearty, lively, perky, robust, sound, strong, vigorous, well. 2 *healthy surroundings.* hygienic, sanitary, wholesome.

heap 1 *a heap of rubbish.* mass, mound, pile, stack. 2 *We heaped up the rubbish.*

to accumulate, to collect, to mass, to pile up, to stack up.

hear 1 *Have you heard this new single?* to listen to. **2** *Have you heard the news about Logan?* to discover, to find out, to gather, to learn.

hearse SEE **funeral, vehicle**.

heart 1 SEE **body**. **2** *the heart of the forest, the heart of the problem.* centre, core, focus, hub, middle.

heart-broken SEE **sad**.

hearth fireplace, grate.

heartless *heartless behaviour.* SEE **cruel**.

hearty 1 *a hearty welcome.* enthusiastic, sincere, warm. **2** *a hearty appetite.* big, healthy, robust.

heat 1 *the heat of a fire.* glow, hotness, warmth. **2** WORDS FOR HEATING THINGS OR FOR BEING HOT ARE to bake, to blister, to boil, to burn, to cook, to fry, to grill, to melt, to roast, to scald, to scorch, to simmer, to sizzle, to smoulder, to steam, to stew, to swelter, to toast. **3** *the heats for a race.* SEE **race**.

heath moor, moorland. SEE ALSO **geography**.

heathen atheist, barbarian, pagan, savage. ! These words are often insulting.

heather SEE **shrub**.

heave *They heaved the sacks onto the lorry.* to drag, to draw, to haul, to hoist, to lift, to lug, to pull, to raise, to throw, to tow, to tug.

heaven 1 paradise. **2** (informal) *Mum says it's heaven to have a hot bath.* bliss, ecstasy, happiness, rapture.

heavenly (informal) *What's that heavenly smell?* blissful, celestial, divine. SEE ALSO **pleasant**.

heavy 1 *a heavy load.* burdensome, massive, ponderous, weighty. **2** *heavy work.* arduous, difficult, hard, exhausting, laborious, strenuous, tough. **3** *heavy rain.* concentrated, considerable, severe, torrential. **4** *a heavy heart.* depressed, gloomy, miserable. SEE ALSO **sad**.

hectare SEE **measure**.

hectic *We had a hectic time doing the Christmas shopping.* active, bustling, busy, excited, frantic, lively, mad, wild.

hedge 1 fence, hedgerow. **2** *to hedge in:* to encircle, to enclose, to fence in, to hem in, to pen, to surround.

hedgehog SEE **animal**.

heed *If you're wise, you'll heed his warning.* to attend to, to follow, to keep to, to listen to, to mark, to mind, to note, to notice, to obey, to observe, to take notice of.

heel 1 SEE **body, foot**. **2** *The dinghy heeled over in the wind.* to lean, to list, to slope, to tilt.

hefty *a hefty man.* beefy, big, brawny, burly, mighty, muscular, strong, tough.

heifer SEE **cattle, young**.

height *the height of a mountain.* altitude, tallness.

heir inheritor, successor.

helicopter SEE **aircraft**.

hell underworld.

hellish diabolical, dreadful, ghastly. SEE ALSO **unpleasant**. ! *Hellish* is often used as slang.

helm SEE **vessel**.

helmet SEE **hat**.

help 1 *You can help each other if you want.* to aid, to assist, to back, to boost, to collaborate with, to co-operate with, to side with, to support. **2** *Give Logan a bit of help.* aid, assistance, backing, boost, co-operation, relief, support.

helpful 1 *a helpful person.* accommodating, benevolent, considerate, constructive, co-operative, neighbourly, obliging, thoughtful, willing. SEE ALSO **kind**. **2** *a helpful tool.* convenient, handy, useful. **3** *a helpful suggestion.* advantageous, informative, instructive, profitable, valuable.

helping *a helping of pudding.* portion, share.

helpless 1 *a helpless invalid.* feeble, impotent, incapable, weak, (informal) weedy. **2** *a helpless ship.*

aground, disabled, drifting, stranded.

hem 1 *the hem of a skirt*. border, edge. **2** *to hem in*: to encircle, to enclose, to hedge in, to surround.

hemisphere SEE **geography, shape**.

hen 1 chicken, fowl. SEE ALSO **poultry**. **2** SEE **bird, female**.

herald announcer, messenger, town-crier.

herb 1 KINDS OF HERB ARE mint, parsley, sage. **2** SEE **plant**.

herd 1 *a herd of cattle*. SEE **group**. **2** *to herd together*. to assemble, to congregate, to crowd, to flock, to gather, to swarm, to throng.

hereditary *a hereditary disease*. handed down, inherited, passed on.

hero, heroine champion, idol, star, superstar, victor, winner.

heroic *a heroic rescue*. bold, brave, chivalrous, courageous, daring, fearless, gallant, intrepid, noble, valiant.

heroin SEE **drug**.

heron SEE **bird**.

herring SEE **fish**.

hesitate *I hesitated before jumping into the cold water*. to delay, to falter, to hang back, to pause, to think twice, to wait, to waver.

hew *to hew down a tree*. to chop, to saw. SEE ALSO **cut**.

hexagon SEE **shape**.

hibernating *a hibernating animal*. asleep, dormant, inactive.

hide 1 *Hide the sweets when Logan's around!* to bury, to conceal, to cover, to put away. **2** *The mist hid the view*. to blot out, to camouflage, to cloak, to mask, to obscure, to screen, to shroud. **3** *The runaway hid in an old warehouse*. to lie low, to lurk. **4** *an animal's hide*. fur, leather, skin.

hide-and-seek SEE **game**.

hideous *a hideous wound*. frightful, ghastly, grisly, gruesome, repulsive, ugly, unsightly. SEE ALSO **unpleasant**.

hide-out den, hiding-place, lair.

hiding *to give someone a hiding*. SEE **punishment**.

hieroglyphics SEE **writing**.

hi-fi SEE **audio equipment**.

high 1 *a high building*. lofty, tall, towering. **2** *a high look-out*. elevated, raised. **3** *high prices*. excessive, exorbitant, unreasonable. **4** *a high rank in the army*. eminent, important, leading, powerful, prominent, top. **5** *a high wind*. great, intense, stormy, strong. **6** *a high reputation*. favourable, good, respected. **7** *a high sound*. piercing, sharp, shrill. **8** *a high school*. SEE **school**.

highbrow 1 *highbrow music*. classical. **2** *a highbrow book*. cultural, educational, improving, intellectual.

high-fidelity SEE **audio equipment**.

highlight *The highlight of our day out was a flight in a helicopter*. best moment, climax, peak.

highly-strung *Our dog yaps because he's highly-strung*. edgy, jittery, nervous, tense, touchy, (informal) uptight.

Highness SEE **royal**.

high tea SEE **meal**.

highway SEE **road**.

highwayman bandit, brigand, robber, thief. SEE ALSO **criminal**.

hijacking SEE **crime**.

hike *We hiked across the moors*. to ramble, to tramp, to trek. SEE ALSO **walk**.

hilarious *a hilarious joke*. amusing, comic, funny, humorous, hysterical, laughable, ridiculous, silly, uproarious, witty.

hill 1 *I climbed the hill*. mountain, peak, rise, summit. **2** *an area of hills*: downs, fells, highlands. **3** SEE **geography**.

hinder *Deep snowdrifts hindered our progress*. to bar, to check, to curb, to delay, to deter, to hamper, to impede, to obstruct, to prevent, to stop.

hindrance *Our heavy rucksacks were a hindrance*. difficulty, disadvantage, handicap, impediment, inconvenience, obstacle.

Hindu SEE **religion**.

hint 1 *I don't know the answer: give me a hint*. clue, implication, indication, inkling, suggestion, tip. **2** *Dad hinted that we might have a trip to London*. to imply, to indicate, to suggest.

hip 1 *Mum's got a pain in her hip*. SEE **body, joint**. **2** *rose hips*. SEE **fruit**.

hippopotamus SEE **animal**.

hire 1 *We hired a bus*. to charter, to rent. **2** *to hire out*: to let.

hiss SEE **sound**.

historic *a historic battle*. celebrated, eminent, famous, important, notable, renowned, well-known.

history SEE **subject**.

hit 1 *Logan's jokes were a hit at the concert*. success, triumph. **2** *I got a hit on the head*. blow, bump, knock. **3** VARIOUS WAYS TO HIT THINGS ARE to bang, (informal) to bash, to batter, to beat, to bump, to butt, to cane, to clout, to collide with, to cuff, to dash, to drive, to flick, to flip, to flog, to hammer, to head, to jab, to jar, to jog, to kick, to knock, to lash, to pat, to poke, to pound, to prod, to punch, to putt, to ram, to rap, to scourge, to slam, to slap, to slog, to smack, to smash, to spank, to strike, to stub, to swat, to swipe, to tap, to thrash, to thump, to wallop, to whack, to whip.

hitch-hike SEE **travel**.

hive apiary.

hoard *Squirrels hoard nuts*. to accumulate, to collect, to gather, to keep, to mass, to pile up, to save, to store, to treasure.

hoarse *a hoarse voice*. croaking, grating, gruff, harsh, husky, rasping, raucous, rough.

hoax 1 *The firemen were angry when they heard that the emergency call was a hoax*. deception, fake, fraud, practical joke, trick. **2** *They realized that someone had hoaxed them*. to bluff, to deceive, to delude, to fool, to hoodwink, to mislead, to take in, to trick.

hobble to limp. SEE ALSO **walk**.

hobby *Mr Brunswick's hobby is water-skiing*. interest, pastime, pursuit, relaxation.

hockey SEE **sport**.

hoe SEE **garden**.

hog SEE **male, pig**.

Hogmanay SEE **time**.

hoist *The crane hoisted the boxes onto the deck*. to heave, to lift, to pull up, to raise.

hold 1 *Hold this rope!* to catch, to clutch, to grasp, to grip, to hang on to, to keep, to retain, to seize. **2** *He held the baby*. to bear, to carry, to clasp, to embrace, to hug, to support, to take. **3** *Uncle George held an important position in the bank*. to have, to occupy, to possess. **4** *The suitcase held all our things*. to contain, to enclose, to include. **5** *The lock gates hold back the water*. to block, to check, to control, to curb, to halt, to keep back, to retain, to stop. **6** *The police are holding a suspect*. to arrest, to confine, to detain, to keep. **7** *Hold that pose while I put a film in the camera!* to keep up, to maintain, to preserve, to retain. **8** *The church holds services every week*. to conduct, to have. **9** *I wonder how long this heat-wave will hold?* to carry on, to continue, to endure, to keep on, to last, to persist, to stay. **10** *to hold out*: *Hold out your hand*. to extend, to reach out, to stick out, to stretch out. **11** *to hold up*: *The traffic jam held up our journey*. to delay, to hinder, to obstruct, to slow down.

hold-all SEE **container**.

hold-up 1 *There was a hold-up at the bank*. SEE **crime**. **2** *My train was late because of a hold-up on the line*. delay, pause, postponement, wait.

hole 1 *a hole in the ground*. abyss, burrow, cave, chasm, crater, excavation, pit, pothole, tunnel. **2** *a hole in a fence, a hole in a tyre, etc*. breach, break, chink, crack, cut, gap, gash, leak, opening, puncture, slit, split, tear, vent.

holiday 1 *a holiday from school*. day off, leave, rest, time off. **2** VARIOUS kinds of holiday are camping, cruise, honeymoon, safari, seaside holiday, tour, trip, vacation, youth-hostelling. 3 KINDS OF HOLIDAY ACCOMMODATION ARE apartment, boarding-house, campsite, flat, guest-house, hostel, hotel, inn, motel, self-catering, villa, youth hostel.

hollow 1 *a hollow space.* empty, unfilled. 2 *a hollow in the ground.* dent, depression, dip, hole, valley. 3 *Lucy hollowed out a pumpkin to make a lantern.* to dig, to gouge, to scoop.

holly SEE **tree**.

hollyhock SEE **flower**.

holster SEE **container**.

holy *The temple is a holy place.* blessed, consecrated, divine, hallowed, heavenly, religious, sacred, saintly.

homage *to pay homage to*: to honour, to praise, to respect, to worship.

home abode, dwelling, residence. SEE ALSO **house**.

homeless *homeless people*: beggars, the destitute, tramps, vagrants. SEE ALSO **poor**.

homework SEE **school**.

homosexual gay, (impolite) queer.

honest 1 *an honest worker.* conscientious, honourable, law-abiding, moral, trustworthy, upright.
2 *an honest answer.* blunt, candid, direct, frank, genuine, open, sincere, straightforward, truthful. 3 *an honest judgement.* fair, impartial, just, unbiased, unprejudiced.

honey SEE **food**.

honeymoon SEE **holiday, wedding**.

honeysuckle SEE **climber**.

honour 1 *Tony had the honour of presenting a bouquet to our visitor.* distinction, fame, importance, renown, respect. 2 *If Logan had any honour, he would own up.* decency, honesty, integrity, loyalty, nobility, principle, sincerity, virtue. 3 *On Remembrance Day we honour those who died in war.* to admire, to pay homage

to, to pay tribute to, to praise, to respect, to show respect to.

honourable *It was the honourable thing to hand over the money you found.* admirable, decent, good, honest, law-abiding, loyal, noble, respectable, upright, virtuous, worthy.

hood SEE **hat**.

hoodwink *Logan was silly to try to hoodwink the head.* to bluff, to cheat, to deceive, to dupe, to fool, to hoax, (informal) to kid, to mislead, to swindle, to take in, to trick.

hoof foot.

hook 1 *to hook a fish.* to capture, to catch, to take. 2 *to hook a wagon on to a train.* SEE **fasten**.

hooligan delinquent, mugger, ruffian, thug, trouble-maker, vandal. SEE ALSO **criminal**.

hoop band, circle, ring.

hoot SEE **sound**.

Hoover SEE **house**.

hop to bound, to jump, to leap, to skip, to spring.

hope 1 *Is there any hope of better weather?* likelihood, prospect. 2 *We hope that we'll win.* to have confidence, to have faith, to trust.

hopeful 1 *We're hopeful that we can win.* confident, optimistic. 2 *There are hopeful signs that we can do well.* encouraging, favourable, promising, reassuring.

hopefully 1 *The cat looked hopefully at the scraps left from dinner.* confidently, expectantly, optimistically.
2 (informal) *Hopefully, I'll be fit to play tomorrow.* all being well, probably. ! Many people think that this is a wrong use of *hopefully*.

hopeless 1 *a hopeless situation.* desperate, impossible, incurable.
2 *a hopeless footballer.* feeble, incompetent, inefficient, poor, useless, weak, worthless. SEE ALSO **bad**.

hopscotch SEE **game**.

horde *a horde of children from the other school.* band, crowd, gang, mob, swarm, tribe. SEE ALSO **group**.

horizontal *Is the snooker table*

horizontal? flat, level. ❘ *Horizontal* is the opposite of *vertical*.

horn SEE **brass, music**.

hornet SEE **insect**.

hornpipe SEE **dance**.

horrible *horrible weather, horrible food, etc.* awful, beastly, dreadful, ghastly, horrid, nasty, terrible. SEE ALSO **unpleasant**.

horrific *a horrific accident*. appalling, dreadful, frightful, gruesome, hair-raising, horrifying, shocking. ❘ You often use *horrible* to describe things that aren't important, but you use *horrific* to describe things that really horrify you.

horrify *The accident horrified us.* to appal, to frighten, to scare, to shock, to terrify.

horror dismay, dread, fear, terror.

horse 1 bronco, cart-horse, colt, foal, mare, mount, mule, nag, piebald, race-horse, stallion, steed. **2** ITEMS OF EQUIPMENT FOR HORSES ARE bridle, collar, girth, halter, harness, horseshoe, rein, saddle, spur, stirrups. **3** WAYS TO RIDE A HORSE ARE to amble, to canter, to gallop, to trot. **4** HORSE-RIDING EVENTS ARE gymkhana, hunting, pony-trekking, racing, riding, show-jumping, steeplechase.

horse-box SEE **vehicle**.

horse-chestnut SEE **tree**.

hose *a water hose*. pipe, tube.

hospitable *The people we stayed with were very hospitable.* friendly, kind, sociable, welcoming.

hospital SEE **medicine**.

hostage captive, prisoner.

hostel SEE **holiday**.

hostile 1 *a hostile crowd*. aggressive, attacking, belligerent, pugnacious, unfriendly, warlike. **2** *hostile weather conditions*. adverse, contrary, opposing, unfavourable.

hot 1 *hot weather, a hot iron, etc.* baking, blistering, boiling, burning, fiery, red-hot, roasting, scalding, scorching, sizzling, sweltering, warm. **2** *a hot temper*. angry, fierce, passionate, violent. **3** *a hot taste*. gingery, peppery, spicy. SEE ALSO **taste**.

hotel SEE **building, holiday**.

hot-pot SEE **food**.

hound 1 SEE **dog**. **2** *The wanted man was hounded by the police.* to chase, to hunt, to pursue, to track down.

hour SEE **time**.

house 1 *Come to my house.* abode, dwelling, home, lodgings, place, quarters, residence. **2** KINDS OF HOUSE ARE apartments, bungalow, chalet, cottage, council-house, croft, detached house, farmhouse, flats, hovel, lodge, manor, manse, mansion, prefab, rectory, semi-detached house, shack, shanty, terrace house, thatched house, vicarage, villa. SEE ALSO **building**. **3** ROOMS IN A HOUSE ARE attic, bathroom, bedroom, cloakroom, conservatory, corridor, dining-room, drawing room, hall, kitchen, landing, larder, lavatory, living-room, loft, lounge, outhouse, pantry, parlour, passage, porch, scullery, sitting-room, study, toilet, WC. **4** ITEMS OF EQUIPMENT IN A HOUSE ARE air-conditioning, barometer, boiler, brush, central heating, clock, double-glazing, duster, fire, fire-extinguisher, freezer, Hoover, immersion heater, incinerator, iron, ironing-board, lighter, mangle, meter, mop, phone, plumbing, radiator, sanitation, scissors, spin-drier, step-ladder, thermometer, thermostat, tray, tumble-drier, vacuum-cleaner, washing-machine, wiring. FOR OTHER HOUSEHOLD EQUIPMENT SEE ALSO **bathroom, furniture, kitchen, tool**. **5** *to house someone*. to accommodate, to board, to lodge, to put up, to shelter.

house-boat SEE **vessel**.

house-trained *a house-trained dog*. clean in the house, domesticated.

hovel cottage, hut, shack, shanty. SEE ALSO **house**.

hover 1 *The hawk hovered over its prey.* to float, to fly, to hang in the air. **2** *After* counterfeit, dummy, duplicate, orgery, likeness, replica, ...duction.

...ure *immature behaviour.* ...sh, childish, inexperienced, ...ile, juvenile, young, youthful.

...iate 1 *I took immediate action to ...e crisis.* instant, instantaneous, ...pt, quick, speedy, swift. **2** *Mrs ...wick talks to her immediate ...our over the fence.* adjacent, ...st, nearest, next.

...iately directly, forthwith, ...ntly, promptly.

...nse colossal, enormous, ...tic, great, huge, large, massive, SEE ALSO **big**.

...rse 1 *to immerse something in ...* to dip, to drench, to drown, to ..., to plunge, to submerge. *...mersed: immersed in your work.* ...rbed, interested, preoccupied.

...rsion heater SEE **fire**.

...grate to settle.

...bile *The car was immobile in the ...* fast, firm, fixed, immobilized, ...ovable, motionless, paralysed, ...re, static, stationary.

...obilize *to immobilize a vehicle.* to ...ple, to damage, to put out of ...on, to stop.

...ral *Everyone disapproved of his ...oral behaviour.* base, corrupt, ...raved, evil, sinful, villainous, ...ked. SEE ALSO **bad**.

...rtal *Some people believe that your ...is immortal.* endless, eternal, ...lasting, undying.

...ovable SEE **immobile**.

...unization SEE **medicine**.

...a mischievous imp. demon, devil, ...cal, rogue, scamp, spirit.

...ct 1 *Was the car damaged in the ...act?* bump, collision, crash, ...ash. **2** *The pictures of the famine made ...rong impact on us.* effect, ...pression, influence, shock.

...le SEE **wound**.

...artial *an impartial referee.* ...ached, disinterested, fair, just, neutral, unbiased, uninvolved, unprejudiced.

impatient 1 *We were impatient to star...* anxious, eager. **2** *The horses were impatient.* edgy, fidgety, restless.

impede *A fallen tree impeded our progress.* to block, to check, to delay to deter, to hinder, to obstruct, to slow down.

impediment SEE **handicap**.

impenetrable *impenetrable forest.* dense, thick.

imperceptible *an imperceptible movement.* insignificant, invisible, microscopic, minute, negligible, slight, small, tiny, undetectable.

imperfect *If the goods are imperfect, ta...* them back to the shop. defective, faulty incomplete, unfinished.

imperfection *Lucy corrected the imperfections in her gymnastic routine.* blemish, defect, flaw, shortcoming, weakness.

impersonate *We laughed when Logan impersonated the vicar.* to copy, to imitate, to mimic, to pose as, to pretend to be.

impertinent *Mrs Angel said it was impertinent to mimic the vicar.* cheeky, discourteous, disrespectful, impolite impudent, insolent, insulting, rude, saucy.

impetigo SEE **illness**.

impetuous *Logan's impetuous dash across the road almost caused an accident.* hasty, headlong, impulsive, quick, rash, reckless, speedy.

implement *gardening implements.* device, gadget, instrument, tool, utensil.

implore *Granny implored us to stay for tea.* to ask, to beg, to entreat, to plead, to request.

imply *Dad implied that we might have a treat at the weekend.* to hint, to indicate, to suggest.

impolite *It's impolite to talk with your mouth full.* discourteous, disrespectful, insulting, loutish, rude. SEE ALSO **impertinent**.

important 1 *important facts, an*

the party, people hovered about for a while. to hang about, to linger, to loiter, to wait about.

hovercraft SEE **vessel**.

howl SEE **sound**.

howler (informal) *to make a howler.* blunder, (informal) clanger, error, mistake, (informal) slip-up.

hubbub *The head could hardly be heard above the hubbub.* clamour, commotion, din, hullabaloo, noise, pandemonium, racket, row, rumpus, uproar.

huddle 1 *The sheep huddled in the corner of the field.* to cluster, to crowd, to flock, to gather, to herd, to press, to squeeze, to swarm, to throng. **2** *The children huddled together to keep warm.* to cuddle, to curl up, to nestle, to snuggle.

hue colour, shade, tinge, tint, tone.

hug *Dad hugged the baby.* to clasp, to cling to, to crush, to cuddle, to embrace, to hold, to snuggle, to squeeze.

huge *Elephants are huge animals.* colossal, enormous, gigantic, great, immense, large, mammoth, vast. SEE ALSO **big**.

hulking *The hulking wrestler towered above us.* bulky, clumsy, heavy, massive. SEE ALSO **big**.

hull SEE **vessel**.

hum SEE **sing**, **sound**.

human beings folk, humanity, mankind, mortals. SEE ALSO **person**.

humane *Is it humane to kill animals for food?* benevolent, kind, kind-hearted, merciful, sympathetic, unselfish, warm-hearted.

humble 1 *humble behaviour.* lowly, meek, modest, unassuming. **2** *to humble someone.* to bring down, to disgrace, to humiliate, to shame.

humbug SEE **sweet**.

humid *humid weather.* clammy, damp, dank, moist, muggy, steamy, sultry.

humiliate *They humiliated us by winning 14-0.* to disgrace, to humble, to make ashamed.

humorous *a humorous story.* amusing, comic, facetious, funny, hilarious, laughable, ridiculous, silly, witty.

humour *You seem to be in a good humour!* mood, state of mind, temper.

hump bulge, bump, lump, swelling.

hunch *I have a hunch that Lucy broke that window.* feeling, guess, intuition.

hundredweight SEE **measure**.

hunger 1 *Did that meal satisfy your hunger?* appetite, desire, greed, longing. **2** *Hunger kills millions of people.* famine, malnutrition, starvation.

hungry *Logan's always hungry!* famished, greedy, (informal) peckish, ravenous, starved, starving, underfed.

hunk *a hunk of cheese.* block, chunk, lump, mass, piece.

hunt 1 *to hunt animals.* to chase, to hound, to poach, to pursue, to stalk, to track down. **2** *We hunted for mum's keys.* to look for, to search for, to seek. **3** *Does the fox enjoy the hunt as much as the hounds do?* chase, pursuit, quest, search.

hunter predator.

hurdle barrier, fence, obstacle.

hurl *He hurled the sword into the lake.* to cast, to chuck, to fling, to pitch, to sling, to throw, to toss.

hurricane cyclone, storm, tempest, tornado, typhoon. SEE ALSO **weather**.

hurried *a hurried decision, hurried work, etc.* careless, cursory, hasty, impetuous, quick, rushed, speedy.

hurry 1 *I hurried home.* to dash, to hasten, to hurtle, to hustle, to rush, to speed, (informal) to zoom. SEE ALSO **move**. **2** *If you want to finish you must hurry.* to accelerate, (informal) to buck up, to quicken, to work faster.

hurt 1 *That wasp sting hurts!* to ache, to be painful, to be sore, to smart, to sting, to throb. **2** *Did the attackers hurt her?* to afflict, to cripple, to damage, to disable, to distress, to harm, to

injure, to maim, to misuse, to pain, to torment, to torture, to wound.

hurtle to dash, to race, to rush, to speed, (informal) to zoom. SEE ALSO **move.**

husband SEE **family, marriage.**

hush 1 be quiet! be silent! shut up! **2** *We tried to hush it up, but everyone found out.* to conceal, to hide, to keep it quiet, to keep it secret.

husk covering, shell.

husky 1 *a husky voice.* croaking, gruff, harsh, hoarse, rasping, rough. **2** *a big, husky fellow.* beefy, big, brawny, bulky, burly, hefty, hulking, muscular, strong. **3** *a team of huskies.* SEE **dog.**

hustle 1 *The gang hustled their victim into a car.* to jostle, to push, to shove. **2** *As we were late, they hustled us to our seats.* to hurry, to rush.

hut hovel, shack, shanty, shed, shelter.

hutch cage, coop, pen.

hyacinth SEE **bulb, flower.**

hydrofoil SEE **vessel.**

hydrogen SEE **gas.**

hyena SEE **animal.**

hygienic *You need hygienic conditions in hospital.* clean, disinfected, germ-free, healthy, sanitary, sterilized, unpolluted.

hymn SEE **church, sing.**

hyphen SEE **punctuation.**

hypocritical *Is it hypocritical for a vegetarian to wear leather shoes?* false, inconsistent, insincere.

hypodermic SEE **medicine.**

hysteria frenzy, madness, mania, panic.

hysterical 1 *The fans became hysterical when the group appeared.* delirious, demented, frantic, frenzied, mad, uncontrollable, wild. **2** *a hysterical joke.* comic, funny, hilarious, laughable, ridiculous, uproarious.

I i

ice 1 KINDS OF ICE ARE black ice, floe, glacier, iceberg, icicle. **2** SEE **weather.**

ice-breaker SEE **vessel.**

ice-cream SEE **food.**

ice-hockey, ice-rink SEE **sport.**

icing SEE **food.**

icy 1 *icy weather.* bitter, cold, freezing, frosty, wintry. **2** *icy roads.* frozen, slippery.

idea 1 *I have an idea.* (informal) brainwave, concept, notion, plan, point, proposal, suggestion, thought. **2** *Have you any idea who will win?* attitude, belief, impression, inkling, opinion, view.

ideal *ideal conditions.* excellent, faultless, perfect, suitable.

identical *identical twins.* alike, equal, indistinguishable.

identify *Did the vet identify what was wrong with the cat?* to detect, to diagnose, to discover, to name, to recognize.

identity *Did you discover his identity?* name.

idiot ass, blockhead, booby, dope, dunce, fool, half-wit, ignoramus, imbecile, moron, nitwit, twerp. ! These words are mostly used informally and are often insulting.

idiotic *an idiotic mistake.* absurd, crazy, foolish, irrational, ludicrous, ridiculous, silly, stupid, unwise.

idle 1 *The machines were idle during the holiday.* inactive, not working, unemployed, unoccupied, unused. **2** *He lost his job because he was so idle.* lazy, slow, sluggish.

idol 1 *a pagan idol.* god, image, statue. **2** *a pop idol.* hero, star, superstar.

idolize *The children idolize their grandfather.* to adore, to love, to revere, to worship.

ignite 1 *The gas fire won't ignite.* to burn, to catch fire, to fire. **2** *I ignited the fire with a match.* to kindle, to light, to set fire to.

ignition SEE **vehicle.**

ignoramus SEE **idiot.**

ignorant 1 *We were ignorant of the facts.* unaware, uninformed. **2** *You'd be ignorant if you didn't go to school.* illiterate, uneducated. **3** (insulting) *He's just plain ignorant!* foolish, stupid, unintelligent.

ignore *He ignored the 'stop' sign.* to disobey, to disregard, to leave out, to miss out, to neglect, to omit, to overlook, to skip, to take no notice of.

ill 1 bedridden, diseased, feeble, indisposed, infirm, pasty, (informal) poorly, queer, sick, unhealthy, unwell. SEE ALSO **illness. 2** ILL PEOPLE ARE invalid, out-patient, patient, sufferer, victim. **3** *ill effects.* bad, evil, harmful, unfavourable.

illegal *Cycling after dark without lights is illegal.* banned, criminal, forbidden, irregular, unauthorized, unlawful.

illegible *an illegible signature.* indecipherable, unreadable.

illegitimate *an illegitimate child:* bastard. ! Nowadays *bastard* is usually insulting.

illiterate *He was illiterate because he never went to school.* ignorant, uneducated.

illness 1 *to suffer from an illness.* ailment, affliction, attack, blight, (informal) bug, complaint, disease, disorder, infection, infirmity, injury, malady, sickness, wound. **2** VARIOUS ILLNESSES OR COMPLAINTS ARE abscess, allergy, amnesia, anaemia, appendicitis, arthritis, asthma, bilious attack, blister, boil, bronchitis, cancer, cataract, catarrh, chicken-pox, chilblain, chill, cholera, claustrophobia, cold, colic, coma, concussion, constipation, convulsion, corns, cough, cramp, dandruff, dermatitis, diabetes, diarrhoea, diphtheria, dysentery, earache, epilepsy, fever, fits, flu, frostbite, gastric flu, hay fever, headache, impetigo, indigestion, inflammation, influenza, insomnia, jaundice, leprosy, leukaemia,

lumbago, mal... migraine, mu... paralysis, pho... pneumonia, p... rabies, rheuma... scurvy, seasick... bifida, stroke,... tonsilitis, tooth... typhoid, typhu... wart, whooping...

illogical *an illog...* irrational, unre...

illuminate to li...

illusion *It didn't...* *an illusion.* conju... dream, fantasy,...

illustrate *The pi...* it. to demonstra... explain, to pictu... show.

illustration 1 di... picture. **2** *This ti...* illustrations of hou... case, example, i...

image 1 *You can s...* *mirror.* imitation,... reflection. **2** *The...* *god's image.* carvi... representation, s...

imaginary *The un...* *beast.* fanciful, fict... legendary, made-... existent, unreal.

imaginative *Tony...* *imaginative.* artisti... beautiful, clever,... inspired, inventiv...

imagine 1 *Can you...* *was like 1000 years a...* create, to dream u... picture, to see, to t... visualize. **2** *I imagi...* *something to eat.* to a... to guess, to presum... think.

imbecile SEE **idiot.**

imitate *Tony can imit...* to copy, to counterf... duplicate, to impers... to reproduce.

imitation *It isn't real...*

copy... fake... repr...

imm... bab... infa...

imm... end... pro... *Br...* nei... clo...

imm... ins...

imm... gi... va...

imm... w... lo... **2** a...

imm...

imm...

im...

im...

important event, etc. basic, big, chief, essential, fundamental, main, major, momentous, notable, pressing, primary, principal, serious, significant, urgent, weighty. **2** *an important person.* celebrated, distinguished, eminent, famous, great, influential, leading, notable, outstanding, prominent, renowned, well-known. **3** *to be important*: to matter.

impose *to impose a penalty.* to enforce, to inflict, to insist on.

imposing *an imposing castle.* big, grand, great, important, impressive, magnificent, majestic, stately, striking. SEE ALSO **splendid**.

impossible *It'd be impossible to swim the Atlantic.* impracticable, impractical, inconceivable, unimaginable.

impostor SEE **deceive**.

impotent *I was impotent to help the dying creature.* helpless, powerless, weak.

impoverished *an impoverished family.* destitute, needy, penniless, poor, poverty-stricken.

impregnable *an impregnable castle.* invincible, strong, unconquerable.

impress *Did the film impress you?* to affect, to influence, to move.

impression 1 *I had the impression you were bored.* feeling, idea, opinion, view. **2** *The film made a big impression on Tony.* effect, impact, mark. **3** *Granny has clear impressions of her childhood.* memory, recollection.

impressive *an impressive occasion.* grand, great, imposing, magnificent, majestic, moving, splendid, stately, striking.

imprison *to imprison a criminal.* to confine, to detain, to gaol, to intern, to lock up, to shut up.

improbable *an improbable story.* far-fetched, incredible, unbelievable, unconvincing, unlikely.

impromptu *an impromptu concert.* spontaneous, unplanned, unprepared, unrehearsed.

improper *improper language.* coarse, crude, inappropriate, indecent, rude, unbecoming, unsuitable, vulgar, wrong.

improve 1 *Lucy's work has improved lately.* to advance, to develop, to move on, to progress. **2** *Has granny improved since her illness?* to get better, to recover. **3** *Has Logan improved his behaviour?* to reform, to revise. **4** *Mr Brunswick wants to improve his house.* to make better, to modernize, to rebuild, to reform, to renovate, to touch up, to upgrade.

improvise 1 *We improvised a play.* to concoct, to invent, to make up. **2** *I didn't have all the ingredients, so I had to improvise.* to make do.

impudent bold, cheeky, disrespectful, impertinent, impolite, insolent, insulting, presumptuous, rude, saucy.

impulsive *When he thought about it, he regretted his impulsive action.* automatic, hasty, impetuous, impromptu, involuntary, rash, spontaneous, sudden, unconscious, unplanned, unthinking.

impure *impure water.* contaminated, dirty, filthy, foul, infected, polluted, unclean.

inaccessible *The South Pole is an inaccessible spot.* cut off, isolated, remote, unreachable.

inaccuracy error, fault, miscalculation, mistake, (informal) slip-up.

inaccurate *It was silly to give an inaccurate statement to the police.* false, incorrect, mistaken, untrue, wrong.

inactive *Hedgehogs are inactive in winter.* asleep, dormant, hibernating.

inadequate *an inadequate supply of food.* insufficient, unsatisfactory.

inanimate lifeless.

inappropriate *an inappropriate gift.* improper, incongruous, irrelevant, unsuitable, wrong.

incendiary bomb SEE **weapon**.

incense 1 SEE **church**. **2** *Logan's bad behaviour incensed her.* to anger, to enrage, to inflame, to infuriate, to madden, to provoke, to vex.

incentive *Mrs Angel doesn't offer us sweets as an incentive to work.* encouragement, stimulus.

incessant *The insects kept up an incessant buzzing.* ceaseless, chronic, constant, continual, continuous, everlasting, interminable, permanent, persistent, relentless, unending.

inch SEE **measure**.

incident *The crash at the crossroads was a nasty incident.* affair, event, happening, occasion, occurrence.

incinerator SEE **fire**.

incite *Some trouble-makers incited the crowd to start fighting.* to arouse, to encourage, to excite, to provoke, to rouse, to stimulate, to stir up, to urge.

inclination *Grandad has an inclination to doze in the evening.* habit, instinct, leaning, readiness, tendency, trend.

incline 1 *That pillar inclines to the right.* to lean, to slant, to slope, to tilt, to tip. 2 *inclined to*: disposed to, liable to.

include *The packet includes everything you need to make a trifle.* to consist of, to contain, to cover, to incorporate, to involve.

incoherent *an incoherent message.* confused, disjointed, disorganized, garbled, jumbled, mixed up, muddled, rambling, unclear.

income earnings, pay, pension, salary, wages.

incompatible *What Logan said today is incompatible with what he said yesterday.* conflicting, contradictory, inconsistent.

incompetent *an incompetent workman.* bad, helpless, (informal) hopeless, incapable, inefficient, unqualified, untrained, useless.

incomplete *Logan's work was still incomplete when the bell went.* imperfect, unfinished.

inconceivable *It's inconceivable that anyone could swim the Atlantic.* impossible, unimaginable.

incongruous *Granny thinks it might*
look incongruous if she wore a miniskirt. inappropriate, odd, out of place, unsuitable.

inconsiderate *It is inconsiderate of them to park in front of our gate.* careless, negligent, rude, tactless, thoughtless, uncaring, unkind.

inconsistent 1 *Our team's performance has been inconsistent this season.* changeable, erratic, fickle, patchy, unpredictable, variable. 2 *What he does is inconsistent with what he says.* conflicting, contradictory, incompatible.

inconvenient awkward, bothersome, troublesome.

incorporate *Our book incorporates the stories we wrote last week.* to consist of, to contain, to include.

incorrect *an incorrect answer.* false, inaccurate, mistaken, untrue, wrong.

increase 1 *They've increased the number of traffic wardens.* to add to, to boost, to build up, to enlarge, to expand, to strengthen, to swell. 2 *The traffic jam increased our journey by an hour.* to extend, to lengthen, to prolong. 3 *Dad increased my pocket-money.* to improve, to raise, to step up. 4 *The price of food seems to increase every day.* to escalate, to go up, to grow, to multiply, to rise.

incredible *an incredible story.* extraordinary, far-fetched, improbable, miraculous, unbelievable, unconvincing, unlikely.

incredulous *Mrs Brunswick was incredulous when Lucy won the competition.* disbelieving, dubious, sceptical, unconvinced.

incriminate *Logan incriminated Tony to avoid taking all the blame.* to accuse, to blame, to involve.

incubate *The hen was incubating her eggs.* to brood, to hatch.

incurable *an incurable illness.* hopeless.

indecent *indecent language.* coarse, crude, dirty, foul, improper, obscene, offensive, rude, smutty, vulgar.

indecipherable *indecipherable handwriting.* illegible, unreadable.

indefinite *He was indefinite about how much it would cost.* confused, general, neutral, uncertain, unclear, undecided, unsure, vague.

indelible *indelible ink.* fast, fixed, permanent.

independence *Do animals in the zoo miss their independence?* freedom, liberty.

independent *Mr Brunswick wants to run an independent business instead of working for other people.* free, private, self-governing.

indestructible *Some plastics are indestructible.* durable, everlasting, unbreakable.

index *an index of library books.* alphabetical list, catalogue, directory, register.

indicate 1 *Indicate which way you are turning.* to make known, to point out, to register, to show. 2 *A red light indicates danger.* to be a sign of, to convey, to communicate, to mean, to stand for, to symbolize.

indication *The spots are an indication of measles.* clue, hint, omen, sign, signal, symptom, token, warning.

indifferent 1 *He seemed indifferent about the result.* cold, cool, half-hearted, unconcerned, uninterested. 2 *The food was indifferent.* commonplace, fair, mediocre, middling, moderate, ordinary, unexciting.

indigestion SEE **illness**.

indignant angry, cross, furious, infuriated, irate, irritated, scornful, upset, vexed.

indigo SEE **colour**.

indirect *an indirect route.* devious, rambling, roundabout.

indispensable *A fishing rod is indispensable to an angler.* essential, necessary, vital.

indisposed *Mrs Angel wasn't here yesterday because she was indisposed.* ill, (informal) poorly, sick, unwell.

indistinct 1 *an indistinct picture.*

blurred, confused, dim, faint, fuzzy, hazy, misty, obscure, unclear. 2 *indistinct sounds.* deadened, dull, muffled.

indistinguishable *The twins are indistinguishable.* alike, identical.

individual 1 *Lucy has her own individual style in gymnastics.* characteristic, different, distinct, distinctive, particular, peculiar, personal, private, separate, special, specific, unique. 2 *Who was that individual I saw you with?* SEE **person**.

indoctrinate to brainwash, to instruct, to teach, to train.

induce 1 *We couldn't induce granny to come to the disco.* to coax, to persuade, to tempt. 2 *What induced your cold?* to bring on, to cause, to lead to, to produce, to provoke.

indulgent *Mrs Brunswick says that grandpa is too indulgent.* easygoing, forgiving, genial, kind, lenient, patient, tolerant.

industrial *an industrial area.* industrialized, manufacturing.

industrious *an industrious worker.* busy, conscientious, diligent, earnest, enterprising, hard-working, involved, keen.

industry *Is there much industry in this town?* business, commerce, manufacturing, trade.

inedible *inedible food.* uneatable.

ineffective *Tony made an ineffective attempt to score.* feeble, futile, unsuccessful, useless.

inefficient 1 *an inefficient workman.* (informal) hopeless, incapable, incompetent. 2 *an inefficient use of resources.* extravagant, wasteful.

inevitable *Disaster was inevitable when the brakes failed.* certain, inescapable, sure, unavoidable.

inexcusable unforgivable, wrong.

inexhaustible never-ending.

inexpensive cheap, cut-price, economical, reasonable.

inexplicable *an inexplicable mystery.* baffling, insoluble, mysterious, puzzling, unaccountable.

infamous *an infamous crime.*
disgraceful, evil, notorious,
outrageous, scandalous, shocking,
wicked. SEE ALSO **bad**.

infant 1 baby, child. SEE ALSO
person. **2** *an infant school*. SEE
school.

infantile *infantile games*. babyish,
childish, immature.

infantry SEE **armed services**.

infatuation love, obsession, passion.

infect 1 *People asked if the spilled acid
would infect the water supply*. to
contaminate, to poison, to pollute.
2 *infected: an infected wound.* festering,
inflamed, poisoned, putrid, septic.

infection *to catch an infection.* ailment,
(informal) bug, blight, disease. SEE
ALSO **illness**.

infectious *an infectious disease.*
catching, contagious.

inferior 1 *inferior rank*. junior, lower,
subordinate. **2** *inferior quality*. cheap,
poor-quality, shoddy, tawdry, tinny.
SEE ALSO **bad**.

inferno blaze, conflagration, fire.

infested *infested with mice.* overrun,
swarming.

infidelity 1 *infidelity to your team.*
disloyalty, treachery, treason.
2 *infidelity to a wife or husband.*
adultery, unfaithfulness.

infinite *Space is infinite.* boundless,
endless, everlasting, immeasurable,
interminable, limitless, unending,
unlimited.

infirm bedridden, elderly, frail, ill,
old, (informal) poorly, senile,
unwell, weak.

infirmary clinic, health centre,
hospital. SEE ALSO **medicine**.

infirmity SEE **illness**.

inflame 1 *to inflame someone's anger*. to
arouse, to enrage, to excite, to
incense, to infuriate, to madden, to
provoke. **2** *inflamed: an inflamed wound.*
festering, infected, poisoned.

inflammation abscess, boil, sore.
SEE ALSO **illness**.

inflate *to inflate a tyre.* to blow up, to
pump up.

inflexible 1 *an inflexible framework.*
firm, hard, rigid, solid, unbending,
unyielding. **2** *an inflexible attitude.*
obstinate, strict, stubborn.

inflict *to inflict a punishment.* to
administer, to impose.

influence 1 *Did the weather have any
influence on the game?* effect, impact.
2 *Parents have influence over their
children.* authority, control, power.
3 *Does TV violence influence you?* to
affect, to control, to dominate, to
impress, to modify, to move, to stir.
4 *Don't try to influence the referee.* to
bribe, to persuade.

influential 1 *an influential person.*
important, powerful. **2** *an influential
idea.* convincing, persuasive.

influenza SEE **illness**.

inform 1 *The shop will inform us of the
cost.* to advise, to notify, to tell. **2** *to
inform against*: to complain about, to
denounce, to report, to spy on, to tell
of. **3** SEE **educate**.

informal 1 *informal clothes.* casual,
comfortable. **2** *an informal party.*
easygoing, friendly, relaxed.

information 1 *Is there any information
about our outing?* announcement,
communication, message, news,
report, statement. **2** *The police are
collecting information.* data, evidence,
facts, knowledge, statistics.

informer spy, tell-tale.

infrequent *The golden eagle is an
infrequent sight in Britain.* occasional,
rare, uncommon, unusual.

infringe *to infringe the law.* to break, to
disobey, to disregard, to violate.

infuriate *Logan often infuriates Mrs
Angel.* to anger, to enrage, to
exasperate, to incense, to madden, to
provoke, to vex.

ingenious *an ingenious plan.* artful,
clever, crafty, cunning, imaginative,
inventive, resourceful, shrewd,
skilful.

ingot *a gold ingot.* lump, nugget.

ingredient component, element,
part.

inhabit *We inhabit a council flat.* to

dwell in, to live in, to occupy, to populate, to reside in.

inhabitant citizen, native, occupant, population, resident, tenant.

inhale *to inhale smoke.* to breathe in.

inheritance *He got a small inheritance from his uncle's will.* bequest, estate, fortune, legacy.

inherited *an inherited title.* hereditary.

inheritor heir.

inhospitable *an inhospitable welcome.* unfriendly, unwelcoming.

inhuman *inhuman cruelty.* bestial, bloodthirsty, cruel, heartless, merciless, pitiless, ruthless, savage, unfeeling.

initial *If you buy this on hire-purchase, the initial payment is £10.* earliest, first, opening, original, starting.

initiate *to initiate negotiations.* to begin, to commence, to embark on, to launch, to open, to start.

initiative *to take the initiative*: to begin, to commence, to open, to start.

injection SEE **medicine**.

injure to damage, to harm, to hurt. SEE ALSO **wound**.

ink SEE **write**.

inkling *I'd no inkling he was coming.* clue, hint, idea, indication.

inlet bay, creek, fiord. SEE ALSO **geography**.

inn hotel, pub, tavern. SEE ALSO **building, holiday**.

innings SEE **cricket**.

innocent 1 *The trial proved he was innocent.* blameless, guiltless.
2 *Sleeping babies look innocent.* angelic, chaste, harmless, inoffensive, pure, virtuous.

innocuous *Grass-snakes are innocuous.* harmless, innocent, inoffensive, mild, safe.

innumerable *innumerable stars.* countless, numberless, untold.

inoffensive SEE **innocuous**.

inquest inquiry.

inquire to ask, to beg, to demand, to enquire, to entreat, to implore, to query, to question, to request.

inquiry inquest, investigation.

inquisitive *It's rude to be inquisitive.* curious, interested, nosey, prying.

insane *an insane idea, an insane person, etc.* crazy, demented, deranged, (informal) dotty, (informal) loony, lunatic, mad, unhinged.

insanitary dirty, unhealthy.

inscribe SEE **write**.

insect 1 VARIOUS INSECTS ARE ant, bee, beetle, blackbeetle, bluebottle, bumble-bee, butterfly, cockroach, crane-fly, cricket, daddy-long-legs, dragon-fly, drone, earwig, fly, glow-worm, gnat, grasshopper, hornet, ladybird, locust, louse, midge, mosquito, moth, nit, tsetse fly, wasp, woodworm. 2 OTHER FORMS OF AN INSECT ARE caterpillar, chrysalis, grub, larva, maggot. 3 OTHER CRAWLING CREATURES ARE centipede, earthworm, slug, snail, spider, wood-louse, worm. These creatures are not proper insects. 4 SEE ALSO **animal**.

insecticide pesticide. SEE ALSO **garden, poison**.

insecure *an insecure foothold.* loose, precarious, rocky, shaky, unsafe, unsteady, wobbly.

insensible *I was insensible for a moment after the accident.* knocked out, senseless, unconscious.

insensitive *It was insensitive to joke about granny's operation.* callous, cruel, hard-hearted, heartless, tactless, thoughtless, unfeeling.

insert *Insert a coin.* to push in, to put in, to tuck in.

inside centre, core, heart, middle.

insignificant *an insignificant improvement.* imperceptible, minor, minute, negligible, small, trifling, trivial, unimportant.

insincere *an insincere compliment.* deceitful, dishonest, false, hypocritical.

insist 1 *Mrs Angel insists on the importance of neatness.* to assert, to emphasize, to maintain, to state, to stress. 2 *They insisted that I went to the* *police station*. to command, to demand, to enforce, to require.

insolent *an insolent stare*. arrogant, bold, cheeky, disrespectful, impertinent, impolite, impudent, insulting, presumptuous, rude.

insoluble *an insoluble problem*. baffling, inexplicable, mysterious, puzzling, unanswerable.

insomnia SEE **illness**.

inspect *We inspected the damage*. to check, to examine, to investigate.

inspection check-up, examination, investigation, scrutiny.

inspector SEE **police**.

inspire *The big crowd inspired us to play well*. to arouse, (informal) to egg on, to encourage, to prompt, to reassure, to stimulate, to support.

install *New central heating has been installed*. to establish, to put in, to set up.

instalment 1 *Have you paid all the instalments?* payment, rent. 2 *Did you see last week's instalment?* episode.

instance *Give me an instance of what you mean*. case, example, illustration, sample.

instant 1 *an instant reply*. immediate, instantaneous, prompt, quick, speedy, swift. 2 *The shooting star was gone in an instant*. flash, moment, second.

instantaneous immediate, instant.

instep SEE **foot**.

instinct *Animals have an instinct to look after their young*. feeling, inclination, intuition, tendency.

institution 1 *Sunday dinner is a regular institution for the Brunswicks*. custom, habit, practice, routine. 2 *an institution for blind people*. establishment, organization.

instruct 1 to coach, to lecture, to teach, to train. SEE ALSO **educate**. 2 *He instructed us to wait*. to command, to direct, to order.

instructive *an instructive book*. educational, helpful, informative.

instructor coach, teacher, trainer.

instrument 1 *an instrument for measuring rainfall*. apparatus, device, equipment, gadget, implement, machine, tool, utensil. 2 *musical instruments*. SEE **music**.

insubordinate *The insubordinate soldier was punished*. defiant, disobedient, mutinous, rebellious.

insufficient *insufficient food*. inadequate, meagre, scanty, unsatisfactory.

insulate *to insulate pipes*. to lag.

insult 1 *Logan's continual chatter was an insult to our visitor*. cheek, impudence, rudeness. 2 *He didn't mean to insult her*. to abuse, to be rude, to mock, to offend, to snub.

intact *Did the glasses arrive intact?* complete, entire, perfect, undamaged, untouched, whole.

integer digit, figure, number.

integrate *So many players were ill that we had to integrate two teams*. to amalgamate, to combine, to join, to merge, to put together, to unite.

integrity *You can trust his complete integrity*. fidelity, honesty, honour, principle, sincerity, virtue.

intellect ability, brains, cleverness, genius, intelligence, mind, reason, sense, understanding.

intellectual 1 *an intellectual student*. SEE **intelligent**. 2 *an intellectual book*. cultural, deep, educational, highbrow, improving.

intelligence 1 SEE **intellect**. 2 *Our intelligence discovered some enemy secrets*. espionage, spying.

intelligent *an intelligent student*. brainy, bright, clever, intellectual, wise.

intelligible *an intelligible message*. clear, comprehensible, logical, lucid, unambiguous, understandable.

intend *What do you intend to do?* to aim, to contemplate, to design, to mean, to plan, to plot, to propose, to scheme.

intense 1 *intense pain*. acute, extreme, keen, severe, sharp, strong, violent. 2 *intense feelings*. burning, deep, eager, earnest, passionate, profound, serious, vehement.

intent *intent on what you're doing.* absorbed, determined, eager, keen.

intention *What is your intention?* aim, ambition, goal, object, objective, plan, point, purpose, target.

intentional *an intentional foul.* conscious, deliberate, intended, premeditated, wilful.

intercept *We intercepted Logan's gang before they got near our den.* to ambush, to attack, to cut off, to head off, to stop, to trap.

interchange *a motorway interchange.* crossroads, intersection, junction.

intercom SEE **communication**.

intercourse SEE **mate**.

interest 1 *Did he show any interest?* attention, concern, curiosity, notice. 2 *What are your main interests?* hobby, pastime, pursuit. 3 *Astronomy interests me.* to appeal to, to attract, to fascinate, to intrigue. 4 *interested*: absorbed, curious, preoccupied.

interface SEE **computer**.

interfere *Logan always interferes in our games.* to be a busybody, to butt in, to interrupt, to intervene, to intrude, to meddle, to molest, to pry, to snoop, to tamper.

interlude *There will be an interlude before Part 2.* break, gap, intermission, interval, lull, pause.

intermediate *an intermediate position.* half-way, middle, neutral.

interminable *Logan asks interminable questions.* ceaseless, constant, continual, continuous, everlasting, incessant, persistent, unending.

intermission SEE **interlude**.

intermittent *My computer has an intermittent fault.* occasional, on and off, spasmodic.

intern *Many foreigners were interned when the war started.* to confine, to gaol, to imprison.

internal inner, inside, interior.

interpret *Can you interpret this old writing?* to decipher, to decode, to explain, to make clear, to translate.

interpreter SEE **job**.

interrogate *The police interrogated him.* to ask questions, to cross-examine, to examine, to question.

interrupt 1 *Please interrupt if you have any questions.* to break in, to butt in, to cut in, to intervene, to intrude. 2 *A fire alarm interrupted the lesson.* to break off, to disrupt, to disturb, to interfere with.

interruption break, gap, pause.

intersect *Two motorways intersect.* to converge, to cross, to divide, to pass across.

intersection crossroads, interchange, junction.

interval 1 *an interval in time or space.* break, distance, gap, lapse, lull, opening, pause, respite, rest, space. 2 *We had an ice-cream in the interval.* break, interlude, intermission.

intervene *Mrs Angel intervened when Logan started quarrelling with Tony.* to butt in, to come between, to interfere, to interrupt, to intrude.

interview 1 *A reporter interviewed the eyewitness.* to ask questions, to question. 2 SEE **television**.

intestines SEE **body**.

intimate 1 *an intimate relationship.* affectionate, close, familiar, friendly, loving. 2 *intimate details.* confidential, personal, private, secret.

intimidate *Logan was in trouble for intimidating the infants.* to bully, to frighten, to make afraid, to menace, to persecute, to scare, to terrify, to terrorize, to threaten.

intolerable unbearable.

intolerant narrow-minded, prejudiced.

intoxicate 1 *intoxicated*: drunk, fuddled. 2 *intoxicating*: alcoholic.

intrepid *intrepid explorers.* bold, brave, courageous, daring, fearless, heroic, valiant.

intricate *intricate machinery.* complex, complicated, delicate, detailed, elaborate, involved.

intrigue 1 *Guy Fawkes took part in an intrigue against parliament.* conspiracy, plot, scheme. 2 *The parrot's swear-words intrigued us.* to appeal to, to arouse the curiosity of, to attract, to fascinate, to interest.

introduce 1 *Dad introduced me to his friend.* to make known, to present. 2 *The DJ introduced the next disc.* to announce. 3 *They introduced a new bus service.* to begin, to bring out, to create, to establish, to initiate, to set up, to start.

introduction *an introduction to a book.* preface, prelude, prologue.

intrude *Please don't intrude during the staff meeting.* to butt in, to interfere, to interrupt, to intervene.

intruder *The intruder ran away when the burglar alarm went off.* burglar, prowler, robber, thief, trespasser.

intuition *I had an intuition that you'd come.* feeling, instinct.

inundate *A tidal wave inundated the town.* to drown, to engulf, to flood, to submerge, to swamp.

invade *A flock of pigeons invaded Mrs Brunswick's cabbage patch.* to attack, to march into, to occupy, to overrun, to raid.

invalid 1 *He's an invalid who spends most of the time in bed.* patient, sufferer. 2 *an invalid passport.* out-of-date, unacceptable, unusable.

invaluable *Your help was invaluable.* precious, useful.

invariable *an invariable rule.* constant, reliable, unchangeable, unchanging, unvarying.

invasion attack, onslaught, raid.

invent *Who first invented a computer?* to conceive, to concoct, to contrive, to create, to devise, to discover, to make up, to plan, to put together, to think up.

invention *a useful invention.* contraption, contrivance, device, discovery.

inventive *Mrs Angel likes Tony's work because it is so inventive.* creative, enterprising, imaginative, ingenious, resourceful.

inventor creator, discoverer, originator.

invest *to invest money.* to save.

investigate *to investigate a topic.* to examine, to explore, to inquire into, to study.

investigation *an investigation into a crime.* examination, inquiry, inspection, research, scrutiny.

invigorating *an invigorating shower.* healthy, refreshing, stimulating.

invincible *We never scored: their defence was invincible.* impregnable, strong, unbeatable, unconquerable.

invisible *an invisible repair.* concealed, covered, hidden, imperceptible, inconspicuous, obscured, undetectable, unseen.

invite 1 *We invite you to join in.* to ask, to encourage, to request, to urge. 2 *inviting*: SEE **attractive**.

involuntary *Blinking is usually an involuntary movement.* automatic, impulsive, spontaneous, unconscious, unintentional, unthinking.

involve 1 *What does a policeman's job involve?* to contain, to include. 2 *The problem of feeding the world involves us all.* to affect, to concern, to interest. 3 *Logan tried to involve Tony in the crime.* to incriminate, to mix up. 4 *involved: involved in your work.* active, busy, employed, occupied. 5 *an involved story.* complex, complicated, confusing, elaborate, intricate.

iodine SEE **medicine**.

irascible *an irascible old gentleman.* bad-tempered, cross, grumpy, irritable, short-tempered, snappy.

irate angry, cross, enraged, fuming, furious, indignant, infuriated, mad, raging, vexed.

iris SEE **flower**.

iron 1 SEE **metal**. 2 *They put convicts in irons.* chains, fetters, shackles. 3 *to iron clothes.* to flatten, to press, to smooth.

ironmonger SEE **shop**.

irrational *an irrational argument.* crazy, illogical, unreasonable.

irregular 1 *an irregular surface.* bumpy, rough, uneven. 2 *irregular intervals.* erratic, random, unequal, variable.